Resistance and Death in the Czenstochower Ghetto
(Częstochowa, Poland)

Translation of
Vidershtand un Umkum in Czenstochower Ghetto

Edited by: Liber Brener

Published in Poland in Yiddish before 1952
by The Jewish Historical Institute of Poland

Translated by Gloria Berkenstat Freund

Published by JewishGen

**An Affiliate of the Museum of Jewish Heritage - A Living Memorial to the Holocaust
New York**

Resistance and Death in the Czenstochower Ghetto (Częstochowa, Poland)
Translation of *Vidershtand un Umkum in Czenstochower Ghetto*

Project Coordinator and Translator: Gloria Berkenstat Freund
Layout: Joel Alpert
Cover Design: Rachel Kolokoff Hopper

Published by JewishGen, Inc.
An Affiliate of the Museum of Jewish Heritage
A Living Memorial to the Holocaust
36 Battery Place, New York, NY 10280

"JewishGen, Inc. is not responsible for inaccuracies or omissions in the original work and makes no representations regarding the accuracy of this translation. Digital images of the original book's contents can be seen online at the New York Public Library Web site."

The mission of the JewishGen organization is to produce a translation of the original work and we cannot verify the accuracy of statements or alter facts cited.

Printed in the United States of America by Lightning Source, Inc.

Library of Congress Control Number (LCCN): 2018965373
ISBN: 978-1-939561-73-2 (hard cover: 254 pages, alk. paper)

Front Cover: Map of Czenstochower
Back Cover: Czenstochower Old Synagogue

JewishGen and the Yizkor-Books-in-Print Project

This book has been published by the **Yizkor-Books-in-Print Project,** as part of the **Yizkor Book Project** of **JewishGen, Inc**.

JewishGen, Inc. is a non-profit organization founded in 1987 as a resource for Jewish genealogy. Its website [www.jewishgen.org] serves as an international clearinghouse and resource center to assist individuals who are researching the history of their Jewish families and the places where they lived. JewishGen provides databases, facilitates discussion groups, and coordinates projects relating to Jewish genealogy and the history of the Jewish people. In 2003, JewishGen became an affiliate of the **Museum of Jewish Heritage - A Living Memorial to the Holocaust** in New York.

The **JewishGen Yizkor Book Project** was organized to make more widely known the existence of Yizkor (Memorial) Books written by survivors and former residents of various Jewish communities throughout the world. Later, volunteers connected to the different destroyed communities began cooperating to have these books translated from the original language—usually Hebrew or Yiddish—into English, thus enabling a wider audience to have access to the valuable information contained within them. As each chapter of these books was translated, it was posted on the JewishGen website and made available to the general public.

The **Yizkor-Books-in-Print Project** began in 2011 as an initiative to print and publish Yizkor Books that had been fully translated, so that hard copies would be available for purchase by the descendants of these communities and also by scholars, universities, synagogues, libraries, and museums.

These Yizkor books have been produced almost entirely through the volunteer effort of researchers from around the world, assisted by donations from private individuals. The books are printed and sold at near cost, so as to make them as affordable as possible. Our goal is to make this important genre of Jewish literature and history available in English in book form, so that people can have the personal histories of their ancestral towns on their bookshelves for themselves and for their children and grandchildren.

A list of all published translated Yizkor Books in the project with prices and ordering information can be found at:
http://www.jewishgen.org/Yizkor/ybip.html

Lance Ackerfeld, Yizkor Book Project Manager

Joel Alpert, Yizkor-Book-in-Print Project Coordinator

JewishGen
Yizkor Book Project

This book is presented by the
Yizkor Books in Print Project
Project Coordinator: Joel Alpert

Part of the
Yizkor Books Project of JewishGen, Inc.
Project Manager: Lance Ackerfeld

These books have been produced solely through volunteer effort
of individuals from around the world. The books are printed and
sold at near cost, so as to make them as affordable as possible.

Our goal is to make this history and important genre of Jewish
literature available in English in book form so that people can have
the near-personal histories of their ancestral towns on their bookshelves for themselves and for their children and grandchildren.

Any donations to the Yizkor Books Project are appreciated.

Please send donations to:
Yizkor Book Project
JewishGen
36 Battery Place
New York, NY 10280

JewishGen, Inc. is an affiliate of the
Museum of Jewish Heritage
A Living Memorial to the Holocaust

Acknowledgements

Thank you to the JewishGen organization for making possible both the on-line publication and the publication of this hardcover edition of this translation.

I also want to thank those who had a part in allowing this project to reach completion:

*Daniel Kazez, president of CRARG (Czestochowa-Radomsko Area Research Group), who contacted me about translating the book.

*David Rose, a CRARG member, who generously sent me his copy of the Yiddish text.

*William Leibner of Jerusalem, who provided translation guidance whenever it was needed.

*Larry Freund, my beloved husband and editor extraordinaire, who read my translations and shared his editing expertise with me.

*Lance Ackerfeld, JewishGen Yizkor Book Project Manager, who as always, made certain that my translations were uploaded to the JewishGen Yizkor Book Translation website.

*Joel Alpert, Yizkor Books in Print Project Coordinator, who conceived of this project to publish in book form material that is already on the web in the Yizkor Books Project.

Special thanks to the National Yiddish Book Center in Amherst, Massachusetts and the New York Public Library for supplying the images used in this book.

Gloria Berkenstat Freund
Translator and Project Coordinator

Brief Summary of the Book

The Germans invaded Poland on Friday, the 1st of September 1939 and entered Czenstochow on Sunday, the 3rd. This invasion was the beginning of the end of the Jewish community, which had existed in Czenstochow for hundreds of years. The Jewish population of approximately 30,000 men, women and children enjoyed an active economic, political, cultural and religious life. All of it was erased.

Resistance and Death in the Czenstochow Ghetto tells the story of the brave but mostly unsuccessful fight for life by the Czenstochower Jews and of their tragic death, of the annihilation of a vibrant community. Their story is important as a historical tale of their existence and as first-hand evidence of what happened to them and to Jewish Czenstochow.

Preface to the Translation and Publication of the Yizkor Book

Translating this book, *Vidershtand un Umkum in Czenstochower Geto* [*Resistance and Death in the Czenstochower Ghetto*], was important to me for multiple reasons. I had already translated another book about the destruction of the Jewish community in Czenstochow, *Khurbn Czenstochow* [*The Destruction of Czenstochowa*]. That book gave a detailed account of the events of the annihilation of the Jewish community and population in that city. However, the book did not provide the names of many of those affected by the dreadful events described in the book; *Resistance and Death in the Czenstochower Ghetto* does.

I believe that it is very important that the names of the Czenstochower martyrs be known as far as is possible. We must never forget who they were, how they lived their lives and the terrible manner in which they died.

On a personal note, translating *Resistance and Death in the Czenstochower Ghetto* was important to me because the book contains the story of my courageous cousins, Moshe Berkensztat and his wife, Rayzl Fajertag Berkensztat, and the story of their tragic deaths at the hands of the Germans.

I dedicate this translation to their memory and to the memory of all of the 30,000 Czenstochower Jews who perished.

Gloria Berkenstat Freund
Translator and Project Coordinator

Geopolitical Information:

Częstochowa is located at 50°48' North Latitude / 19°07' East Longitude

Major city, 60 miles NW of Kraków, 67 miles SSW of Łódź.

Alternate names: Częstochowa [Pol], Chenstochov [Yid], Tschenstochau [Ger], Čenstochová [Cz], Chenstokhova [Rus], Chenstokhov, Chestokhova, Tshenstokhov

Yiddish: טשענסטאָכאָוו. Russian: Ченстохова. Hebrew: נסטוחובה'צ.

Region: Piotrkow

Jewish population: 11,764 (1897), 25,588 (1931)

Period	Town	District	Province	Country
Before WWI (c. 1900):	Częstochowa	Częstochowa	Piotrków	Russian Empire
Between the wars (c. 1930):	Częstochowa	Częstochowa	Kielce	Poland
After WWII (c. 1950):	Częstochowa	Poland		Poland
Today (c. 2000):	Częstochowa	Poland		Poland

Nearby Jewish Communities:

Olsztyn 7 miles ESE
Mstów 8 miles ENE
Kamyk 9 miles NNW
Kłobuck 11 miles NW
Aurelów 13 miles NE
Truskolasy 13 miles WNW
Miedzno 14 miles NNW
Janów, 15 miles ESE
Żarki 16 miles SE
Przyrów 17 miles E
Myszków 18 miles SE
Gidle 20 miles NE
Nowa Brzeźnica 20 miles N

BALTIC SEA

LITHUANIA

RUSSIA

Vilnius ●

POLAND

BELARUS

GERMANY

● Poznan

Warsaw ●

● Lodz

● **Czestochowa**

● Prague

● **Zabrze**

CZECH REPUBLIC

● Krakow

●**Jordanow**

UKRAINE

SLOVAKIA

250 miles

0

0   250 Km   500 Km

POLAND - **Current Borders**

Map of Czestochwa located in Poland

Notes to the Reader:

We apologize ahead of time for the poor quality of images in the book. Often these images had been scanned from the original Yizkor books which were of poor quality to begin with, being copies of old photographs. Each transfer results in loss of quality. We have done the best we could given the original material and the resources and technology at hand. Even though images often appear of higher quality on computer screens, that does not transfer to high quality images in print. A reader can view the original scans on the web sites listed below.

Also please note that all references within the text of the book to page numbers, refer to the page numbers of the original Yizkor Book.

In order to obtain a list of all Shoah victims from Czestochowa, the reader should access the Yad Vashem web site listed below; one can also search for specific family names using family name option. These lists are continually updated by Yad Vashem, so it is worthwhile to periodically search these lists.

There is much valuable information available on this web site, including the Pages of Testimony, etc.

http://yvng.yadvashem.org

A list of this book and all books available in the Yizkor-Book-In-Print Project along with prices is available at:

http://www.jewishgen.org/Yizkor/ybip.html

Explanation for the Cover Design

The Czestochowa Ghetto was set up by Nazi Germany for the purpose of persecution and exploitation of local Jews in the city of Czestochowa during the German occupation of Poland. At the beginning, the approximate number of people confined to the ghetto was around 40,000 Jews, and in late 1942, at its peak and before the mass deportations, at 48,000 Jews.

Most ghetto inmates were transferred by Holocaust trains to their deaths at the Treblinka extermination camp. In June 1943, the remaining ghetto inhabitants launched the Czestochowa Ghetto uprising, which was extinguished by the SS after a few days of fighting.

The front cover is an image from the book and is a map of Czestochowa. I have merged a partial list of the the names of the Czestochowa murdered into the map to serve as a remembrance to those who suffered and those who died.

The photo on the back cover is of the old synagogue in Czestochowa (public domain). The exact date of the start of the construction of the *Old Synagogue (Stara Synagoga)* is unknown, but the building was expanded in 1872 and then renovated in 1928-29. It was ransacked by the Germans in September 1939, and then completely destroyed by them during the liquidation of the *Small Ghetto* in 1943.

As in most European Jewish communities, places of worship were central to the lives of the Jews of Czestochowa and it is fitting that this photo reminds us of the lives, community, and culture, that were lost with the annihilation of this city and its beloved people.

We must remember this once thriving community of Jewish inhabitants before the total devastation and destruction of their lives by the Nazis. We must remember the 40,000 murdered Jews from this community. We must remember. We must never forget.

Never again.

Rachel Kolokoff Hopper
December 23, 2018

Yiddish Title Page of Original Yizkor Book

ל. בּרענער

ווידערשטאַנד און אומקום אין טשענסטאָכאָווער געטאָ

ייִדישער היסטאָרישער אינסטיטוט אין פּוילן

Translation of the Title Page of Original Yizkor Book

L. Brener

Resistance and Death in the Czenstochower Ghetto

Jewish Historical Institute in Poland

Table of Contents

The First Tortures   2

The Judenrat and Its Authority   10

The Ghetto   21

Forced Labor   30

Jews Would Escape from the Collection Point   37

The Jewish Police   42

The Economic Situation of the Jews in the Ghetto   48

Special Help   51

Cultural Activity   62

The Underground Movement in the Ghetto   70

Demographic Relationships   79

On the Eve of Liquidation   85

The Large Liquidation   91

The Small Ghetto   106

The Resistance Movement in the Small Ghetto   133

In the HASAG Camp   156

Underground Work in HASAG and in the Koniecpoler Forests   175

The Last Days of the Czenstochower *HASAG* Camps   184

List of Jewish Doctors in Czenstochow Who Perished During the
German Occupation   187

Map of Czestochowa   190

Names Index   191

Family Notes

Introduction

This work by Liber Brener, *Viderstand un Umkum in Czenstochower Ghetto* [Resurrection and Destruction in Ghetto Czestochowa], is an expansion and reworking of a diary which the author continued for a long time in the ghetto and in the camp. After the liberation, L. Brener restored his memories and verified and completed them with a series of German, Polish and Yiddish documents as well as testimony from other Jewish survivors of the Czenstochower ghetto. The subjective element, those who themselves lived through it and, as matter of fact, the specific nature of the events – places a seal on the book and is the reason that the author does not pretend to have exhaustively [covered everything] and answered every problem that emerged in connection with the events in the large and small Czenstochower ghettos and in the *H.A.S.A.G.* camp.* As a matter of fact, this book does not pretend to be a thoroughly rigorous scientific study. Therefore, Brener's book presents itself as an important and worthwhile material collection, which will serve as a basis for research and scientific synthesis by the future historian of the ghettos and resistance movement and as a source for creating materials for illuminating those basic problems for which this book does not give a completely clear answer.

*[Translator's note: *H.A.S.A.G.* is the acronym for a German metal goods manufacturer, Hugo Schneider Metallwarenfabrik Aktiengesellschaft. A *H.A.S.A.G.* factory was established in the Czenstochower ghetto and "employed" forced labor or prisoners from concentration camps.]

The First Tortures

Czenstochow was one of the first cities in Poland that was occupied by Hitlerist troops. On the 3rd of September 1939, the German military marched into the city. The streets were already covered in placards with various notices from the German military regime on that same day after eight o'clock in the morning. The population cautiously began to appear on the streets to read the demands. The next morning, the German soldiers went through the street and gave the population cookies and chocolate. The people began to feel at ease and to think that "the devil was not as frightening, as it had been painted." Therefore, they began to appear in the streets more boldly and more often. On the same day at 11 o'clock in the morning, the Germans opened fire on the people in every street without any "explanation." Many houses were also shot up. After this "foreplay," the Germans began to chase the people from the streets and residences. Thousands of people with raised hands were driven to the squares: in front of the cathedral (Katedralna Street), in front of the church, "Swientego Zygmunta" [Saint Zygmunt] (New Market, today Dusznicka Square), in front of Brast's factory (Strazaca Street) and to the large square in front of city hall. All of the enumerated squares were surrounded with machine guns and by armed soldiers. The Jews who had been brought together had to lay immovable on their stomachs for hours and they were shot at by machine guns, rifles and automatic weapons. Later an order was issued: "Stand" and they began to chase the hordes of people. Those running were shot at again. The people who found themselves in front of the cathedral were driven into the cathedral. Those who were located at the New Market were driven into the church, "Swientego Zygmunta."

Those who were on Strazaca Street were driven into Brast's factory and those who were on the square in front of the city hall were driven into the church, "Swientego Jakuba [Saint James]." It has not been determined exactly how many fell then as victims. Rumors went around that approximately 120 men had fallen in the square in front of the Brast factory, more than 100 at the cathedral, more than 50 at the city hall and approximately 30 men fell in front of the church, "Swientego Zygmunta." In addition, there were hundreds of victims who had been shot, in the streets and in the courtyards. Meanwhile, the Germans chased people to the designated places. There were many Jews among the hundreds shot and wounded. Many Jews were buried in the courtyard of the artisans' synagogue on Garncarska Street. On this spot, murdered people were slid into a large pit together with cows and horses, which had accidentally met with German bullets during the shooting.

This day entered the history of Czenstochow as "Bloody Monday." When someone wanted to designate the terms of a certain event, he would not express himself in any other way then, "This was still before Bloody Monday," or "This was already after 'Bloody Monday.' The then city commissar, Drahaberg, who was chosen as city commissar over Czenstochow and as county chief over the area of Czenstochow by Ridiger, (chief of the civilian managing committee) had a large share in "Bloody Monday."

"Bloody Monday" was the horror-day for the entire Czenstochow population for a long time. There also was much talk about the appeal of the priest, Zimniak, who, at the request of the occupiers, appeared in the city on the same day. "The appeal was directed "to the residents of the city of Czenstochow. I appeal to all residents of Czenstochow that they should not spread any panic and avoid provocations, which could bring the strongest punishments to the entire city, which according to the rules of war could lead to [punishment] including the death penalty." Signed: Vicar-General A. Zimniak – Suffragan Bishop, Czenstochow, the 4th of September 1939.

Going to the execution in the Olszyna Forest

On the morning of Tuesday, the 5th of December 1939, those who were 50 and older were freed. The remaining were taken to the military barracks and a number of them were also imprisoned in jail on Zawodzie Street, where many went through physical and moral pain.

Before the execution

On Wednesday the Germans began to free those detained and left several dozen men as hostages, who were held responsible if the city population possibly came out against the Germans. The German guards often made each hostage feel as if their life had been abandoned.

The permanent torture of the Jews began right after "Bloody Monday." The masses of Jews were driven each day to work, where they had to endure various troubles. Women, men and children and young people were forced to cover the pits with their bare hands, to carry bricks without purpose from one spot to another and also do other heavy physical labor under the blows of rifle butts and whips. At work, everyone had to remove all of their outer coats or jackets and throw then to one side. Under rain and, later, under snow, we had

to work this way until late at night. As soon as we were released from work, we
had to grab an overcoat and run away. Rarely did someone have his [or her]
own clothing. Men often grabbed women's and children's coats, women
grabbed men's coats and children heavy overcoats of adults. In general, many
did not grab something for themselves and would run from the workplace
entirely without an overcoat. Kriger, the chief of the Gestapo in Czenstochow
at the time, particularly excelled in torturing people at work. He would often
demand that the Gestapo premises be cleaned and that women who excelled
with musical capabilities should be sent to him personally. He would force
them to clean his house up to the highest floors and then he, himself, played a
pianoforte while they worked. Kriger also demanded that the *Judenrat* should
assure that two open graves on the Jewish cemetery would always be ready for
Jewish criminals. The graves were often filled and fresh graves had to be
prepared. However, this alone did not satisfy the members of the Gestapo and
they would often carry out arrests among Jews, sending them to jail and
sending them to the Olsztiner woods with larger groups of Poles, where they
were executed and buried on the spot. Among the members of the Gestapo, a
certain Szabelski, a *Volks-Deutsch* (a Volks-Deutsch, a former policeman, at
the time of the *Sanacja**), showed particular sadism and savagery. This
murderer was feared for a long time not only by the Jews, but also by the
Poles whom he tortured no less than the Jews.

*[Translator's note: A *Volks-Deutsch* was an ethnic German living in Poland. The *Sanacja*
was a nationalist political movement in Poland that emerged after the 1926 coup that brought
Józef Piłsudski back to power. The *Sanacja* was authoritarian and opposed parliamentary
democracy.]

* * *

Catching [Jews] for work became a daily phenomenon. The appearance of a
Jew in the street was connected to the danger of being caught for work and
beaten returning late. When walking in the street, everyone moved along at
the walls in order to be able to hurry into a gate and disappear in a moment of
danger. In addition, no one was secure at home, not knowing if he would be
successful in passing the day without pain.

On the 14th of September 1939 (the first day of Rosh Hashanah) hordes of
Hitlerists appeared in the thickly populated Jewish neighborhood and drove
the Jews out of all of the houses to work. This drive to work was accompanied
by various curses. The torturers would shout, "Lazy people, they wanted the

war," and then beat with murderous blows. Dante-like scenes were played out at the bridge that connected the center of the city with the Zawodzie suburb. Groups of Germans with rifles ready to shoot stood on both sides of the river. One division of Germans forced the Jews with blows from the rifle butts to crawl into the water fully dressed and pick out stones from the ground with bare hands. In a similar manner at a second place near the *Czenstochowianka* (textile factory), the Germans forced the Jews to drag out heavy, long beams from a destroyed bridge and to pull out the nails with their teeth. The 24-year old Yudl Granek[1] was shot for not wanting to carry out the order. This was the first bloody victim at work, which was to serve as a warning for everyone that no one shall dare to turn away from carrying out his orders.

Jews were grabbed in the streets; they were pulled from their residences and from the hiding places in the attics and cellars. No one knew where he was being chased, when he would return, how he would return and, in general, if he would return home again. Often after an entire day of work and pain, the same one would be pulled out of bed at night and driven to work again. Mostly the crowds who were driven to work had to march in rows and sing. Those who could not sing also moved their lips in order that the torturer, God forbid, might not notice that someone dared to not carry out their demands.

On a frosty Friday night of January 1940 the gendarmes of police battalion 72, which was stationed in the Narutowicz Synagogue, under the leadership of Chief Ambras and his close accomplices, *Hauptwachtmeister* [warrant officer] Cangrel and Kabak, surrounded several streets thickly populated by Jews and shouted: "*Juden raus* [Jews out]!" They started to enter the Jewish residences.

Thousands of men, women and mainly young girls were pulled from their beds and driven half naked to the large square in the new market. After holding them for hours in the cutting frost, the wounded, severely beaten and frozen people were allowed to go home. Those remaining, who had not had the "luck" to be beaten, wounded or to have frozen limbs, were sent to the large building of the Narutowicz Synagogue. Here, everyone was forced to undress completely naked. The officers as well as the simple gendarmes bullied them in a sadistic manner. The gendarmes carried out gynecological "examinations" of the women. In the morning a number of the Jews there were freed and those remaining were harnessed to various work. The next day, in the evening, they were allowed to go home. Five men did not return then and every trace of them disappeared.

* * *

The eviction of the Jews from their residences began as soon as the Germans took Czenstochow. Later, the frequent removal from individual houses as well as from entire streets began, which were made *judenrein* [free of Jews]. No one was certain if he would be there in the morning where he had just settled anew the night before. The eviction of the Jews from their residences took place in the following manner: All of the Jewish residents of these houses were driven out into the courtyard and were held there for as long as it took the Germans to loot everything they wanted from the residences. Then the Jews could remove what the Germans allowed and then leave their houses, not having any designated spot to go to live. The evicted Jews had to leave the furniture and other household items in the apartments they left.

Besides the fact that Jewish possessions were stolen during the deportations, individual Germans would visit Jewish residences on "their own" and take everything that pleased them. The first time, the still naïve Jews who were freed sought justice from the organs of the German regime, for which several paid with their lives. This happened to a certain Jew, Pelta from Ostrow and his wife, who had asked General Barimhercik that her household things, which the gendarmes of police battalion 72 had taken on the 28th of December 1939 from her residence, be returned.[2]

On the 25th of September 1939 the first day after Yom Kippur, uniformed young Germans began to demolish the old synagogue on Mirowska Street.

Many young *Volks-Deutsche* and other scoundrels actively took part in the demolition and looted everything that was found in the synagogue. This "sacred" handiwork lasted for three full days. On the fourth day only the walls of the synagogue remained. Even the doors, windows and floors were torn out.

On the 25th of December 1939 (*Boże Narodzenie* – Christmas) a pogrom was carried out against the Jews under the direction of the gendarmes and police battalion 72. When it started to get dark, hundreds of scoundrels left for the Jewish neighborhood and attacked the Jews who were in the street with wild screams, tossed stones at them and beat them with ice skates and sticks[3]. Many of the beaters also began to rob the shops and residents. In the course of one hour 1,000 windowpanes were knocked out and three shops were entirely looted.[4] Simultaneously the only Jewish cigarette kiosk owned by Kawa, the war invalid, was set on fire. Wild scoundrels, (probably German gendarmes who had changed their clothes) began to scream that Jews had hidden a weapons storehouse in the Jewish synagogue on Wilson Street (the so-called "German Synagogue"). Under this pretext the gendarmes blew up the synagogue and began to demolish the inner spaces. At around nine o'clock in the evening, the young scoundrels set fire to the synagogue and for a long time the gendarmes threw grenades into the fire until the entire building was enveloped in flames.

During the time that the tongues of fire rose to the sky, the same gendarmes arrested 20 men, among them two Jews on whom they threw the blame for the events. Early in the morning 19 of the arrestees were freed and the twentieth, a certain Stanislaw Dergowski, 16 years old, they brought to the State Court for taking part in the looting.[5] As a punishment it was ordered that the curfew hours were lengthened.[6]

In the morning of the 26th, the *S. S. Hauptscharführer* [squad leader], Ditman, sent a report to the security police of the Radom district about this pogrom. The report ended with the statement that "The largest number of those people who carried out this unrestrained behavior should be considered as lower people who search for such opportunities to rob and plunder." Ditman writes further in his report: "It cannot be ruled out that on New Year's Eve similar events will happen again."[7] The then chief of police battalion 72 (the actual leader of the pogrom) sent out a sizeable report. Among other words written in the report: "The hostile mood of the Jews can be seen in the fact that Jewish businessmen use New Year's Eve in order to raise the prices, as well as the fact that the number of Jews in Czenstochow keeps growing through constant emigration."

In the same report is also written: "This strengthening of the fire in the synagogue in many areas at once makes it impossible to carry out a search there for ammunition."[8] In the report, again from the city chief to the chief of the Radom district, it is said, that the pogrom was carried out by former students and this probably was the result of the sermons at the Jasna Góra [monastery in Czenstochow, home of the "Black Madonna"] during the service that took place on the 25th of December.[9] Thus appeared the official clarifications by the Germans, who themselves had organized the pogrom and carried it out with the help of the young outcasts. The purpose of the German pogrom provocations was three-pronged: to terrorize the Jewish population and to throw fear into the Poles one by one; second – to dirty the name of the Polish people abroad; third – the old well-known method of "divide and rule."

The majority of the documents given below are from the occupation, collected and hidden by the author. There are now partially found in the Archives of the Jewish Historical Institute in Warsaw, partially in a private archive.

The *Judenrat* and Its Authority

On the 16th of September 1939 the expert on Jewish matters with the Gestapo called to him Moshe Asz, Rabbi Nukhem Asz's son, and ordered that he give a list of former Jewish social workers who would also now be involved with Jewish matters. Moshe Asz gave the names of several former municipal community workers. On the same day, after the indicated men were ordered to appear in the premises of the Trade Bank on Pilsudski Street no. 3, where this speaker [the Gestapo Jewish expert] accepted them in the presence of two more Gestapo members. In the course of three hours, he kept "persuading" those called that the Jews are a people only of criminals, that they are hiding a large number of weapons in order to murder Germans and, to their knowledge, in Czenstochow itself the Jews had already murdered two German soldiers. He repeated several times in his long "speech" that the Jews did not have any hope of mercy from the Germans. According to his understanding it would be necessary to cleanse the entire Lublin area of non-Jews and move all of the Jews from all occupied areas here. He said that a Jewish state would be created there. In the end he declared to the Jews who stood before him: "Nevertheless, you know that a German regime exists here, what kind of relationship we have with the Jews is certainly known, so know that from today on and further, the Jews must support themselves and generate income!"

The Jews tried to make him aware that they did not see the possibilities for this because most prosperous Jews had left Czenstochow as soon as the war operation began; he began to curse them and shouted: "If you have less you'll eat less!" Right there he designated a council of six men: Moshe Asz, Leib Bromberg, Nusan-Dovid Berliner, Ahron-Josef Krojcer, Leib Kapinski and Dovid Koniecpoler.[10] He gave them five minutes in which to agree and to divide among themselves the functions of the chairman, vice chairman, secretary and treasurer. This council of six, on the order of the same member of the Gestapo, had to provide the number of Jewish workers and tradesmen that were demanded by the German regime organs. The council would also have to cover all of the expenses that would be connected with carrying out the work that the German municipal organs would decide.

On the 1st of October 1939, Kapinski, the chairman of the council of six, was called to the city chief. Here he was given notice that all of the Jews from Berlin, from all of Germany and from all of the cities and *shtetlekh* [towns] around Czenstochow that were annexed to the Reich would be brought to Czenstochow and the *Judenrat* would need to house them in the streets that run from the train bridge (the end of the First *Aleje*) up to the bridge over the Warta River (in 1941 these streets were designated as the Jewish ghetto). As a result Kapinski received an order that on that same day he had to put together a *Judenrat* [Jewish council] of 24 people who would have to deal with all of the Jewish matters and also with quartering all of the Jews transferred to Czenstochow. That day the council of six called together a meeting of about 100 Jews from the almost 25,000 who then lived in Czenstochow, who elected a *Judenrat* of the following 24 men: Leib Kapinski (a manufacturer, a Zionist community worker, a former managing committee member of the cultural society, *Lira* and a managing committee member of the Hebrew-Polish *gymnazie* [secondary school], Moshe Asz (rabbinate official), Nusan-Dovid Berliner (partner in an exchange bank), Mordekhai Beserglik (merchant), Ziskind Brandliewicz (teacher), Yehiel Gerichter (Zionist), Wolf Icek (Zionist), Nakhman Grynfeld and Josef Klajnplac (rabbinate members], Josef Braniatowski (lawyer), Leib Bromberg (manufacturer, *Mizrakhi* [Religious Zionist], Dovid Koniecpoler (a Zionist, an artisan activist), Ahron-Josef Krojcer (merchant), Jakob Lewit (manufacturer, vice president of *Mizrakhi* in Czenstochow), Shmuel Lewkowicz (engineer, house owner), Maurici Nojfeld (vice president of the Merchants and Manufacturers Union), Shmuel Niemerowski (president of the small merchants union), Natan Rodal (lawyer), Zelik Rotbard (merchant, Zionist), Jakob Roziner (bookkeeper, Democrat), Mikhal Ruczewicz (merchant), Adam Slonimski (*gymnazie* lecturer, assimilated), Gershon Szafir (Zionist, *kehile* [organized Jewish community] council man, *gymnazie* lecturer), and Wilhelm Czeriker (manufacturer).

The presidium of the *Judenrat* consisted of the following five members: L. Kapinski – chairman, L. Bromberg – vice chairman, N. D. Berliner – treasurer and presidium members without offices – Nojfeld and Gerichter.[11] The members of the *Judenrat* divided the various functions among themselves and started to organize their work.

During the second half of the month of November 1939 the then city chief, Dr. Wendler, ordered all members of the *Judenrat* to report to him immediately. As soon as they entered the building of the city chief they were surrounded by gendarmes and members of the Gestapo and placed in two rows. Then Wendler appeared and announced to them that the Jewish population must pay a 1,000,000 *zlotes* contribution over the course of 10 days. If this were not carried out during the designated term, 100 Jews would be shot. One group of members was freed in order to gather the designated sum and the second was taken to the city jail as hostages. In the course of the 10 designated days the freed members of the *Judenrat* taxed the Jews for this purpose and simultaneously carried out negotiations with Wendler that he decrease the sum of the contribution placed [on the Jews]. The *Judenrat* did not succeed in putting together the designated sum and it did not succeed in "softening" Wendler's heart. Therefore, on the 10th day all of the wives of the hostages were arrested and they were taken to a special camp with their husbands, which had been prepared for them in the city itself. On the 14th day they succeeded in ransoming [the hostages] with money and objects. The contribution was reduced to 400,000 *zl.*, which the *Judenrat* had to pay in installments.[12]

* * *

The authority and tasks of the *Judenrat* kept increasing. Therefore, the *Judenrat* created even more divisions. During 1940 the following divisions were active at the *Judenrat*: 1. Division of General Matters (presidium).

In the beginning, the leader of this division was Pohorille and, later, Gitler, the lawyer; 2. Chief Secretariat – the leader was the lawyer, Dr. Leib Asz, his representative – Avraham Fogel; 3. Request Office, leader – the lawyer Leon Gajzler; 4. *IRU (Inspekcja Ruchu Ulicznego* – traffic inspection) (Jewish police), leader – M. Galster; 5. Housing Office, 18 officials worked there under the leadership of Bernard Kohlenberger; 6. Requisition Office, under the leadership of the same Kohlenberger; 7. Trade and Artisan Division with eight officials. Leaders: M. Prafart and lawyer Ester Epsztajn; 8. Food Supply Leaders – former bank director – Pruszicki; 9. Registration and Statistics. This division arose in the month of January 1940. Employed here were 11 officials under the leadership of the lawyer, Marian Haspnfeld and Maurici Safirsztajn. At the end of 1940 these divisions under the same leadership grew into eight sections that employed 63 officials; 10. Division for Forced Labor, which fell upon various sections in which 102 officials were employed under the leadership of Moshe Kapinski; 11. Punishment Division, under the leadership of D. Kasman and two other officials: the lawyer M. Renenweter and Y. Rifsztajn; 12. Finance Division, leader Maurici Kacinel; 13. Social Aid, which employed 178 officials under the leadership of N. Radal; 14. Courts Commission. At the general meeting of all lawyers and apprentice lawyers that took place on the 26th of December 1939, it was decided to create this commission that would work to reconcile conflicts among the Jews and also serve with legal advice. This commission began its activities in January 1940. The chairman of this commission was the lawyer M. Konarski, representative – W. Rajchman and secretariat, W. Krakower and A. Radal. Twenty-six lawyers belonged to this commission during the first three months of 1940; at the end of 1940, the commission consisted of 35 members. Twenty-one male lawyers and two women, of them 16 were from Czenstochow and seven from other cities (refugees). Apprentices – five local and five refugees and two judicial apprentices. This division was independent and the *Judenrat* did not have any great influence there. In addition to the offices mentioned, still others existed at the *Judenrat*: a technical division, an economic division, a division for training in the trades and a division for religious matters.[13] All of these enumerated offices of the *Judenrat* were active during the entire course of time until the great expulsion (September 1942). At the end of 1940, the *Judenrat* selected Pohorille as the organizational chief who had supervision over all the offices, and Gitler as his representative.[14]

The *Judenrat* needed to be concerned not only with the internal life of the ghetto, but it also had to carry out all of the demands and orders of the German administrative organs, as well as from every other German office that was located in the city. Municipal construction work had to be carried out at its own cost and only using Jewish craft-specialists and with Jewish workers.

The *Judenrat* had to provide everything they needed to all Germans and their families who were already in Czenstochow: with skillfully remodeled and beautifully furnished homes, with linen, bedding, crockery, wallpaper and other things. Even the cleaning, furnishing and arranging the house of the former Akser *gymnazie* as a "down house" for Germans (house of shame – a brothel), to which women specially were brought from Germany, had to be organized by the *Judenrat* and paid for by the Jewish population. In order to carry out everything else that the Germans demanded, as well as to cover the costs connected with the internal work, the *Judenrat* placed heavy taxes on the Jewish population and requisitioned from Jewish residences not only what was needed by the Germans in a given moment, but much more, in order eventually to be ready to cover further orders. At the proposal of the *Judenrat*, the city chief ordered the arrest of the Jews who refused to pay the designated taxes and they would be held there until they paid the demanded tax sum. The circumstances of the contribution and the activity of the *Judenrat* in general, which the Jewish population felt still more, convinced a certain number of members of the council that they absolutely did not serve the Jewish population as they imagined in the beginning, but that they were a tool in the hands of the Germans at the expense of the Jews. Therefore, they began to turn away from the work, During the course of several months, the presidium of the *Judenrat* removed the following members for sabotaging the work: Asz, Razine, Beserglik, Brandlewicz, Broniatowski, Grynfeld, Klajnplac, Niemirowski, Ruszewicz and Szafir and one more (Y. Lewit), who traveled abroad. Appointed in their place were: Wolf Anisfeld (Zionist), Dovid Borzykowski (merchant), Maurici Galster (expeditor), Jeremy Gitler (lawyer, Zionist), Shmuel Kac (master tailor), Maurici Kacinel (independent), Moshe Kapinski (manufacturer), Bernard Kurland (proxy for a large firm), Shiman Paharille [alternately spelled Pohorille] (lawyer), Maurici Prapart (merchant) and Hilary Zandsztajn (estate owner). In addition to those, Shmuel Wajnrib (merchant), who was a man from the Gestapo and, therefore, was the liaison between the *Judenrat* and the Gestapo, was designated. Thus, at the beginning of 1940, the *Judenrat* consisted of 25 members.[15]

The composition of the presidium also changed. In the first quarter of 1940, the presidium of the *Judenrat* consisted of the following seven members: Leib Kapinski, Leib Bromberg, Dr. Shiman Pohorille, Nusan-Dovid Berliner, Yehiel Gerichter, Jeremy Gitler and Zelig Rotbart [alternately spelled Rotbard].[16] Bromberg died in 1941. The remaining composition of the entire council and the presidium remained until the large liquidation of the Czentochow Jewish community.

* * *

Edicts from the German regime organs appeared very often. One more severe than the other and decrees from the *Judenrat* appeared more often that reflected the orders of these regime organs. The response and reaction of the Jews to various edicts was not always the same. One of the first official edicts was the order to wear armbands. A decree was issued on the 15th of December 1939 that Jews from 14 years of age on must wear a white armband with the blue Star of David of 10 centimeters on the right arm over the elbow. It was not easy to become accustomed to this new "style." They were somewhat ashamed as if they had committed a crime in public. However, the feeling of shame little by little disappeared and they began to assert: "Why should we be ashamed, let those who thought it up be ashamed." Later, when one met Jews from the *shtetlekh* around Czenstochow with yellow Stars of David patches on their chests and on their backs, it was believed that we somehow were special because we had been humiliated less. It was not easy to accustom oneself to this and people would often forget to put the band on the arm before going outside in the street and this caused much pain. The Germans started to chase the "insubordinates," who would then pay for their "nerve" with money, with jail, or with both penalties together. In order to avoid such "surprises," a note hung in almost every house at the door to the outside with the inscription: Attention, arm-bands! A large blue Star of David had to hang in the window of every Jewish shop so that the non-Jewish customers would know which shops belonged to Jews. These arrangements were accepted indifferently by everyone because the non-Jewish population that had always bought from the Jews did not pay attention to this and the Jews were happy that the Germans would not come to shop.

On the 8th of April 1940, the city-chief supported by a decree of the 24th of January 1940 about the duty to report Jewish estates, ordered the Jewish population to register their movable and immovable possessions.

The city-chief announced that all Jews estates, as well as the possessions of converts and non-Jews who had Jewish husbands or Jewish wives, were included. A second edict from the city-chief about the same matter was published on the 7th of May 1940. All of these decrees did not make a great impression on the Jews in Czenstochow because after the beginning of March 1940 almost all Jewish possessions had been confiscated, all Jewish shops, except those selling produced goods, were already locked and the keys were located in the offices of the city-chief. Jews were not permitted to have more than 2,000 *zlotes* and, later, only 500.[18] The remainder of one's money had to be paid into the *K.K.O.* (Communal Savings Fund) for a savings account from which he had the right, only formally, to take up to 100 *zl.* each week for a livelihood. About six weeks later, on the 15th of April, the *Judenrat* created a requisition office, which was led by the then leader of the housing office, Bernard Kohlenbrener, who disregarded any sentiment. This institution requisitioned 6,964 pieces of furniture and other household articles from the Jews just from the 15th of April until the 5th of August 1940 and then during September.[19] On the 14th of June 1940 the city-chief ordered that the *Judenrat* gather together various metals up to three kilograms per family, or tin up to one and a half kilos from a family.[20] The *Judenrat* demanded of all administrators that in the course of 48 hours they gather from among the tenants in the houses that they manage, the demanded metal.[21] The Jews did not take this edict very seriously and the *Judenrat* increased the time for presenting the metal three times. Finally the *Judenrat* had to add a certain amount of metal from stores that were located in their warehouses. However, all of the enumerated demands and many others caused the poverty among the Jewish population to be felt even more. It is worthwhile mentioning that the bread ration per person allotted by the German and Austrian powers amounted to an average of 50 grams.[22] Later, the bread ration reached up to 100 grams per person, but not consistently.[23] The situation again became more dreadfully worse. There was suffering today and fear of tomorrow.

* * *

Because of frequent ousters from residences, houses, as well as entire streets, the *Judenrat*, in the first days of its work, created a housing office in which 18 officials were employed.

The leader of this office was Kohlenbrener, who with his elegant and beautiful German quickly found favor in German eyes and, therefore, used his influence personally for himself. The housing office hardly helped the poor and impoverished Jews, who were forced to seek a roof over their head. The refugees wandered around refugee points in so-called "refuges." The "refuges" were located in the synagogue on Mirowska Street 9-11, *Hakhnoses-Orkhim* [institution to help the poor and visitors] on Garncarska Street number 65, Artisans School on Garncarska no. 86, in a residence at the Old Market no. 18, in the prayer house on Berka Joselewicza Street no. 10, on Pilsudski Street no. 17, in the former premises of the Bund and in the former premises of the Zionist organization in *Aleje* Wolnosci no. 3-5. After a time, there were also "refuges" in the First *Aleje* no. 12 in the former premises of the artisans and in the premises of the *Makhzekei haDas* [those who inforce the law – an organization to improve education and observance] on Nadrzeczna Street.[24]

* * *

Czenstochow became an important location during the Second World War, where refugees arrived from various cities in Poland. The number of Jews, who amounted to 28,485[25] before the war, strongly increased during the years 1940, 1941 and 1942. Exactly how many refugees were in Czenstochow is not known. It is only known how many refugees arrived in the first 10 months of 1940 because until then the *Judenrat* did not cause difficulties for the refugees with registration and settling in Czenstochow. However, seeing that more poor refugees were arriving, the *Judenrat* carried out certain selections in order to avoid an excessive burden, in registering the newly arrived.[26] On the basis of an edict from the city-chief, the city hall did not register the newly arrived Jews. It is written in the second volume Statistical Yearbook *(Rocznik Statystyczny)* of the *Judenrat* of 1940: the food division maintains only the residents who are registered with city hall. As reported by the statistical office of the *Judenrat*, 3,252 refugees arrived in Czenstochow. Among the refugees were 1,791 men and 1,461 women. Of them, 676 were children up to 14 years old and 154 old people over 66.[27] A large number of these refugees came from Lodz, 1,116 men; from Krakow – 771; from Warsaw – 106; from Radomsk – 283 and the rest came from other cities in Poland, such as Gdansk, Lublin, Kielce, Radom, from *shtetlekh* and villages around Czenstochow and from various other cities and *shtetlekh* in Poland. Not all of the refugees came from the places from which they arrived. Many of them had changed their places of residence several times during the war.[28] Former residents, who left Czenstochow at the beginning of the war, had arrived. Three thousand former residents returned just during the time from the 1st of January 1940 to the 31st of December 1940.[29] Several also came, who had family or acquaintances here with whom they expected to receive a temporary refuge.

Many refugees came to Czenstochow during the course of the years 1940 and 1941, about which we can draw the following facts:

On the 20th of January the inner managing committee in the district in Radom asked the city-chief about the possibility of Czenstochow taking those deported from the territory within the boundaries of the German Reich. On the 8th of March 1940 Wendler answered that Czenstochow had already taken 5,173 forced evacuees and in addition there were 16,000 refugees still present from earlier. On the 14th of May an order came that the Radom district would have to take 20,000 additional refugees and Jews, as well as 500 gypsies. On the 18th of July, the General Government demanded a report from the city-chief about the number deported to Czenstochow. On the 25th of July Wendler sent an answer that the city was over-populated because there were now 14,035 homeless people that had appeared, among them 6,224 Poles and 7,811 Jews. In addition, Wendler reported that there were no arrivals mentioned that can be evaluated: Poles from four to five thousand and Jews from 12 to 15 thousand. It was recorded in Wendler's notes from a "service discussion" and it was discussed there, that 38,000 people would be evacuated, among whom would be found 10,000 Jews from Vienna, from the 1st of February 1941 to the 30th of April of the same year from the incorporated parts of the Reich and from other parts of the area of the Reich.[30] Exactly how many of all of the refugees actually arrived in Czenstochow and how many of them were Jews is unknown. However, it was known by every resident of Czenstochow that during the entire time of the occupation, that in one arrival in Czenstochow of Jewish refugees, there were both illegal and deported, that the Germans sent in from the cities and *shtetlekh* that they made *judenrein* [clean of Jews].

In the month of February and March of 1941 2,300 Jews were deported from Plonsk and Bodzanow to Czenstochow. At the end of February 1941, 780 Jews from Plonsk were held on the train-line between Konicepol and Zloty-Potok, from where they escaped and came to Czenstochow. The Germans brought 1,200 Jews from Bodzanow and 500 Jews from Plonsk to Czenstochow; they were held on the ramp during the 7th and 8th of March and finally permitted to enter the city when the city-chief gave this his agreement.[31] However much larger the number of Jews grew, the Germans shrunk the Jewish living area in the city. At the beginning of 1940 the Jews, who lived here before the war in almost all 400 streets of the city, were pushed into only 84 streets. During the first half of 1941 the Jews were pushed into only 28 streets that were designated as the ghetto for the Jews in Czenstochow.

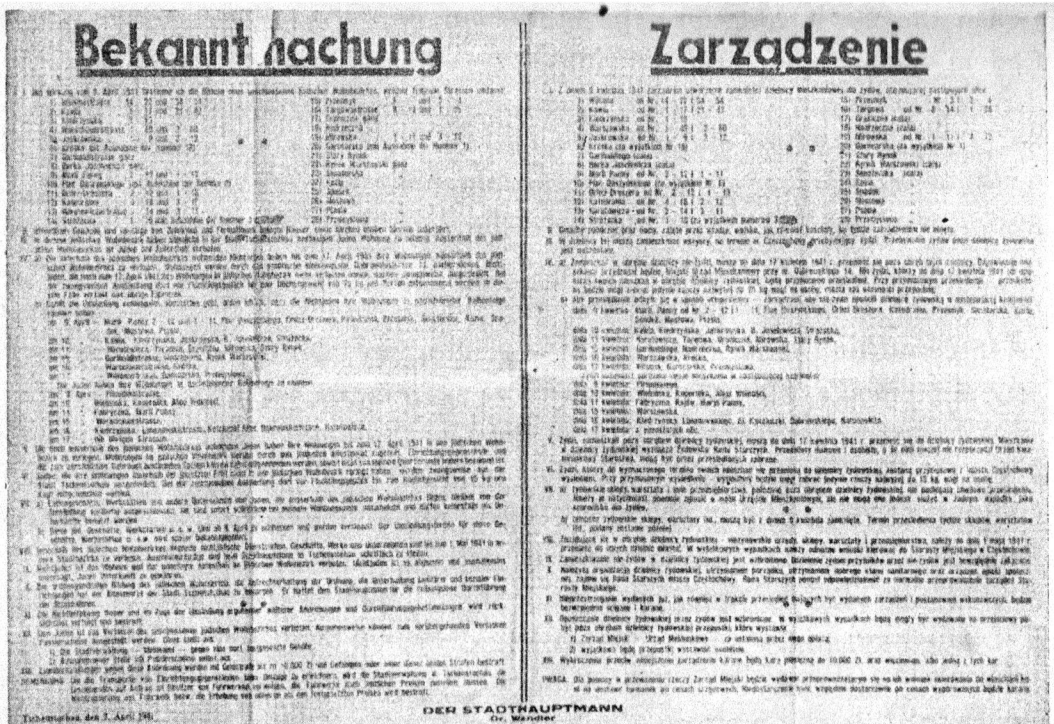

Ordinance issued by the city chief in German and Polish

Footnotes

1. Reported his time by eyewitness Birenholc.

2. Personal written requests to the Judenrat [Jewish council] by the Barenhercyk and Pelta families.

3. Written report of Police Battalion 72 on the 26th of December 1939.

4. Written report of the city chief on the 17th of December 1939.

5. Written report of the Gestapo on the 27th of December 1939.

6. Written report of the city chief on the 26th of December 1939.

7. Written reports of the Gestapo and Police Battalion 72.

8. Written reports of the Gestapo and Police Battalion 72.

9. Written reports of the Gestapo and Police Battalion 72.

10. Reports of the time by eyewitnesses Moshe Asz and Jakov Rozine.

11. Statistical Book of *Judenrat* [Jewish council] Volume I.

12. Reports of the time by Jakov Rozine.

13. Statistical Book of *Judenrat* [Jewish council] Volume I, II and III.

14. Statistical Book of *Judenrat* [Jewish council] Volume I page 12.

15. Statistical Book of *Judenrat* [Jewish council] Volume I page 11.

16. Statistical Book of *Judenrat* [Jewish council] Volume I page 11.

17. Statistical Book of *Judenrat* [Jewish council] Volume II pages 228, 259.

18. Statistical Book of *Judenrat* [Jewish council].

19. Statistical Book of *Judenrat* [Jewish council] Volume I page 68.

20. Statistical Book of *Judenrat* [Jewish council] Volume II page 250.

21. Statistical Book of *Judenrat* [Jewish council] Volume II page 250.

22. Written message from the *Judenrat* [Jewish council] to the city chief.

23. Letter from the city chief to the *Judenrat* [Jewish council].

24. Statistical Book of *Judenrat* [Jewish council] Volume III pages 406-412.

25. Report of the Evidence Division of the City Managing Committee no. A-891/I/47.

26. Statistical Book of *Judenrat* [Jewish council] Volume II page 126.

27. Statistical Book of *Judenrat* [Jewish council] Volume II pages 163-165.

28. Statistical Book of *Judenrat* [Jewish council] Volume II pages 167-168.

29. Statistical Book of *Judenrat* [Jewish council] Volume II page 135.

30. Report from the city chief.

31. Daily report of the city chief of the 24th of March 1941 no. 41/17.

The Ghetto

On the 22nd of February 1941, Kadner, the then representative of the city chief, sent to Dr. Lash, the chief of the Radom District, two plans for arranging a ghetto for Jews in Czenstochow. The first plan provided for a surrounding fence of brick with iron and barbed wire. It also required 14,000 workdays; this was connected with a cost of 190,000 *zlotys*. The second plan provided a wooden surrounding fence with iron and barbed wire, for which was demanded 7,000 workdays and this was connected with a cost of 120,600 *zlotys*. Kadner based these plans on a specially worked out plan of the 15th of February 1941 from the municipal construction office.[32]

On the 29th of March 1941, a *Dienstbesprechung* [official meeting] took place at [the office of the] chief of the Radom District, Dr. Lash, with the county chiefs of the Radom District, at which Lash reported about the "thorough and energetic preparations to attack the Soviet Union" and simultaneously announced that on the 5th April 1941 the entire Radom District had to carry out a *Judenaktsia*" [action against the Jews] of creating a Jewish "residential area."[33] On the same day the *Judenrat* also reported that on the basis of the order of the regime the following streets had become prohibited to the Jewish population: Alee from house number 26 on the even side and 27 on the odd side and higher, Kosciuszko Street, Kilinski Street, Waszyngton Street, the entire even side of Alee-Wolnosci, Pilsudski Street and Sobieski Street.[34]

On the 9th of April 1941 a decree from the city chief, Dr. Wendler, was published about a closed residential district for Jews. This edict was printed on large red placards and directed: "On the 9th of April 1941 I order the creation of a closed residential quarter for Jews which includes the following streets: Wilson Street from number 14 to 22 and from 34 to 54; Kawia Street from number 1 to 17 and 21 to 43; Krakowska – from number 1 to 9 and from 2 to 12; Krotka Street except number 16; Garibaldi Street, Berka Joselewicza Street; the first Alee from number 2 to 12 and from 1 to 11; Dazcinski Square except number 8; Orlicz-Dreszer Street from number 2 to 12 and from 1 to 13; Katedralna – from number 4 to 18 and from 3 to 17; Narutowicz Street from number 2 to 14 and from 3 to 11; Strazacka – from number 1 to 19 except number 3; Przesmyk – from number 2 to 4 and number 3; Targowa from 8 to 14 and from 1 to 25; all of Nadrzeczna Street, Mirowska – from 1 to 11 and from 4 to 12; all of Garncarska Street except number 1, the old market, Rinek

Warsawski, Senatorska, Koczospadek, Mostowa, Ptusza and Przemyslowa." It says further in the edict that the movement of all of the Jews into the enumerated streets and the withdrawal of the Poles from the mentioned streets would last until the 17th of April. The Jews who do not carry out the edict during the designated term will be deported from the city and will not have the right to take more than 25 kilos of baggage each. The Poles who live in the designated ghetto streets will be withdrawn by force and will not have the right to take more than 25 kilos each with them.[35] The number of Polish families that needed to withdraw from the ghetto reached 255, which numbered 3,309 souls.[36]

On the 17th of April 1941 the Jewish policemen, who were placed at all of the border points of the ghetto, did not let out any Jews from it without written permission from the German regime organs. Even the members of the *Judenrat* had to show such permission when crossing the border points of the ghetto.[37] However, the complete closing of the ghetto was drawn out until the 23rd of April 1941.

On the 23rd April 1941, posts with large yellow panels with the inscriptions turned to the ghetto in German, Polish and Hebrew were erected at several border points: "Closed residential district. Death penalty for leaving ghetto." It is not known exactly how many Jews were in Czenstochow then. According to what was provided by the Division of Evidence and Statistics of the *Judenrat*, officially there were 32,744 Jews.[38]

According to an attached note to Wendler's decree (written by hand), 2,100 Jewish families that numbered 9,600 souls and 35 non-Jewish family members had to move into the ghetto. According to the same note there were then 35,591 declared Jews and 1,500 undeclared. At that time in the circle of the *Judenrat* there was talk that during the creation of the ghetto, there were almost 40,000 Jews. So about 40,000 Jews were pushed into the poorest city quarter.

* * *

For the Jews, moving through the ghetto streets was connected with pain and insults. Many Germans, mainly military men, would come into the ghetto in order to observe the "amazing sight." Jews received blows for "impertinence" in walking on the sidewalks, for not taking off their hats for a German. It was never known how it was best to act in order to avoid blows.

On the 25th of April 1941 the city chief (probably at the intervention of the *Judenrat*) turned to the military commandant [indicating] that "soldiers are taking pleasure in strolling in the ghetto." ... "This running around the ghetto from pure curiosity" – he wrote in this application – "is not only unworthy, but also dangerous and, therefore, it is forbidden."[39] Four days later, the 29th of April, the commandant alerted the soldiers that because of the threatening danger of contagion from a typhus epidemic only servants were permitted to enter the ghetto.[40] The plague of "curious" visitors did not end.

On the 4th of May 1941 the city chief received a demand from Radom to present a detailed report of the ghetto created for Jews up to the 10th of May.[41] A detailed report came from Wendler, which covers six sides of typewritten pages about the matter, how he assembled the ghetto. Among other things, he praises himself: "...the typhus epidemic that was brought here with the last Jewish transport (he meant the Plocker and Bodzanower – L.B.), is at an end. I believe that there will be no new cases if I am not sent any further repugnant transport, totally lousy and dirty Jews sent to the city because those other county and city chiefs do not want to take them.[42]

The Jews from various cities also came to the enclosed ghetto. According to the order of the city chief of the 5th of August 1941, the result was that on the 1st of July 941 of the general number of the Czenstochow population, which then was made up of 164,567 [people], there were 37,667 enrolled Jews.[43]

According to the statement of the magistrate, 37,371 food cards for Jews were given out at the end of 1941. In the same statement it was noted that for various reasons up to 20 percent of the Jews were not registered and did not received food cards.[44] According to this, it appears that there were more than 40,000 Jews in Czenstochow at the end of 1941. Therefore, the crowdedness in the ghetto was felt not only in the residences, but also in the streets. On orders from the Germans, the Jewish police began to be occupied with regulating the movement in the ghetto alleys. They chased the small traders who mainly consisted of the young and children; they did not permit gathering in the streets; they did not allow sitting on the benches in the part of the First *Aleje* that belonged to the ghetto and, in the evenings, dispersed those strolling. A curfew was added to this that always was earlier for the Jews than for the non-Jewish population in the city. Every night, before the designated curfew, the Jewish police began to chase them from the streets and then the horse drawn ambulance of the *Schutzpolizei* ["protection police"] would appear. The gendarmes started chasing after the Jews across the ghetto streets like dog beaters. Every Jew who was not in his house by then was dragged into the ambulance and taken to be guarded at a "place for the night." In the morning, those caught had to pay a penalty and then were sent to work.

Zusammenstellung der ung. Materialienmassen und Baukosten.

L. N.	Vorgesehene Arbeit.	der Einer	Anzahl		Alternative 1. Materialienbedarf				Alternative 2. Materialienbedarf				Ung. Baukosten	
			gem. d. Alt 1	gem. d. Alt 2	Holz. m³	Eisen kg	Stacheldraht l. m.	Mauer m³	Holz m³	Eisen kg	Stacheldraht l. m.	Mauer m³	Alt. 1 zl.	Alt. 2 zl.
1.	Hölzener Zaun 3.o m hoch mit den Pfosten ⌀16cm und Brettern 2.5 cm stark	l. m.	2362	1772	500	—	750	—	400	—	5400	—	94 480	70 800
2.	Pfosten ⌀ 16 cm je 2.5 m mit Stacheldrath	l. m.	550	550	40	—	13200	—	40	—	13200	—	ohne Sta- cheldrath 3 500	ohne Sta- cheldrath 3 500
3.	Vergitterung der Öffnungen auf dem Abschnitt A-B	l. m.	—	556	—	—	—	—	—	20000	—	—	—	97 300
4	Vergitterung einzelner Öffnungen	m²	76	76	—	250	—	—	—	2500	—	—	9 120	9 120
5.	Mauer 3 m hoch 30 cm stark	l. m.		408	—	—	—	122	—	—	—	216	5 500	10 000
	Zusammen				540	2500	20700	122	440	22500	18600	216	112 600	190 800
													120 000	200 000

Bemerkungen: 1) gemäss der Alternative 1 Abschnitt A-B ist mit der hölzerner Umzäunung vorgeschen
gemäss der Alternative 2 Abschnitt A-B ist mit der Vergiterung aller Öffnungen und Ver- mauerung der Strassen vorgesehen
2) die in der Alternative 1 vorgesehene hölzerne Umzäunung des Abschnites A-B ist leichter und schneller zu erledigen.
Die Arbeitsdauer beträgt nach Alternative 1 ca 7000 Arbeiter-tage; nach Alt, 2 bis 14000.

Tschenstochau, den 15. 2. 1941 J.   St. Bauamt

Notifications: *Compilation of materials and building costs
***Notice *Elders Council in Czenstochow**

The ghetto was located on the east side of the city. This region was connected to the suburbs of Zawodzie and Rakowa from the center of the city. The Polish population, which lived in these suburbs, therefore had to walk through the ghetto and this permitted Jews to maintain contact with the Poles, which the German Police Directorate could not bear. On the 11th of August 1941 the German Police Directorate turned to the city chief with a proposal that a notice board be placed on the outside in German and Polish at all border points of the ghetto, without exception, with the inscription: "*Yidisher Wohnbezirk* [Jewish Residential Area], non-Jews are forbidden to remain in this residential area. Violations will be severely punished." Understand that the city chief agreed with a provision that only the word *Zeichen-Gefahr* [sign of danger] should appear on the board.[45] On the 15th of August 1941, 30 such signs were erected at all of the border points of the ghetto and no Poles were allowed to go through without special permission.

OBWIESZCZENIE

Na skutek zarządzenia Władz zamknięte zostały dla ludności żydowskiej następujące ulice:
        N. M. Panny od nr. 26—27 w górę,
        Al. Kościuszki,
        Kilińskiego,
        Washingtona,
        Al. Wolności strona parzysta,
        Pułaskiego,
        Sobieskiego.
    Osoby, zamieszkałe na tych ulicach, lub mające tam swe sklepy,
warsztaty, lub miejsca pracy, mogą zgłosić się po przepustki do Wydziału Rejestracji i Statystyki, ul. Katedralna 7, front II piętro, pokój
Nr. 1, w dnie powszednie w godzinach 9—12 i 15—17. (W soboty tylko
od 9 do 12) lub do Wydziału Administracyjnego Zarządu Miejskiego.
    Koszt przepustki wynosi Zł. 10.—.
                     Przewodniczący Rady Starszych
                     (—) w. z. Dr. Sz. Pohorille
Częstochowa, dnia 29 marca 1941 roku.

                                      23. 12. 1941

Dr. W./Gä. —
              An
      den Herrn Staatsanwalt beim Sondergericht
                      in Tschenstochau.
    In der Anlage übermittle ich 4 Gnadengesuche des Altestenrates
von Tschenstochau mit der Bitte um Weiterleitung an die für die Begna-
digung zuständige Stelle, den Herrn Generalgouverneur in Krakau.
    Meine persönliche Stellungnahme geht dahin, dass ja durch das Ge-
richt die Einwendungen wohl vollkommen geprüft worden sind. Ich
stelle jedoch amtlich fest, dass erst nach dem Straffälligwerden der Ge-
suchsteller am Ausgang des Ghettos in deutsch, polnisch und hebräisch
die Androhung der Todesstrafe angebracht werden konnte. Es war
jedoch zweifellos vorher schon bekannt was dem Juden blüht, der
widerrechtlich das Ghetto verlässt.
4 Anlagen.

                                        26. Juni 1941

Dr. W/Br/447/41
          Herrn
          Gouverneur Dr. L a s c h
                       R a d o m
    Sehr geehrter Herr Gouverneur!
    Ich habe eine Reihe von Berichten bekommen, dass gegenwärtig die
jüdische Propaganda auf dem flachen Lande eine ganz intensive ist
und dass die Juden, die ja nur in den grossen Städten in Wohnviertels
zusammengeschlossen sind, während sie in den Landstädten ungeniert
wie bisher hausen, durch das Flache Land ziehen und dabei nicht nur
schieben und wuchern, sondern auch Propaganda machen. So wird den
Polen Angst eingeflösst vor einer langen Dauer der kriegerischen Aus-
einandersetzung mit Russland. Es wird auch der Gedanke in die Masse
geworfen, dass dieses grosse russische Reich mit seinen unerhörten Men-
schenmassen eben vielleicht doch siegen würde und wenn schon nichts
anderes erreicht wird, so zumindest das eine, dass der Bauer mit seinen
Produkten zurückhält, aus dem Zloty flüchtet und damit die Ernährungs-
lage immer schwieriger gestaltet wird. Es müsste im gegenwärtigen
Zeitpunkt, und das bitte ich Sie, Herr Gouverneur, zu erwägen, eine
absolut strenge Zusammenfassung aller Juden erfolgen, die Einweisung
in geschlossene Wohngebiete, gleichgültig ob das nun in irgendeinem
Gebiet erfolgt, jedenfalls müsste in jeder Kreishauptmannschaft eine
jüdische geschlossenes Wohnviertel bestehen, damit das Herumziehen
der Juden radikal unterbunden wird.
                        Heil Hitler Herr Gouverneur!
                            Ihr ergebener

Polizei — Direktion
— Abt. V. Tgb. Nr. 5037/41
Tschenstochau, den 11. 8. 1941.
An den Herrn Stadthauptmann
hier. Betr.: Absperrung des jüdischen Wohnbezirks.
Bezug: Ohne.

Die Erfahrung hat gezeigt, dass die Absperrung des jüdischen Wohnbezirks durch Ordnungsleute des jüdischen
Ordnungsdienstes allein nicht genügt. Diese Ordnungsleute
haben zwar bisher- im ganzen gesehen- gewährleistet, dass
Juden den Wohnbezirk ohne Passierschein nich verlassen,
es war jedoch nicht gewährleistet, dass sich Nichtjuden im
jüdischen Wohnviertel nicht unbefugt aufhalten.

Ich halte es daher für dringend erforderlich, dass die
Grenzen des jüdischen Wohnbezirks auch nach aussen er-
kennbar werden und schlage deshalb vor, dies durch Auf-
stellung von Schildern nachzuholen.
Wortlaut der Schilder: (deutsch und polnisch)
Jüdischer Wohnbezirk
Nichtjuden ist der unbefugte Aufenthalt in diesem
Wohnbezirk verboten.
Zuwiderhandlungen werden schwer bestraft.
Der Stadthauptmann
Grösse der Schilder: 60 mal 40 cm
Farbe: gelbe Grundfarbe, schwarze Schrift.

Insgesamt werden 30 Schilder benötigt. Bei der Berech-
nung dieser Zahl bin ich davon ausgegangen, dass die Haupt-
einfallstrassen recht **und links** beschildert werden.

Ich halte dies deshalb für erforderlich, um einmal mit
Nachdruck auf den Sperrbezirk hinzuweisen und zum an-
deren sollen diese Schilder die Absperrung im Hinblick auf
die Lage des Wohnbezirks z. Zt. nicht durchführbarer ist.

Schliesslich wäre noch zu erwägen, ob es nicht möglich
ist, die verhältnismässig geringe Zahl der restlichen jüdischen Wohnhäuser in der Kathedralnastrasse von den jüdischen Familien zu räumen, sodass diese Strasse aus dem
jüdischen Wohnviertel herausgekommen werden könnte.
Dies hätte den Vorteil, dass der gesamte Fahrverkehr in
Richtung Olstyn und Rakow nicht mehr das jüdische Wohnviertel zu berühren brauchte. Diese Massnahme läge nicht
zuletzt im Interesse der Schleichhandelsbekämpfung.

Ich bitte, die Aufstellung der Schilder zu genehmigen
und werde alsdann ihre Aufstellung von hier aus veranlassen.

Dr. W/Br   18. August 1941.
1) Schreibe

An die
Polizeidirektion
im Hause
Betr.: Absperrung des jüdischen Wohnbezirks.
Bezug: Ihr Schreiben vom 11. August 1941 Abt. V Tgb. Nr
5037/41.
Ich bin absolut damit einverstanden, dass Ihrem
Vorschlag entsprechend Schilder angebracht werden. Ich er-
suche nur unter der Aufschrift „Jüd'scher Wohnbezirk" noch
anzubringen das Wort „Seuchengefahr". Sonst bin ich mit
dem Wortlaut vollkommen einverstanden.
Was die Freimachung der Katedralna anlangt, so
bitte ich um Ihre Unterlagen wieviel Familien, bzw. Köpfe
hier für die Umsiedlung in Frage kommen. Es ist Tatsache,
das die Freimachung wenigstens hier nicht durch das Ghetto leisten zu müssen. Wenn Sie die notwendigen Unterlagen
haben, bitte ich um Rücksprache.

ÄLTESTENRAT in TSCHENSTOCHAU || RADA STARSZYCH w CZĘSTOCNOWIE

MARIENALLEE 11.   "ALEJA 11.

Tel. 13-47. Zentrale || Centrala
13-56 Technische Abt. || Wydz. Techniczny.
13-46 Arbeitseinsatz || Wydz. Robót Przymus. (Marienallee 9)

Nr 4281/42   Tschenstochau, 17 Juni   1942
                         Częstochowa,

An den

    Herrn Stadthauptmann

        in Tschenstochau.

      In Befolgung des Scheibens von 11, VI. 1942 legt der Aeltestenrad nachstehende Unterlagen in zweifacher Ausfertigung vor:

      1.— Eine Statistiche Übersicht über die Belegung des jüd. Wohnbezirkes in Tschenstochau

      2. — Einen Lage-plan des jüd. Wohnbezirkes nach geschlossenen Häuserblocks geordnet als Ergänzung der Statistischen Übersicht. Die Häuserblocks sind durch entsprechende Farbennuancen abgezeichnet und besonders numeriert.—Die Numerationen des Lageplanes und Statistischen Übersicht sind gleichlautend.—

      3 — Einen Lage plan des jüd. Wohnbezirkes mit Häuserbezeichnungen schlechthin.
2 Beilagen.

               Der Vorsitzande des Aeltestenrates.

DO ODCZYTANIA NA ODPRAWACH CODZIENNYCH!

OKÓLNIK

      Zarządzam i przypominam, że obowiązkiem każdego funkcjonariusza Żydowskiej Służby porządkowej, pełniącego służbę na wylotowych punktach dzielnicy, jest żądanie okazywania przepustek lub innych dokumentów, upoważniających do opuszczenia dzielnicy.

      Odnosi się to również do znanych osób oficjalnych — aż do p. Prezesa Rady Starszych włącznie.

               Częstochowa, dnia 8. sierpnia 1941 r

However, in order for the Poles who lived in the suburbs of Zawodzie and Rakowa to be able to have a connection to the city center, Strazacka Street and a part of Katedralna were cut off from the ghetto, and they connected to the city center from the streets that bordered on the named suburbs. However, the decreased ghetto area became thickly populated with almost 1,500 Jews who again lost the roofs over their heads.[46]

On the 24th of December at the start of the evening, Germans in uniforms and civilian clothing attacked the ghetto streets and without a reason beat every Jew that they met. Jews who wore fur coats or coats with fur collars had to take them off in the street and then they were allowed to go home. The account of the fur coats immediately spread through the ghetto and the people arranged a "night watch." We sat the entire night behind firmly closed doors and curtained windows and released with the smoke [burned] old inherited furs, silver foxes, expensive otter collars, as well as new modern Persian lamb and skunk coats. Not all Jews knew that they should burn everything, not all Jews wanted to burn the furs because they believed that they would be left with something. Early in the morning the *Judenrat* announced that by virtue of the decree of the regime all of the Jews must give up their furs and every piece of fur that they possessed. The *Judenrat* also received an order from the city chief that it needed to gather the fur goods and to engage Jewish artisans at its own expense, who were to renovate and adapt the furs to the needs of the German army. Many Jews hid their furs in attics and cellars and even buried them. Several made connections with Polish acquaintances and smuggled out the furs; others sold their furs for *groshns*. There were also those who were not very worried about this decree and believed that the edict about taking the furs would pass and they could be used later. There were several who failed to obey in the last cases, for which they paid with their lives. The *Oberleutnant* [lieutenant colonel] of the gendarmerie, Frankowski, who came from the Poznan area, was in charge of the action of confiscating the furs from the Jews. There were three large rooms filled with confiscated furs. The rooms were locked and guarded by the Jewish police until the prominent men chose the most expensive and the nicest furs for themselves, for their lovers in Czenstochow itself and for their wives and children somewhere in Germany. The *Judenrat* had to organize Jewish furriers who remodeled the remaining furs according to the instructions of the city chief.

Thus, new blows that upset and made life repugnant came all the time.
The blows came often and were even more exact. However, we became
accustomed to each affliction. We shook off each precise blow and again pulled
the heavy, cruel wagon of life, waiting full of agitation about what morning
would bring.

Call to the Jewish population – notice about forced labor

Forced Labor

The *Judenrat* had to provide a certain number of workers and tradesmen for various *platzowkes* [temporary labor camps] every day. In addition, Jews were caught in the street and taken away for various labor and Jews also would be removed from their residences for the same purpose. The labor office was created at the *Judenrat* at the end of 1939 so that it could direct this matter.

On the basis of the ordinance of the general governor on the 26th of October 1939 about the forced labor for Jews, the city chief demanded on the 9th of March that all Jews (as well as converts to Christianity), who were born in the years 1914 to 1923 inclusively register with the *Judenrat*..[47] On the 2nd of April 1940 came a second demand signed by Wendler that those Jews born in the years 1879 to 1925 also must register..[48] On the 11th of May 1940 a decree from the city chief's office was again published, signed by Kadner, that the summoning of Jews for forced labor had begun..[49] In July 1940 the German labor office, making use of the 10 Jewish officials, took over the organization of forced labor of the Jews. This office then had in its possession the files of all of the Jews aged from 12 to 60..[50] The labor office that existed at the *Judenrat* was subjugated to the German labor office. The illusion of the *Judenrat* that the Jewish division for forced labor would control the chaotic situation of grabbing people in the streets and would alleviate the situation was quickly turned upside down because this division was simply converted into a work branch of the German office in the city and from time to time the *Judenrat* and its labor office sent out the Jewish police across the ghetto in order to provide the number of Jewish workers demanded by the Germans.

During the course of both periods of registration, 8,330 men registered. Among the registrants were men who had no children – 38.3 percent; fathers of only one child – 32.7 percent; fathers who had two children – 19.1 percent; the remaining had three, four, five, six, seven and eight children. There were six fathers of seven children and one father of eight children, who was 39 years old..[51] The registered were divided into six groups: merchants, traders, manufacturers, unqualified workers, students and private officials were counted in the first group; artisans in the second group; building workers, water installers, concrete workers, bricklayers, painters, tinsmiths and so on in the third group. Agricultural workers and gardeners in the fourth group; doctors, lawyers, teachers in the fifth; technicians with higher education in the sixth. The general total of the registration was the following: merchants – 50.4

percent; artisans – 40.96 percent; free professions [medicine, law] – 3.97 percent; building artisans – 2.67 percent; agricultural workers – 1.07 percent and technicians – 0.93 percent..[52] All of those perfectly capable of working were 64.3 percent; less capable – 22.5 percent. The largest number of the healthy were in the third and fourth groups..[53]

The first time the workers were sent to forced labor at the local *platzowkes*. There were 120 such workplaces. The largest *platkowkes* were: German Police, swimming pool and sport place, city chief's office, military, German school, railroad, city hall, Polish police, delousing institution, airport, district administrator's office, immigration central, municipal theater and post office. At the beginning everyone had to work one day a week. Those who wanted to be freed from the work had to pay four *gildn* for the day of work. No one was supposed to provide a substitute on his own. The labor office of the *Judenrat* chose substitutes from among those who presented themselves for work for the purpose of earning money. Such workers received 24 *zlotys* for six days of work a week, from which four *zlotys* were subtracted for the other day of the week that had to be given for forced labor. The motivation for this action by the *Judenrat* was that each must carry identical duties..[54] Each received an order on the designated workday on which it was shown: when, where, at what time and with which work tools the given person had to appear. Because of the great and growing need, the labor office of the *Judenrat* gave notice for more Jews for paid work as demanded by the German labor office. For this reason, no difficulties were made for those who wanted to pay for their day of forced labor. .[55]

On average, in 1940, 2,624 forced laborers were employed, in 1941 – 4,798 and from the 15th of December 1941 to the 22nd of September 1942, 7,595 men were employed daily for forced labor in the local *platzowkes*.

Besides providing workers for the *platzowkes* in Czenstochow itself, the *Judenrat* had to provide a certain number of workers for the labor camps of Przyrów (near Czenstochow), Cieszanow and Wereszyn (near Lublin). Three hundred Jewish workers, who had to regulate the river there and drain the swamps, were sent out to Przyrów in June 1940..[56] Everyone who had been chosen by the Jewish labor office to be sent out to Przyrów had an order that asserted: "Order to forced labor in the water management committee. On the basis of the decree of the 26th of October, 1930, you are ordered to report at the assembly place on Pilsudski Street, nos. 13-15, 5:30 in the morning. They must take a blanket, a pillow, a spoon, a deep dish and a cup with them." It was signed by the Jewish Forced Labor Command. This group of 300 men consisted of men from 18 to 35. They lived in the synagogues and barracks; they worked for 10 hours a day and received food three times a day. In the morning, up to 30 *deka* [10 units] of bread and coffee; a little cooked food during the day. The first transport of workers was held in Przyrów for two months; after this term, because of the need, a number voluntarily remained longer and the number that was lacking was up to 300 men. The Jewish labor office again provided them by force..[57] At first the security service strongly mistreated the workers. They would beat everyone who appeared under them as they worked. The workers were forced to sing while marching to and from work. Little by little they succeeded in making the hearts of the guards "softer" with [the payment of] money and life in that camp became bearable. The Jewish residents of Przyrów also did everything to ease the life of those forced laborers, helping them with food and arranging better living conditions.

At the beginning of August 1940, the *Judenrat* was ordered to present 1,000 workers to be sent to Wereszyn and Cieszanow (Lublin area) for the labor camps there. The first transport consisted of 450 men, the second – of 460. Both transports consisted of men up to 30 years of age..[58] The transports were taken to Lublin in freight wagons accompanied by gendarmes.

In Lublin, they were surrounded by members of the *S.S.* who immediately treated them with blows when they climbed out of the wagons and they were taken to barracks in which there already were thousands of Jews from other cities. During the march to the barracks, those accompanying those who were taken from the transport removed one of them and placed a brass fireman's hat on his head, gave him a trumpet and ordered him to march in front and play. Everyone marching after him had to sing based on his rhythm. After this, the entire transport of Jews from Czenstochow who were there earlier were taken to the barracks in Belzec, where there were other transports of Jews and Gypsies. From there, everyone again was driven on foot to Cieszanow. Mordekhai Lewkowicz, one of the survivors of this transport, relates: "...we had to run uphill, then we had to go downhill slowly. Whoever stopped on the road was shot immediately. We were driven into a building ruin in Ruskie Piaski, where dozen of Jews who had been shot lay. From there we were then driven on foot to Cieszanow, where we were yoked to murderous work..." In addition to the beatings during work, they bullied them after work. The members of the *S.S.* loved to create a "spectacle" during the work. They often would take someone out from among the workers and place a stick in his hand and force him to climb a tree. He had to direct with the stick from there. Every worker had to stand around the tree, look at the "director" and sing or moo like a cow. A certain German major, Dolf, would ride around on a horse every day among the crowd of workers, flogging them with a small whip, or shooting at each one who dared straighten his back or rest for a second. Lewkowicz (today he is a factory worker who lives in Czenstochow. He survived the Cieszanow labor camp) says "During the work we sometimes had to stand in water up to the waist and dig out sand from the ground with our bare hands. Once returning from the work, one of us, he was named Kohn, turned to the *S.S.* man who guarded our barracks, asking for permission to go out to take care of his natural needs. The other one smiled and gave permission. When Kohn stepped over the threshold, a shot from a rifle was heard. Kohn ran back in with a hand that had been shot through from which blood ran and he hid. At once, *S.S.* men arrived and began looking for the one who could no longer work. We cried and begged them to give him his life.

Nothing helped. Kohn crawled out of his hiding place and himself cried and begged them to let him live because of his old mother. Nothing helped; he was dragged out of the barracks and shot. The same night three more Jews were shot. We were ordered to bury them and to place wooden crosses on their graves. In the morning, leading us to work, we were shot at. I do not know how many fell. A young man from Radom named Lipszic, who I later buried myself, fell next to me. *Erev Sukkous* [the eve of the Feast of Tabernacles] we were brought to Radom. From outside Radom, a number of us were sent back to a camp in Ostrow near Hrubieszow. I was among those sent back and fell into another, worse misfortune up to now. On the way, one of us committed suicide. In Ostrow we worked at draining the swamps, smoothing the roads and building highways. Once, a labor security service member forced us to bury alive a young man from Czenstochow, the son of Kawan, the war invalid. He was saved, by chance, by the arrival of some German accompanied by the chairman of the Hrubieszow *Judenrat* and Bernard Kurland of Czenstochow."

We quickly learned in Czenstochow about the terrible situation of this deportation from the fathers and mothers who, risking their lives, followed their children. Meanwhile, a parents committee was created that began to provide food packages for the deported. The food packages would be given to the Jewish police and they would send the packages to the camps. Groups of parents and relatives of the deported besieged the *Judenrat* building daily, cried, pleaded, screamed and demanded the rescue of their children and parents; the office of the *Judenrat* was besieged with written pleas from parents that in this way cried out their pain. In a request to the *Judenrat* of the 14th of November 1940, a certain Fantofel wrote: "...I am tailor by trade, I am 83 years old and my wife is blind. We have been supported by our two sons: the 27-year old Avraham, a hairdresser, and the 20-year old Moshe, a locksmith. They were sent out with the first transport. Avraham was caught in the street when he came home from work. Our situation is catastrophic and without a way out. My son, Moshe, is very sick there and he is not permitted to go to the doctor's commission. He was very sick when he returned from Pryzow. Therefore, I turn with the fervent request that we be saved and that an effort be made that at least the sick Avraham should be freed.

" The parents of those deported did not rest. They chose a delegation from among themselves that traveled on it own initiative to Cieszanow and Warsaw in order to do something for their children on the spot.

From day to day, the situation of the deported became worse. They fell from suffering; they fell from exhaustion, they fell because the work security service and the camp leader Dolf felt like playing with the prisoners. They died of dysentery and typhoid fever. Many, having nowhere else to turn, escaped from there. Parents and relatives were not satisfied with asking and making scenes at the *Judenrat*; they also were not satisfied with the lack of any great accomplishments by their delegation. Selling the last things they possessed, many of them, risking their own lives, went to the camps to ransom their children from the Germans. No satisfaction came from this and the scenes of the suffering of the fathers and mothers at the *Judenrat* kept being repeated. In a letter of the 22nd of November 1940 Dovid Borzykowski (member of the *Judenrat* presidium) wrote to the *Judenrat* messenger, Bernard Kurland: "...after having sent an earlier list of people as a result of the parents many time making scenes at the *Judenrat*, I concluded that this is useless. Yet, to calm them and assure them that I have written about their matters, I must prepare such a list. Alas, I must do the same thing now".... [59] This letter affirms that although the *Judenrat* did try to do something for those who had been sent out, it was a result of individual efforts by the parents. In the same letter Borzykowski wrote further: "...with pain we must inform you that a large group again set off for Hrubieszow last night. Alas we could not stop this movement; we will take all necessary steps so that this abnormal situation ceases..." Efforts to hold in check the pressure at the *Judenrat* by the parents to save their children actually were weak. Several dozen workers were ransomed and brought home. However, a greater number remained. After two months of suffering in this camp that had swallowed dozens of victims, after efforts by the *Judenrat*, after superhuman efforts by the parents and relatives, they succeeded in extracting those remaining from this camp. However, on the return to Czenstochow, three wagons of workers were stopped and they were taken to Osow to another camp. As it turned out after this, the German administration of the Osow camp only freed the detained

Jews from Radom from this camp for a large ransom. The bullying of the Jews in the Osow camp was still very terrible, as in the camps in the Lublin area. Several escaped from there, risking their lives both while escaping on the road home and arriving in Czenstochow and also being in Czenstochow where they were searched for as deserters from work, even before they arrived.

Avraham Pantofel, one of the poor Jewish workers upon whose fate it fell to take part in every misfortune that the edict of forced labor brought with it, and was also was taken to the labor camp in the Lubliner area, explains: "In Osow, we were held 70 men to a barrack. We got undressed to go to sleep on the first days, but when the 'wake-up calls' began and we were flogged terribly for even being a few minutes late, we began to sleep in our clothing and even in our boots. The "wake-up-calls" would come between two and three o'clock at night. As soon as we heard the scraping [shoes] of our hangmen, we had to go outside and stand in rows. As soon as everyone was standing, they began to chase us. We had to run in this way until five o'clock in the morning. At five o'clock we were given bread and coffee. No one could drink the coffee, but we used it to wash ourselves. We were full of lice. Each of us would go through the delousing on the open field while emptying ourselves of their natural needs; each one would then place his shirt, his pants and jacket in front of him and scrape off the lice from them. Our clothes were completely torn from the work and we did not receive any others. Therefore, we had to work naked and barefoot. Several went around completely naked, covered with something, a piece of rag on only the very front of the body. One, a certain Niedziela from Wielun, who did not have a piece of rag on him, went around completely naked. Our foreman, the Ukrainian Tarashenko, would keep us at work until late at night and at every opportunity he beat us. After work, each of us received a dish of soup. If Tarashenko caught someone with a second portion of soup, he forced him to take a pickaxe in his hand and spring like a frog with it." Pantofel also said that in only one barrack, in which there were 70 men, more than 50 were sick with typhus. (Pantofel today lives in Czenstochow and works in a hairdresser cooperative.)

It is a characteristic of the conditions in this camp that the municipal office of the *Judenrat* even indicated in the *Rocznik Statystyczny* [statistical yearbook]. On page 320 of this book is written among other things:

"...the working conditions at the new place, Osow, were much harder than previously in Cieszanow. We lay the Klinkowa highway in the marshes. The situation was even worse because the workers, exhausted from the two months of labor, did not have any strength for further work."

The last group of workers, physically exhausted and sick, was freed during the second half of December and sent in groups of five to Czenstochow, where they again fell under the edict of forced labor.

On Yom Kippur 1940, the Germans under the leadership of state-inspector of education, residency and sport, Fritz Grieshammer, attacked the Jewish synagogues and drove the Jews in their *talisim* [prayer shawls] to the sports area on Pulawska Street where they had to work cleaning the sports area until late at night.

Jews Would Escape from the Collection Point

One case was when 76 of 82 captured Jews escaped and only six men remained. This was on the night of the 6th and 7th of June, 1941. The work office at the *Judenrat* received a demand that it provide a larger number of Jews who were being sent to Demblin to work. Jewish police caught 82 men and they guarded them in the house of prayer at *Aleje* no. 1. Those held knocked a hole in the wall of the women's synagogue to the courtyard and lowered themselves with a rope. This case so shocked the *Judenrat* that it created a special investigation that was led by Pohorille himself. Only six men, who with a heartache hoped for some kind of miracle, had not succeeded in escaping then... and they were sent away.[60]

At the end of August 1941, 1,400 men were caught and they were confined in the munitions factory in terrible conditions. The factory halls were too small for such a large number of men. Therefore, many did not have the "good fortune" to lie on the floor under a roof and had to lie on the bare earth at the factory location. A miserable "cattle trade" began.

It drew money from the German control office, German gendarmes, the Jewish labor office, the leadership of the Jewish police and the Jewish and Polish police, who guarded the place. A certain number actually was freed by the money-taker; a second group was freed because their families provided substitutes. The substitutes were needy Jews who were ready to be sent out to difficult and dangerous work for a certain sum. they believed that with the money they received for this they could alleviate the need and hunger of their families and those closest to them.

Six hundred Jews who at the same time were held on Srebrna Street in seven old buildings found themselves in a similar situation. With the intervention of *T.O.Z.* [*Towarzystwo Ochrony Zdrowia* – the Association for the Protection of Health, known as the Jewish Health Organization] and the German labor office about the danger of the threat of epidemics among those held in these collection points and after the constant written notices of the leader of the sanitary division of *T.O.Z.*, Dr. Adam Walberg, about the same matter, those who did not have with what to be ransomed, were freed after they had been held there for three and a half weeks.

At the beginning of July 1942, *Shabbos* at around 11 in the morning, the Jewish police spread the dismal news all through the ghetto streets that all men aged 14 to 60 needed to appear at the square of the new market and in the First *Aleje* within half an hour. The ghetto became agitated. The men said goodbye to their wives and children. Grown children said goodbye to their old parents and to younger brothers and sisters. A cry carried through the streets: "May we return soon." Thousands of Jews were drawn to the square. Almost everyone held some sort of paper in his hand that would testify that the possessor of it was employed at a "temporary labor camp." No one had any luggage with him; he would not be sent away. The large square at the new market, the old market and the First *Aleje* were covered with *Schutzpolizei* [order police], members of the Gestapo and *Granat-Policja* [Blue Police – Polish police in the Nazi-occupied area of Poland known as the General Government] and also the members of the *Judenrat* and the Jewish policemen.

All of the assembled Jews stood in long rows, in groups according to the "temporary labor camp," in which they were included. Higher police and members of the Gestapo controlled each group and the representatives of the *Judenrat* gave the Germans various information.

Every movement of the thousands of Jews was watched by the strolling police and Gestapo officers and with the city chief of that time, Dr. Franke in the lead. Everyone was freed after a three-hour wait and was sent in groups to the work places. The ghetto breathed easier. However, an hour had not passed and the Jewish police, at the order of the *Schutzpolizei*, demanded that a certain number of workers from the "temporary labor camps" appear in the courtyard of the *Judenrat* that was located at *Aleje* number 11. More than 2,000 men appeared, of which a certain number were sent home. Those remaining were taken to the former metal factory, *Metalurgia* on Krutka Street. For three days, those held there were tortured with threats of being sent out to Germany to camps; many were terribly beaten by the Germans without reason. All efforts to learn about the further fate of those held had no result. Several of those being held made it out over the roof and smooth walls to Kawia Street and escaped from there. Everyone was freed after three days. This ostensible mobilization of the Jewish labor force further increased the unease that had begun to spread in the ghetto after the spring of 1942 when the terrible news of the explosion in Warsaw burst like lightning in the ghetto. In the morning, the feeling of insecurity seized everyone like an electrical storm. The question of working one day a week ceased to exist. The ransoming of oneself from work with money stopped. Everyone made an effort to belong to a temporary work place where they would work continually and in this way be "covered" and not be threatened with deportation. However, until this moment, when everyone went to great lengths to work in "temporary labor camps," that is, until about the 20th of August, 1942, people were caught in "special *aktsies*" in addition to the mentioned *aktsies*, carried out mostly at night by the Jewish police. They grabbed people in order to fulfill the needs of various "temporary labor camps." The Jewish police carried out 15 such *aktsies* just from the 18 of June to the 19th of August 1942.[61]

The leadership of the Jewish police wrote among other things in a letter of the 15th December 1941, no. 8091, to the president of the *Judenrat* about the results of the "snatchers": "Among those caught are very often found ragged ones, full of lice."[62] Therefore, the police proposed that the *Judenrat* should arrange for a special isolation hall where those caught could be held. These comments from the police characterize which strata of the populations suffered the most from the "snatchers."

Do

Kierownictwa Żydowskiej Służby Porządkowej

w miejscu

W związku z odnośnym rozporządzeniem Władz, Rada Starszych prosi Kierownictwo Żydowskiej Służby Porządkowej o wydanie polecenia podwładnym funkcjonariuszom, aby w czasie przetransportowywania jeńców rosyjskich przez miasto nie dopuszczali do gromadzenia się ludności żydowskiej na trotuarach i przed bramami, gapiów rozpędzać a opornych pociągnąć do surowej odpowiedzialności.

Wobec upomnienia Władz w tym kierunku uważamy sprawę tę za nader pilną, przeto prosimy o wydanie odnośnego polecenia natychmiast.

Przewodniczący Rady Starszych

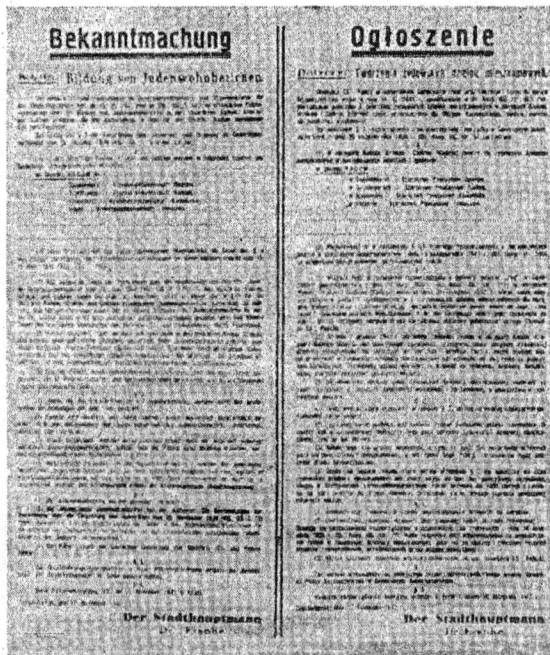

21. Febrar 1941

Ka/Br
1) Schreibe
An den
Chef des Distrikt Radom,
Herrn Gouverneur Dr. L a s c h,
R a d o m,
Sehr geehrter Herr Gouverneur!
In der Anlage übermittle ich den gewünschten Plan 1 : 1000 mit der Einzeichnung des besprochenen Ghettoverlaufes. Die Zeichnung bringt zwei Möglichkeiten zum Ausdruck: den Abschluss des Viertels durch Vergitterung der nach der Strasse zu führenden Öffnungen (Fenster, Türen, u. s w.) mit Eisengittern, wobei der Bürgersteig nicht ins Ghetto fallen würde. Ich habe diese Lösung einmal angeschnitten, weil die Aufstellung des Zaunes am Bordstein des Bürgersteiges immer den Nachteil mit sich bringt, dass, wie man es in Litzmannstadt sehen kann, die Juden auf den Bürgersteigen herumlümmeln, während die Arier in die Gosse treten müssen. Die zweite Lösung sieht die übliche Zaunführung am Rande des Bürgersteiges vor, mit eben dem obengeschilderten Nachteil. Die erste Lösung ist teurer und würde wohl auch af grösserte Materialschwierigkeiten stossen, da das Eisen unverhältnismässig schwierig zu beschaffen sein wird.
Bevor ich mich nun an die zuständigen Stellen um Beschaffung des Materials wenden kann, wobei ich mich auf den mir gewordenen Auftrag berufen muss, darf ich Sie um schriftliche Übermittlung des Auftrages zur Einrichtung des Judenghettos bitten.

Heil Hitler!

2) Wvlg.

An
den Herrn Staatsanwalt beim Sondergericht
in Tschenstochau.
Beiliegend übermittle ich ein Gnadengesuch des jüdischen Ältestenrates, Tschenstochau, mit der Bitte um Weiterleitung. Es ist mir bekannt, wann die Straftat begangen wurde, ob vor oder nach der Beschrifung de Tafeln am Ausgang des Ghettos. Sollte dies nachher schehen sein bin ich nicht der Meinung, dass man den Verurteilten begnadigen soll. Unbeschadet der Feststellugen des Gerichts im jeweiligen Einzelfall bin ich der Meinung, dass bei den Juden schwer unterscheidbar ist, ob nicht neue Tricks versucht werden. Wenn bekannt wird, dass mit armen Juden Ausnahmen gemacht werden, wird das Verbot wahrscheinlich noch öfters überschritten werden.

I. V.

3. Februar 40.

I. An das
Polizei-Batl. 72
in Tschenstochau.
In der Anlage erhalten Sie Abschriften von 2 Eingaben des Judenrates, die mir mit der Bitte übergeben wurden, zu gestatten, dass die Leichen der beiden Toten exhumiert und auf den jüdischen Friedhof beigesetzt werden dürfen. Da ich erl. P. allein nur leider verpflichtet bin, dem Judenrate diese Frage zu entscheiden, bitte ich um Ihre Stellungnahme. Wenn auch die Schriftstücke nicht so abgefasst sind, so weiss doch nach meiner Überzeugung der Judenrat, dass es sich in beiden Fällen um die Erschiessungen in der Narutowicza-Schule handelt.

Der Stadthauptmann

II. Zum Akt.

עס האַנדלט זיך וועגן פעלטמען פון אַמסטוװ און גנענדל באַרעמהערציק

This is a matter about Pelta from Amstow [Msztow] and Gnendl Baremhercik

The Jewish Police

On the 1st of May 1940, with the blessing of the German *Schutzpolizei*, an administrative body under the name *IRU* (*Inspekcja Ruchu Ulicznego* [traffic inspection] – in Polish) was created by the *Judenrat*. Chosen for the headquarters of this administrative body were: chief commandant – M. Galster, assistants – A. Helman, Borzykowski, Y. Landa, M. Cederbaum, Z. Jaracinski and Y. Sztarkman. There were 45 functionaries at the beginning and a few weeks later – 72.[63] At first the *IRU* was occupied with regulating the movement of the Jews in the ghetto; they did not permit strolling the main streets of the city, did not permit sitting on the benches of the *Aleyes*, did not permit them to gather in the streets, did not permit them to stand in the streets in large groups and so on. Later they began to patrol regularly at 24 designated points: in 10 streets of the area with a dense Jewish populations and at 14 sections of the *Judenrat*.[64] The functionaries also were occupied with escorting food products for Jews, with maintaining order during the distribution of these products, supervising the sanitary situation and the prices in the Jewish shops, [maintaining] order at the collection spots for refugees ("asylums"), assisting in the evacuations and removal of Jews from their residences, making sure that Jews were not found in the ghetto streets when the Russian prisoners-of-war were brought through, as well as carrying out all special decrees from the president and of the *Judenrat*.[65] The attitude of the Jewish population to the *IRU* deteriorated and the leader of the *IRU*, Galster, was particularly despised. Jews would joke: "So, we already have autonomy" – and would add – "woe to the autonomy that we received from the Germans!"

The activities of the *IRU* began to be seen differently from the moment when the ghetto arose and the *IRU* was changed into a Jewish *Ordnungsdienst* [police force].

On the 21st of April 1941, Wendler, the city chief, sent a decree (to the *Schutzpolizei*, Polish *Granatowa policja* [Polish police of the General Government], the Security Police, to Battalion 310 and to the *IRU* under the heading: "Service Instructions for the Jewish Ghetto Police in Jewish Residential Areas in Czenstochow." This decree begins as follows: In connection with setting up a Jewish residential area in the city of Czenstochow, the Jews must themselves maintain calm and order there; for this purpose, a Jewish *Ordnungsdienst* was created. The *Judenrat* was responsible for the equipping and support of this administrative body.

After this introduction come nine points in which are listed the authority, tasks and responsibilities of the *Ordnungsdienst*, as well as the uniforms and the ranks. The rank of each *Judenrat* man could be recognized according to the stars, or buttons, that he wore on his hat and by his yellow armband. The leader wore four silver stars, his representative – three, a sector leader – two and his office representative one silver star. A group leader wore three yellow metal buttons, a section leader – two yellow buttons and an ordinary keeper of order – one yellow button.[66] The first time the policemen showed themselves in the street they were ill at ease in their police uniforms and hats and the far greater majority of them would try to draw little attention to themselves and this "attire." Children ran after him, when someone appeared in the street in such "attire," as they did in the good old times with the *Purim shpilers* [actors in Purim plays]. Most of the time, adults would greet them with a mocking smile. Little by little this attitude disappeared. The *Ordnungsdienst* became a natural phenomenon. Peace was made with the idea that they had a certain amount of power that we must consider... The policemen themselves got accustomed to their role; they felt they had a little bit of power and this strongly impressed many of them.

In addition to the authority that *IRU* had earlier, the *Ordnungsdienst* also had to guard the border points of the ghetto and assure that Jews did not leave the ghetto without special permission; they also were occupied with finding and handing over those who had escaped from forced labor, with compelling the payment of the taxes placed by the *Judenrat*, with assisting during the requisition of furniture both by the Germans and by the *Judenrat*, with assisting in deportations and with carrying out special *aktsias* of grabbing people for work who normally did not work in the temporary labor camps. Such special *aktsias* were particularly felt during the last months before the large deportation that took place during the second half of 1942. The "special *aktsias*" would be carried out by the police at an announcement from the Jewish labor office, which at the demand of the German labor office, or of other German government organs, had to provide a certain number of workers for a local temporary labor camp. The police would carry out such special *aktsias* for snatching [people] mostly at night. However, the police were not always successful in such *aktsias* because many Jews already had their hiding places where, in moments such as these "visits," they would disappear. The year 1942 was rich in such *aktsias*.

On the 27 of June 1942, 79 policemen took part, who provided 107 Jews; the 2nd of July – 30 policemen, who delivered 31 men; the 8th of July – 16 policemen, who provided one worker; the 10th of July – 12 policemen who provided 16 men; the 11th of July nine policemen who provided nine men; the 16th of July – 12 policemen who provided 60 men; the 17th of July – 10 policemen who provided 30 men; the 22nd of July – four policemen who put together a mix of a certain number of people without regard to gender from those who had hidden, escaping from temporary labor camps; the 30th of July – 15 policemen who provided 76 men; the 1st of August – 30 policemen who provided 25 men; the 4th of August – 24 policemen who provided 72 men; the 12th of August – the entire police reserve who provided 51 men; the 13th of August – the same reserve, who provided 65 men; the 14th of August – 28 policemen who provided 52 men.[67] Such actions no longer took place after the 16th of August because, due to the uneasy mood that spread in the ghetto everyone went to great lengths to be employed at a temporary labor camp so they were included among those who were needed as [members of] the labor force.

At the direct communication of the *Judenrat*, the police would seal residences of Jews who hid from work, or because they had not paid the taxes that had been placed on them or money penalties. Decrees were issued to seal 76 residences just from the 18th of June until the 16th of August 1942.[68] At the direction of the trade and handworkers division of the *Judenrat*, Jewish police also would seal Jewish shops that had not paid any rent up to that time. Because of the increased amount of authority, the number of police functionaries was increased from 72 to 150 in 1942 – to 250.[69] As soon as the ghetto was established there were not many people who wanted to be policemen. However, little by little the situation changed so much that in order to enter the police one had to pay even larger sums of money in a bribe because being a policeman meant one no longer had to pay various taxes, was freed from forced labor, from the terror and from various other torture racks and insults. Although not all policemen carried out their duties with zeal, the earlier indifference and later mocking attitude of the Jews toward the policemen changed into a relationship of open enmity and contempt. There were more and more cases where policemen were publicly attacked and insulted.

September 1942. No sooner had the murderous liquidation of the Jews begun in Czenstochow then all of the policemen and their wives and children were allowed into store houses at Garibaldi Street 18 where the Jewish doctors and their families were also permitted [to enter] (they were not permitted to bring any other family members with them). Here they had to wait until all of the "selections" occurred and thus avoid the deportations. Only a small group of policemen and several members of the *Judenrat* were permitted to assist during the carrying out of the "selections." After the first "selection" a number of policemen were sent to the ammunition factory, "HASAG" [Hugo Schneider AG – a German metal goods manufacturer] where they no longer were policemen but they took on the functions of foremen. A number of them also were sent away with the transports to Treblinka. Only 50 policemen remained, who had special protection from the Germans or from the officers of the Granat police [*Granatowa policja* – Polish police during the German occupation]. These 50 policemen, on the order of the chief Degenhart, took part during the further "selections." They also went through the courtyards of the ghetto and called the hidden Jews out of their bunkers. On these occasions, several of them found hidden Jewish possessions in the bunkers and mainly valuable items, jewelry and in this manner they became rich. However, among the 50 policemen there were, all told, several exceptions who did not chase after riches and tried to help during the "selections" so that Jews were found on the side that was designated as not to be deported, but this was mostly for those who were close to them and well known to them.

The greater number of the 50 policemen tumbled down the abyss after the whole deportation, when a new ghetto that was called "the small ghetto" was created for those remaining. Drunk from the impulse and from the opportunity to get rich from the remaining hidden Jewish possessions, believing that their families would certainly remain alive after they loyally served the Germans, they were true slaves of the *Schutzpolizei* at a cost to the several thousand still surviving Jews. During the deportation of older Jews and mothers with children in the small ghetto, they keenly searched, dragged out and presented the victims demanded of them by the *Schutzpolizei*.

At the end of July 1943, after the liquidation of the small ghetto, some of the 50 policemen and their wives and children were sent, along with other surviving Jews, from the small ghetto to the "HASAG" camp that was organized in the ammunition factory of Pelcery [a former textile factory] and the rest remained for use by the *Schutzpolizei* to clear away the murdered as well as to clean out the little bit of remaining Jewish possessions in the small ghetto.

On the 19th of July 1943, during the "selection" of the Jews that was carried out in the "HASAG" camp at Pelcery, all of the policemen and their wives and children, without exception, and several hundred more Jews were thrown into a bunker (only one woman and her one and a half year-old son hid). In the morning, they and approximately 300 more Jews were annihilated at the Jewish cemetery, where a large mass grave had earlier been prepared.

Footnotes

32. Letter from the city chief to Dr. Lasz in Radom of the 21st February 1940.

33. Notes from city chief (typewritten).

34. Letter from the *Judenrat* [Jewish council] to the Jewish police of the 29th of March 1941, no. 41/828.

35. Letter from the *Judenrat* [Jewish council] to the Jewish police of the 29th of March 1941, no. 41/828.

36. Report of the city chief of the 8th of May 1941.

37. Announcement by Majznerowicz, the Polish leader of the Jewish Police on the 8th of August 1941.

38. Statistical Book of *Judenrat* [Jewish council] Volume II.

39. Two letters from the city chief to the military commander calling him to a talk with General Zibert about "closed residential district" for Jews of the 25th of April 1941.

40. Statistical Book of *Judenrat* [Jewish council] Volume II.

41. Two letters from the city chief to the military commander calling him to a talk with General Zibert about "closed residential district" for Jews of the 25th of April 1941.

42. Order of the Military Commandant in Czenstochow about "Entering the Ghetto through the *Wehrmachtgeherike* [people working for the German army]."

43. Written demands from Dr. Gutt in Radom of the 2nd of May 1941 to the city chief in Czenstochow.

44. Letter from the city chief.

45. Written report from Wendler (city chief).

46. Statistical Report of the Evidence Division of the city managing committee of the 8th of February 1947.

47. Letter from the *Judenrat* (Jewish Council) to the Jewish police.

48. Statistical Book of *Judenrat* [Jewish council] Volume II pages 182, 189 and 190.

49. Statistical Book of *Judenrat* [Jewish council] Volume II pages 182, 189 and 190.

50. Statistical Book of *Judenrat* [Jewish council] Volume II pages 182, 189 and 190.

51. Statistical Book of *Judenrat* [Jewish council] Volume III page 291.

52. Statistical Book of *Judenrat* [Jewish council] Volume II pages 195, 203 and 206.

53. Statistical Book of *Judenrat* [Jewish council] Volume II pages 195, 203 and 206.

54. Statistical Book of *Judenrat* [Jewish council] Volume II pages 195, 203 and 206.

55. Statistical Book of *Judenrat* [Jewish council] Volume III pages 317. 319 and 324.

56. Statistical Book of *Judenrat* [Jewish council] Volume III pages 317. 319 and 324.

57. Statistical Book of *Judenrat* [Jewish council] Volume III pages 317. 319 and 324.

58. Statistical Book of *Judenrat* [Jewish council] Volume III pages 317. 319 and 324.

59. Statistical Book of *Judenrat* [Jewish council] Volume III pages 317. 319 and 324.

60. Letter from Borzykowski to Kurland (typewritten) with a handwritten postscript by Advocate Faharille.

61. Day report of the Jewish police (police book).

62. Letter from Majznerowicz (Polish commander of the Jewish police) to the Judenrat [Jewish council].

63. [Jewish council] volume I pages 42, 43.

64. Statistical Book of the Judenrat [Jewish council] volume I pages 42, 43.

65. Statistical Book of the Judenrat [Jewish council] volume I pages 42, 43.

66. "Service Instructions for the Jewish Housing Service" of the city chief, Dr. Wendler.

67. Day report in the police book.

68. Day report in the police book.

69. Written order of the police commandant.

The Economic Situation of the Jews in the Ghetto

In order to have an accurate idea about the economic situation of the Jews in the ghetto, it would be necessary to orient oneself in the economic structure of the Jewish population in Czenstochow at that time. Alas, this could not be exactly established because a considerable movement of the population to the ghetto took place that led to the specific situation of the Jews under the German occupation. Yet, we will try to describe the economic life according to what each of us saw and could observe.

The economic situation for the Jews in Czenstochow was very difficult during the first weeks after the outbreak of the war. Hundreds of families were hungry and waited for some kind of miracle. Little by little they began to adjust to the newly created conditions and began to look for income, not waiting for donated help. The Polish population was permitted to enter the Jewish area. This gave many Jews the opportunity to carry out business, artisans to do certain work and to sell their articles and so on. The same thing took place later in the large ghetto. As was said, the Polish population was permitted to go through the ghetto. This enabled the Jews to carry on an illegal barter trade with the Polish population in the ghetto, too. They sold jewelry, household goods, clothing, linens, furniture and even bedding and lived off this. Secret small house factories arose that made soap, candles, shoe polish, washing soda and so on. There also were those who constructed *zharnes* (hand mills to grind kernels). The explanation for this is that it was easier for the peasants to smuggle kernels into the ghetto than flour.

Jews bought the kernels, ground them in the small hand mills, gave it to the bakers to bake and received a kilo of bread for a kilo of flour. The baker received the surplus that remained after baking. The main sellers of the finished goods were children. The *Judenrat* declared that only 1,194 out of 3,800 boys of school age registered under the notice about the registration of children of school age (based on the decree of the 31st of August 1940 about the school system of the General Government). This was only 31.41%. Of 3,776 girls of school age only 1,249 registered, which consisted of 33.1%. The greatest number of registered children missing were those who were born in the years 1931-1933, and this consisted of 60.1% of the number of boys of this age and 59.2% of the number of girls.[70] That the percent of those registered was smaller among the older school ages was because the far greater majority of them were the breadwinners for their families.

Several former manufacturers carried on business again through the German-nominated commissar for their former factories (Jewish factories and larger enterprises were, on the basis of a decree from Ridiger, confiscated in the second half of September 1939).[71] There were commissars who could not cope without the previous owners and the manufacturers made use of this to draw a livelihood from the [factories] and, simultaneously to maintain watch over their possessions. Shops and merchants had their little bit of merchandise "stolen" from their confiscated businesses with copied keys, or under the pretext "airing" the goods from the sealed businesses, they extracted some of the goods in partnership with the German guards. This all was sold or traded with the peasants for food and, meanwhile, they lived. There also were Jews who carried on trade and industrial undertakings legally on a small scale and drew a livelihood from it. A number of Jews who had to live from their work were employed in various "temporary workplaces" and were paid up to four *gildn* by the *Judenrat* for a day's work.[56]*

*[Translator's note: "56" is the footnote number that appears here. The preceding number was "71" and the next number is "72."]

The fact that a certain number of Jews found a way to obtain a livelihood made it possible to help refugees, the sick, the old, orphans and in general, the poor. However, this situation also provided to the *Judenrat* and all of its divisions the opportunity to seize direct and indirect taxes. The indirect taxes were designated for the hospital, old age and orphans house.

The Judenrat declared with an unfair perspective that all Jews must carry identical burdens. Therefore, this tax was even extracted from the poorest, who were forced to pay taxes equal to that of the richest. Buying a food card, taking allocations of coal or soap, everyone had to buy a stamp for two zlotes on which was printed: "Utilitati et Soluti [Utility and Health]." [72]. (Lawyer Shimon Pohorille, the organization chief of the Judenrat, had great love of making use of Latin expressions.) In comparison with the General Government area, the economic situation, in general, was bearable here. This gave rise to Czenstochower Jews trying to bring their relatives from other cities and mainly from the Łódź ghetto from which there was terrifying information. Such permission had to be obtained from the city chief who provided each request with an answer, written on the other side of the request to the Judenrat that the request of "Old Testament Believer" so-and-so is refused. No one received permission to enter. However, the news about the Czenstochower "heaven" spread, tore through the ghetto fences and the Jewish population, against the will of the Judenrat and, chiefly, against the will of the city chief, kept growing in the number of illegal and half-legal refugees from cities and shtetlekh.

A very small number of refugees did not need material help. The much larger majority had to ask for such help. However, the activity of the aid institutions in Czenstochow [in this situation] was to alleviate the need in a minimal way in comparison to the need. But this situation did not last long and the possibility of aid decreased. The administrative division at the city chief's office that was led by Volksdeutsch Zawada and by S.A.-man [member of the Sturmabteilung – Storm Detachment, a paramilitary group] Schleecht found their servants in the city itself and acting with them as partners, they "took care" that the confiscated Jewish businesses would be more quickly liquidated. The large Polish commercial firms Trawinski, Majewski and Miszkewicz first made wide use of the "good heartedness' of the German administrative division. Laski, a former auxiliary to Wendler, received the right to clear out all of the Jewish shoe shops, as well the leather and leather haberdashery businesses. Wendler's lover, Mrs. Maszewicz, received the broadest right to empty all of the Jewish businesses that pleased her and even the artisans' workshops.

She opened a store with the stolen goods, a private "merchandise" house, for which the Jewish artisans had to provide everything that she demanded. Wendler allocated to her the entire building of the former Jewish Merchants and Manufacturers Bank at the Second Alija number 2 for the organization of a "department store."

One can get an idea about the need that reigned in the ghetto from what the statistical official at the Judenrat stated in the Statistical Yearbook (Rocznik Statystynczny, volume 3, published in 1941) about the number of Jews who turned to the social aid [office] at the Judenrat for help. According to the number given there, the figures in the file are for 14,960 people who turned to it for support. These were 4,058 families, of whom, 651 families originated in Czenstochow and numbered 2,169 souls. Because the ghetto consisted of only a few streets, there was no sewer system; because of the crowding in the residences and because of hunger, infectious diseases began to spread in the ghetto at a rapid rate. Spotted typhus, stomach typhus and dysentery had their fat harvest, mainly among the mass of refugees. The epidemic of spotted typhus first broke in the "asylum" for refugees from Łódź that was located in the artisans' school at Garncarska Street no. 6. The need led to the increase in the plague of robberies of linen and food. Informers also played a significant part in the fact that the Jews were impoverished. Among the informers who carried the information of what someone owned and with what he was occupied was Eliash Szeftel who received a concession to run a tavern that was visited by Germans and particularly German functionaries from the administrative office, who he provided with information about Jewish possessions, Yehuda Meir Beser from Zawiercie and Yakov Rozenberg from Łödź, who also took part in similar denunciations as Szeftel and, therefore, had special certificates from the security police to move freely outside the ghetto without the Star of David armbands.[73] These informers made a fortune both from the portion that they received from the Germans of what was taken from the Jews at their instructions and from what they received from Jews, whom they had earlier handed over to the Germans, to be saved from German hands.

The need kept deepening from day to day, the density kept spreading. This strongly affected the general situation in the ghetto and particularly the natural increase in the population.

Special Help

After the month of June 1939, after the famous visit by [Reich Minister of Propaganda Joseph] Goebbels to Gdansk, when the rumors increased about the nearness of war, commerce in Czenstochow, and particularly in Jewish trade, began seriously to cloud over. The first who began to feel this situation were the Jewish transport workers (wagon drivers, porters with hand carts and porters [who carried the goods on their] backs), who lost the opportunities to earn their poor daily sustenance, and were left without the means to live. Serious need was seen among the same strata during the first days after the outbreak of the war. At the end of September 1939, thanks to the initiative of Yakov Rozine (for many years a leader of *TOZ* [Society for the Protection of Jewish Health in Poland]) and Mendl Asz (son of the former Czenstochow rabbi, Nachum Asz), interest was inspired in this matter by a large group of former communal workers who worked with true devotion to alleviate the need of a large number of Jewish families who were threatened with starvation. Yitzhak Czanszinski (Pseud. "Doctor"), who gave the first, large sum of money for this purpose, was a particularly active coworker in this area. Natan Rodal, Cesha Kazak* and later Jakob Tempel, also gave their full energy for the aid work. Many Jews responded to the first appeal to help those people who lost property in fires and this made it possible for every family in need to receive its first help in the form of 10 *gildn* and a meter of coal. The aid activities of the above-mentioned group of workers expanded even more, because every honorable Jew who had the slightest ability to do so willingly taxed himself for this purpose. At the beginning of 1940 a section for aid work was created at the *Judenrat* that took over the actual leadership of the aid work. Natan Rodal and his coworkers Cesha Kozak and Yakob Tempel were at the head of this section.

*[Translators note: Cesha's surname is spelled Kazak and Kozak in this paragraph.]

Holiday money collections, winter aid collections were carried out in the ghetto and six kitchens were also created where lunches were given out free or for a small payment. The first kitchen was created on the 31st of January 1940 in a house of prayer at Nadrzeczna Street 30. An average of 825 lunches were given out here daily for a payment of 10 *groshn* for a lunch.

The second kitchen was opened on the 19th of March 1940 on Katedralna Street in the former premises of the *Makkabi* [international Jewish sports organization]. Up to 1,000 lunches were given out here daily, also for a payment of 10 *groshn*. The third kitchen was opened on the 5th of April 1940 in the *mikvah* [ritual bath] building on Garibaldi Street, no. 18 and gave out 1,025 lunches entirely without cost. The fourth kitchen was opened on the 7th of April 1940 at *Aleje* no. 12 in the former premises of the artisans. Up to 1,030 lunches were given out daily here without cost. At the same time, the fifth kitchen (intelligentsia kitchen) opened at Piłsudski Street no 11. This kitchen served the officialdom and the members of the diplomaed intelligentsia. Here, up to 450 lunches for the payment of from 70 *groshn* up to 1,10 *gildn* per lunch were given out daily. The sixth kitchen was opened in May 1940 on Piłsudski Street no. 17 in the former premises of the Bund. Here up to 1,040 lunches would be given out daily, some for 10 *groshn* and some free. In addition to this the labor office at the *Judenrat* managed a field kitchen that would serve coffee and bread to workers at several temporary workplaces where there was forced labor every morning.[74] In addition to the kitchens five and six, which served the intelligentsia and the forced labor, the lunches in the remaining kitchen consisted mostly of turnips with water, but this also was good fortune for the hungry residents in general and for the refugees in particular because in addition to 50 grams of bread that would be distributed daily to men, this lunch was the only additional food for them that was supposed to quiet the hunger.

In the course of the year 1940 the social protection [office] reported giving out more than 90,000 *gildn* in monetary support. Clothing, underwear, shoes and bedding was also collected from among the Jewish population, from which a part was sent to Radomsko for the Jewish hospital and for those suffering from need there and the remainder was distributed in Czenstochow itself.[75]

From time to time the department for social aid would embark on appeals to the Jewish population about the aid for those suffering from need. On the 28th of November 1940 the winter aid committee sent an appeal to all the Jews in which the following message [appeared] as well as others: "for thousands of Jews there stands the maelstrom of hunger and cold; Jewish society cannot remain indifferent to the exceptional need. The efforts of all of society is necessary to ease the fate of the large masses who are hungry and suffer from the cold!" The purposes of the emerging winter-aid-committee were further discussed in this appeal.

The appeal ended with the words: "Remember that those who give a donation are always more fortunate than those who are forced to make use of the donation."

The first time, a number of the better-situated [members of the] Jewish population were drawn to social help with sympathy and willingly taxed themselves for every necessary purpose. Many even voluntarily took part in the collection work. However, the mood and the relationship toward everything with a connection to the *Judenrat* sharply changed at the end of 1940, and naturally – also toward the provision of social aid that was a program of the *Judenrat*. In addition to this, the material conditions of the Jews changed for the worse. The people became dejected by the constant persecutions by the Germans and the constant taxes that the *Judenrat* kept placing on the Jewish population. This all caused an indifference to the need and suffering of others. The voluntary payment for aid purposes kept decreasing. The *Judenrat* constantly increased the direct and indirect taxes to cover the increasing void at the department of social aid. The indirect taxes fell mostly on the shoulders of the poorest because to redeem their portions of bread, potatoes and coal, each one had to buy special stamps.

A commission for Łódź Jews (Łódź Sub-Committee) also existed for the division of social aid and carried on special aid activities for the poor refugees from Łódź[76]. The Łódź refugees, Jaroczinski and Babiacki, who had a modest manner, were at the head of this committee and did a great deal with limited means for the people from their home.

The aid work also was carried out by the society, *Dobroczynność* [charity], with the lawyer M. Hossenfeld at its head. *Dobroczynność* ran an old age home for 188 men, an orphan house for 150 children and the Jewish hospital during the first years of the occupation.[77]. A refugee aid committee also existed that had to ease the situation of those who suffered the most. The activity of this committee was based on the funds that were collected among the population in the ghetto, on funds that flowed in from special markets. And from the aid from the "Joint" [Distribution Committee] that would be sent from time to time for this purpose. However, the aid from the committee for the refugees was minimal; hunger and dirt reigned there. The only concrete aid from the refugee committee was the kitchen that gave out 250 relatively nutritional lunches for the refugee children up to the age of three.[78].

Yakov Temple and Mrs. Lipintka ran this kitchen.

A separate chapter in the history of social aid was the activity of *TOZ* [*Towarzystwo Ochrony Zdrowia Ludności Żydowskiej w Polsce* – Society for the Protection of Jewish Health in Poland] in Czenstochow. At the initiative of Yakov Rozine, the former leader of *TOZ*, and of the writer of these lines as his representative, *TOZ* began its activity again in the second half of September 1939. At first the two former nurses from *TOZ*, Hanka Birnbaum and Genya Windhajm, appeared voluntarily without any reward; later Chana Janowska (wife of the well-known Hebrew teacher in the city) was added. The pediatrician Halleman and the internist Dovid Blumenfeld voluntarily reported to work in *TOZ*. In addition to the former *TOZ* official Junya Rozen (the daughter of Doctor Rozen), Motek Kusznir and Cesha Czanszinska voluntarily reported as officials without any prospects of reward. A few weeks later, more young people and the young surgeon, Leyzer Glatter, reported for *TOZ* work. At the beginning, only three dispensaries were active: internist, pediatric and surgical. But *TOZ* was much better positioned for the difficult tasks. It especially had to take care of the health of those working because only a small number of these were able to carry out the fierce work they were forced to do. Every day brought with it hundreds of battered, mutilated and frozen limbs. In addition, more poor people came to the location along with a large mass of refugees from various cities in Poland who needed immediate and constant medical help. Therefore, *TOZ* had to quickly increase the scope of its activities. At the beginning of 1940 both former *TOZ* chairmen, lawyer Mendl Konarski and Doctor Adam Walberg, 19 doctors and five nurses as well as dozens of young people were working. New dispensaries arose, such as: anti-tuberculosis, laryngology, dentistry, oculist, a laboratory and a milk-drop-off point for suckling [babies] and tuberculosis patients. From the end of 1940 to the large deportation, 31 doctors and eight nurses worked at *TOZ*. In addition, about 200 medics and sanitary workers, who were schooled in sanitary courses arranged by *TOZ* during the occupation, as well as all Jewish doctors without exception who were in Czenstochow, were active at the sanitary locations of *TOZ*. They had the task of fighting the plague of infectious diseases.

Dr. Walberg headed these locations. For a long time *TOZ* was also in contact with the Jews in the surrounding *shtetlech*, such as: Klobuck, Krzepice, Truskolasy, Panki, Pristan, Pajczeno, Kamyk, Miedzno, Mstow, Przyrow, Janow, Olsztyn, Lelow, Brzeznica, Poraj, Zarki and Myszkow. A *TOZ* committee was organized in each *shtetl* that was involved with aid work there. In addition to medical help, each *shtetl* received food products, linens, furniture and shoes for children. Later, certain sums of money were sent to the mentioned *shtetlech* from what was designated by the Joint [Distribution Committee] and the *TOZ* central in Warsaw. Besides this, a package collection was carried out for the Jews in the Łódź ghetto. Jews in Czenstochow would send certain sums of money through *TOZ* to the *TOZ* divisions in Klobuck and Krzepice, which then belonged to the Reich, and [*TOZ*] would buy food products with the money and send them to the Jews in Łódź whose [names] had been submitted by their relatives in Czenstochow. This all would be taken care of with self-sacrifice through Jewish and Polish messengers who were delegated by the *shtetlech*. During all the time that the aid action for the *shtetlech* was carried out, there was only one failure with Chada, the managing committee member from Klobuck *TOZ*, who also was active there in the work of *TOZ*. Chada was caught smuggling himself to Czenstochow by the Germans who gave him to the "mercy" of their dogs. By chance, this case did not end in death and Chada perished later with the majority of Jews from Klobuck in the death camps. This *TOZ* activity in the small *shtetlech* was interrupted during the month of April 1941 when the ghetto in Czenstochow was created and we were fenced in with a chain by the German murderers. In the field of *TOZ* aid work in the area of child care, *TOZ* activity clearly moved forward. The feeding stations for children aged from three to fifteen was the most important work in this area. Breakfast for nearly 600 children was given out the first time. Because the need kept growing as well as because still more new refugees arrived, *TOZ* had to care for and feed even more children. In July 1940 *TOZ* fed 2,008 children.[79]. It also ran a "consultation location for mother and child." In addition to the normal work in the consultation location, it was possible to distribute prepared food portions for 351 nursing mothers.[80]

The *TOZ* officies were located in several streets in Jewish territory.

There were on Berka Joselewicza Street: an internist office for adults, internist office for children of school age, laryngological office, anti-tuberculosis office, dentistry, x-ray and sun-lamp office and an internal apothecary. At the First *Aleje* 6: internist dermatology office and for venereal diseases, surgical office, sun-lamp, consultation location for mothers and children, consultation location for pregnant women and healing location for those sick with trachoma. At Katedralna Street 6: location to fight epidemic diseases. At Przemysłowa: day-care center and kitchen for children of school age, "drops of milk location" for nursing and milk distribution for children up to the age of three and for the sick.

The *TOZ* activity was associated with a colossal expense. Therefore, *TOZ* was forced to borrow money for its purposes from the Czenstochower Jews, to be returned after the war. Czenstochower *TOZ* borrowed with similar conditions not only for its local needs, but also for the Joint [Distribution Committee] and *TOZ*-central in Warsaw, which turned to the Czenstochower *TOZ* workers. Czenstochower *TOZ* also organized house committees that would collect weekly payments among the tenants of a given house. Smaller sums of money also flowed in from the sale of objects that the children would make in the *świetlices* [day care homes]. The children would make baskets, slippers, bags, bread plates and other things in the *świetlices*. All of this would be exhibited in the shop on Warszawer Street where Griliak's apothecary warehouses were located before the war. Here the displays would be sold and the money would be used for club purposes.

A significant donation would often flow in from the presentations of the amateur dramatic group and chorus that existed at *TOZ* and from the children's performances of those educated at the day care homes (*świetlices*).

A division of *Z.S.S.* (Jewish Social Self-Help) arose during the month of May 1941 that was supposed to subsidize all charitable Jewish institutions that carried on certain activities. The result of this initiative was that help from the Joint [Distribution Committee] ceased and the help from *Z.S.S.* was minimal. The *Z.S.S.* division in Czenstochow took over the direction of the old age home in which approximately 150 young children from the *TOZ* day care homes were located. Furthermore, the activity of *Z.S.S.* resulted in that on the 18th of July 1941 all of the remaining kitchens: the kitchen that served the forced laborers and gave out 1,150 lunches daily; the kitchen at *Kwarantanna* [quarantine] at Garibaldi Street 18 that gave out up to 600 lunches a day; the "intellectuals' kitchen" and the kitchen of the religious Jews almost supported themselves. Of the 2,008 children in the *TOZ* day care homes, only 1,400 children began to make use of the food supply and from August 1941 – only 1,200 children.

There was no peace between the *Judenrat* and *TOZ* during the course of the time of occupation up to the deportation. The first open conflict arose in December 1939. Members of the *Judenrat* inspired the Gestapo "to take an interest" in *TOZ*. In January 1941, the specialist for Jewish matters at the Gestapo summoned a representative of *TOZ*, asked about *TOZ* activity and admonished him for not being obedient to the *Judenrat*. A representative of *TOZ* was called to the Gestapo twice more during the same month, where he heard the same admonition as the first time. The relationship between *TOZ* and the *Judenrat* grew even more aggravated. Representatives of the Joint [Distribution Committee] in Warsaw tried to quiet the atmosphere, but without success.

At the end of February 1941, Kander, the representative of the city chief, called the representatives of *TOZ*, Konarski and Walberg (Walberg received a slap from Kander then in the waiting room "without cause.") and in the presence of the *Judenrat* chairman, Kapinski, ordered that *TOZ* cease its independent activity and become a program of the *Judenrat*. The *TOZ* chairman, Konarski, was so upset by this case that he had a severe nerve attack on the same day, after which he became paralyzed. A month later Konarski again began to take part in *TOZ* work, but only from time to time, because he remained a cripple [paralyzed] in his hand and foot. Konarski suffered to the point of despair by the time he was driven with thousands of Jews to the train wagons that took the Jews to Treblinka. While still in Czenstochow, Konarski received a whip over his head from a German because he could not get into the train wagon, and dying, was thrown into the train wagon.

The day after Kander's demand, *TOZ* sent out a leaflet in Polish. This leaflet was written in the form of a death notice and was spread in great numbers among the Jewish population in Czenstochow itself and from there sent to Jewish communal institutions in Poland. In this way *TOZ* made known the abominable act that the *Judenrat* had committed against an institution that carried out aid work among the Jews. The contents of the leaflet were more or less this:

Czenstochow, 28 day of Shvat, year 5701 [21 February 1941]

Protection Station for the Orphaned in Czenstochow

"When God abandons people

To cruel pain,

He then gives them into their

Brothers' hands."

The Holy Memory of Dr. *TOZ*

On the 28th day of Shvat in year 5701, 7:30 at night at Sobieski Street (seat of the city chief – L. B.) Dr. *TOZ*, well-known to us in the city, well loved and highly valued by all sections of society, suddenly died at a time of flourishing.

In the last moment of the agony of death, he found himself in full consciousness, taking account of the reasons for his premature death. The chairman of *Rasta* [*Rada Starszych* – council of elders] (chairman of the *Judenrat* – L. B.), who gave his last Judas-kiss on the lips of the dying person, who still tried to whisper his strong urge for life for the good of the tens of thousands of poor and sick Jews, to which he always hurried with aid in their moments of suffering, as well as for the thousands of hungry children for which he did not spare any spoon of warm cooked food.

He went through life quietly, calmly, honestly, happily and did not waiver in his deeds, proud of his actions, always with thought for the poor, hungry and sick.

Characteristic of his young life was the serving of those in need without any concern for himself.

He left at a time when he was most needed – when thousands of the sick yearned to find themselves under his protective wings, when hundreds of children stretched out their pale little hands for a piece of bread.

Jewish society painfully feels this loss!

The city, in which he was born and became beloved, will long hold his activity in its grateful memory!

Information about taking out the remains and burial in the pantheon of most deserving was shared by the chief of the *Rasta*, the Herr Pocholera (Pohorille – L. B.).

Hypocritical and ostensible friends of Doctor *TOZ* in Czenstochow are asked not to express any sympathy.

Honor the untarnished memory of Dr. *TOZ*!

"Those closest"[81].

On the 22nd of March 1942 the presidium of the *Judenrat* decided to take *TOZ* into its hands. The next day, the 23rd, Borzykowski, Kurland and Gerichter, the members of the *Judenrat*, reported to the *TOZ* office at Katedralna Street 6 and took over the *TOZ* agenda. On the 25th of March the former teacher at the Jewish *gymnazie* [secondary school], Dr. Mering, reported and declared that he had been designated by the *Judenrat* as commissar of *TOZ*. The *TOZ* managing committee was disbanded.

Sheet music: Club Hymn – "Come quicker, dear children…"

Footnotes

70. Statistical Book of Judenrat [Jewish council] Volume II page 178.

71. [Jewish council] Volume II page 178.

72. Statistical Book of Judenrat [Jewish council] Volume II page 225.

73. Official letter from the Exchange Office in Krakow to the security police in Czenstochow.

74. Statistical Book of Judenrat [Jewish council] Volume III pages 373, 391 395 and 417.

75. Statistical Book of Judenrat [Jewish council] Volume III pages 373, 391 395 and 417.

76. Statistical Book of Judenrat [Jewish council] Volume III pages 373, 391 395 and 417.

77. Statistical Book of Judenrat [Jewish council] Volume III pages 373, 391 395 and 417.

78. Letter from *TOZ* [Society for Safeguarding Jewish Health] to the *Judenrat* [Jewish council] and to the Provisions Commissar in the City Hall.

79. Letter from *TOZ* [Society for Safeguarding Jewish Health] to the *Judenrat* [Jewish council] and to the Provisions Commissar in the City Hall.

80. Letter from *TOZ* [Society for Safeguarding Jewish Health] to the *Judenrat* [Jewish council] and to the Provisions Commissar in the City Hall.

81. From the archive of the Jewish Historical Institute in Warsaw.

Cultural Activity

The entire Jewish cultural life in the city shattered as soon as Czenstochow fell under the German occupation. All libraries, all schools and *gymnazies* [secondary schools] were shut at once. Because of the persecutions and edicts that kept pouring out on our Jewish settlement, everyone at first was concerned with saving themselves from physical death. A consultation among progressive cultural workers took place at the end of 1939 to bring about a change in this situation and cultural activity began, half legal and half illegal. Naturally not all worker activists immediately had the opportunity to take part in the cultural activities. The worst situation was among the well-known communist activists because the former agents of the Polish secret police, principally Wiesalowski and Pietrowski ("Pietrik") severely persecuted the communists in general and the well-known communist activists in particular. Despite this, the cultural work in Czenstochow began during the first months of the occupation. Already at the beginning of 1940 the cultural work also took on another form. The studying young people, younger children and older ones, began to think about not losing any time. There then were 208 teachers and 7,576 children and young people of school age in Czenstochow.[82] There arose illegal plots by young people, who under the leadership of their former *gymnazie* professors carried on continued learning courses. There were also groups of children who continued the courses of elementary school. Only the children of better-situated parents benefitted from all of this, those who were able to pay the teachers. It was worse teaching the children of the poor.

Therefore, the underground activists decided to convert the feeding stations at *TOZ* [Society for the Protection of Jewish Health in Poland], from which 600 children benefitted (later – 2,008 children) into a children's club, day care houses – where the children in addition to eating three times a day, also received education and instruction. The author, as a former teacher at the *YSO* [Jewish School Organization] school, was assigned the task of organizing and leading this club. Kindergarten teachers – Laja Wajnberg, Ruszka Gelber, Saba Ginsberg and Rywka Waczecha – were the first ones to appear for work in the day care houses. In addition, more than 60 young people, mostly young women, threw themselves into this important work with enthusiasm and self-sacrifice. Sala Sziwak, Jadzia Mass, Ira Szterenzis, the two sisters, Polya and Dasza Szczekacz, Aviv Rozine, Yitzchak Fajner, Lili

Krisztal, Stefa Haftke, Rusia Landau, Sosza Opatowska and the 16-year old Praszkewicz stood at the head of this group of young people.

With their dedication and temperament, the young people transformed the day care houses into warm, light homes not only for the children who were fed there, but for all Jewish children who were in Czenstochow without exception.

The children here were divided into groups according to the level of their knowledge and according to their age. They continued the elementary education in such a manner. A course in hand work was given. A certain young woman, Mrs. Mendelson, an artist who came from a Czenstochow family, headed this course. Every *Shabbos*, collective discussions were held about the problems of educating children, which were led by the writer of these lines and by Professor Lonja Rozencwajg so that the new, young, inexperienced educators would have a certain professional approach to their duties. In addition to this, the new educators would share their impressions of the week's work at these collective discussions. Master lessons were also given in which coworkers in the day care houses took part. It was first in 1941 that several professors from the Jewish *gymnazie* [secondary school] began to help in the educational work. Of them all, the one who most distinguished herself was Lonja Rozencwajg, who so took her new task to heart that she quickly won the trust and love of every young club leader and actively worked with them until the liquidation of the ghetto. She, with the greatest number of young educators and almost all of the children from the *TOZ* day homes, then perished in Treblinka.

The children's performances that would illegally take place every two months were the brightest rays in the dark ghetto life. The appearances of the children brought a bit of a holiday into the impoverished lives. The appearances by the children took place in Yiddish and Polish. The songs by Peretz, Reisen, Mani Leib [Brahinsky] and many other Yiddish writers that were sung in the children's clubs and at the children's performances entered every Jewish home where there were still children. A club hymn also was created.

Club Hymn

Come quicker, dear children,
To enter the day care house;
Here it is still always joyous,
Here it is always beautiful.

Everything here is decorated
With delicately fragrant flowers;
We are led
To the blue skies.
We learn, we work,
Here we are not alone,
So come, dear children,
Come here quickly.

    The teachers watch here,
Their gazes watch us;
After all, here is our home,
Here is our luck.
We become cautious,
On the narrow paths,
We are led
Over thorny ways.
We learn, we work,
Here we are not alone,
So come, dear children,
Come here quickly.

The underground activists were not satisfied with only cultural work for children, they also were involved with cultural work among adults. An amateur dramatic group and chorus of adults were under the leadership of Jakob Razine, Ester Razine, Brener, Fiszl Blumenkranc, Leib Srebrnik and Jeszaja Bornsztajn under the *TOZ* mantel. Mrs. Razine was the theatrical director and Srebrnik was the orchestra conductor. Approximately 120 women and men took part in the chorus and amateur dramatic group. The performances took place in the former cinema room at *Aleje* no. 12. Machl Birncwajg and Noach Kurland took care of all of the ideas on the technical side – Leibl Kusznir, with the decorative part. The appearances of the amateur dramatic group and chorus would take place almost every month, mostly with separate programs and from time to time together. Their appearances in the ghetto were the most elevated events in internal ghetto life because the days on which their performances would take place in the ghetto were filled with exhilaration and a holiday spirit.

In addition to serious works from our classics, the amateur dramatic group would perform actual scenes from past Jewish life and from ghetto life. The images were gathered and reworked by the Czenstochow poet, Fiszl Blumenkranc, who perished tragically. A one-act play, *Zbaszyn,** in which was mirrored the tragedy of a mother who lost her only child during a deportation, was one of the strongest things that Blumenkranc wrote and was presented by the amateur drama group. The large movie room was always overflowing although the performances were illegal. Jeszajale Bornsztajn (we called him the "Czenstochower Dzigan" [Simon Dzigan was a comedic Polish-Jewish actor]), who awoke so much laughter with his appearances that we would forget our dark surroundings for a second.

The underground workers published a periodic illegal newspaper under the name *Rasta* [*Rada Starszych* – council of elders] under Walberg's editorship and with the participation of Konarksi, Roziner, Brener, both of the Fogel brothers and Mendl Asz. Sura Chliwner (née Okrent), Motek Kusznir, Datner (a son-in-law of the Fogel family) and Uzer Blechsztajn took care of the technical side of the publishing. Leibl Kusznir was employed on the artistic side of the illustrated publications. The life of the Jews under the German occupation, the cruel activities of the Gestapo, security police and city leadership was reflected in *Rasta*, as well as the sad role of the *Judenrat* and of the Jewish police.

It is worthwhile to remember the caricatures from *Rasta*:

1. "Homage to the Jews" with the chairman of the *Judenrat* on the throne, and all of the members of the *Judenrat* and their devoted officials swear allegiance to him. In the foreground, one official carries a flag with the inscription: "The health of the *Judenrat* matters the most."

2. Bottles of whiskey corked with police hats and from each bottle another member of the *Judenrat*, who would frolic in the food halls, is looking out.

3. "Hocus-Pocus" – the treasurer of the *Judenrat* throws small papers in the air; the papers are turned into money that falls into his pocket.

4. "I have never in my life danced" – a caricature in which Dr. Zondsztajn dances in front of the *Judenrat* (Zondsztajn came from Czenstochow, studied in France and Germany for many years,

thought a great deal of himself and his medical knowledge, strongly flattered the *Judenrat* and helped it in its actions against *TOZ*).

5. "Potatoes" – wagons of potatoes in the footlights, masses of the hungry are standing in the distance with empty sacks looking with pleading eyes in the direction of the full wagons of potatoes, at which stood the former bank director, Pruszicki, now food supply official at the *Judenrat*. With a shovel, he scrapes [potatoes] down into the sacks that members of the *Judenrat* hold. Words from his mouth gravitate to the hungry crowd: "There are now no potatoes for you!"

6. A dog with the head of the *Judenrat* emperor. Opposite him – Walberg with a *TOZ*-insignia and a letter about a subsidy in his hand. Words drift from the treasurer's mouth in Walberg's direction: "If I do not want to give, will you report it to the *Rasta*?"

7. The dermatologist's office at *TOZ* – Walberg sits in a doctor-like easy chair; opposite him, the *Judenrat* member, Jeremy Gilter as a patient with an outstretched hand full of ulcers. From Walberg's mouth drift down the words in Gitler's direction: "This hand will never again be clean."

8. "Evening prayers" – Dr. Kacinel (then commandant of the Jewish police, who was well known for his bad relationship with the Jewish population) is on his knees and with a pitiful gaze looks at a picture of his wife hanging in the bedroom.

9. "Roman Rights" – a codex book surrounded with the body of a snake, which has the head of the organization chief of the *Judenrat*, Pohorille. All of the caricatures in the project were executed by the editorial board; Walberg reworked them, marked them and then Leib Kusznir, who had shown much interest and talent, photographed them in dozens of copies. Two Poles helped in spreading *Rasta*: a certain Kozlowski, who hid the finished samples outside the ghetto, and a certain Kruzler, who would receive the finished examples from Kozlowski, take them to Warsaw and from there send them by mail in the form of letters to the addresses that were given to him.

The "Workers Council," which carried on separate cultural activities among their members for a time, also made a beautiful contribution in the area of cultural work. The council organized frequent readings, lectures and conversations among their members. An amateur drama group was active at the council for a time under the professional leadership of Maks Chraport and Orbach (both were active in the area of amateur drama groups in Czenstochow before the war), who were simultaneously active in the drama group at *TOZ*. The Workers Council's drama group appeared in *Dos Groyse Gevins* [Sholem Aleichim's "The Lottery"] and later joined the general group to strengthen the general cultural work.

The library that was run in the greatest secrecy had a significant influence on cultural life in the ghetto. The library numbered approximately 25,000 books and in the month of February 1940 was smuggled from the Second Aleje no. 20 to Nadrzeczna Street to the librarian, Rayzele Berkensztat, who was engaged in giving out books for hundreds of readers, groups and amateur theater groups until the month of July 1941 when she was arrested by the Gestapo and the library was confiscated. The *Judenrat* first of all turned to the state chief for permission to carry out language courses for the young people from 14 to 18. The city chief permitted this and, on the 9th of December, the *Judenrat* opened a carpentry and locksmith course for men and a tailoring course for women. The carpentry and locksmith course lessons began on the 16th of March 1941 in a room with 46 attendees and the tailoring course began during the first half of May 1941 in a room with 37 attendees. The mentioned courses were run under the directorship of Prusicki. The courses did not have any longevity; they ran for about four months. Official examinations were carried out and the courses closed. The reasons that led to the closing of the courses remained a secret known only by a number of members of the *Judenrat*. The *Judenrat* tried to receive permission to run a Jewish theater. On the 5th of July 1941, Kapinski turned to the city chief with a written request for permission for theater performances and concerts. The request was motivated by the fact that since before the outbreak of the war, a large number of actors, musicians and singers, who were living in need and had no other employment lived in Czenstochow. The performances and concerts would serve as a source of income for the needs of the *Judenrat*.[83] The following answer came from Wendler on the 22nd of July: "The request is rejected. The actors, musicians and singers should look for other employment; their previous employment is no longer being considered."

On the 9th of January 1942, the *Judenrat* again made a similar request, indicating that the *Judenrat* would facilitate several undertakings to create the means for supporting children and others suffering from need.84. Again receiving a refusal, the *Judenrat* gave up the idea of organizing events.

At the same time that the *Judenrat* tried to get permission from the Germans and they [the *Judenrat*] attacked *TOZ* in all areas of its activities, *TOZ* opened sanitary courses led by Doctor Walberg three times a month. The first was visited by 50 attendees; the second course had 54 attendees and the third – 100. The last course ended in the month of March 1941. The *Judenrat* tried to compete and wanted to open a dental technician course with the help of *Z.S.S.* [Jewish Social Self-Help – a social welfare committee], but it remained only an attempt.

The young people and the leadership of the "day rooms" increased their activity. Private children entertainments took place often in the "day rooms" themselves along with public appearances with social content. Among others, a children's opera, *Lialkes* [Puppets], was performed in which it is shown that puppets revolt against their "string-pullers" [puppeteers]. The performance, which made a colossal impression in the ghetto, evoked great bitterness in *Judenrat* circles.

There was not one public children's appearance that did not begin with the marching of hundreds of children singing "Mir kumen on" [We are coming]. The activity of the chorus and the amateur dramatic group also became more intense. Everyone who could make some kind of contribution came willingly to this work. Among others who joined was Jakubowicz, a young man, a refugee from Warsaw (his father was a ticket seller at the Kaminski Theater) who showed talent and became one of the most important pillars in the group (Jakubowicz survived after the liquidation of the ghetto, moved to the "small ghetto" and became a commemorator in song of our great tragedy. He taught himself to write Yiddish, described everything himself, alone appropriated melodies for his poems and at his own initiative carried out literary evenings).

Members of the former *Lira* chorus joined as chorus members, such as: Henrik Edelist and his young son, Ludwig; the strong bass of Grabiner, the well-known old singer, echoed again. Young male and female soloists appeared of whom the tailor Boruch Baum's daughter, the 18-year old Guta, who became the darling of the crowd, Roma Nodelberg of Łódź, Poznanska – a granddaughter of Rabbi Nochum Asz and Slowaka Zitenfeld, excelled. Many of the young people did not know any Yiddish.

However, they learned it and worthily fulfilled the duties that they willingly took upon themselves. The assimilated Wanda Kapiecka, the well-know pianist-teacher in Czenstochow, also placed herself at the service of *TOZ*. She herself appeared in concerts and prepared her former students to appear publicly. Among her students, the very talented pianist Gliksman excelled (Miss Gliksman had the opportunity, thanks to her external appearance, to stay on the "Aryan" side in Warsaw after the expulsion, taking part in the military underground organizations and after the liberation of Czenstochow, marched into Czenstochow as an officer in the Koœciuszko Division*).

*[Translator's note: the Tadeusz Kościuszko Infantry Division was part of the Polish armed forces organized in 1943 by the Soviets.)

In addition to the joint cultural work, both the communists and the Bundists and the left Zionist groupings carried out separate political and cultural work among their members and sympathizers. This intensive cultural work in all fields included the majority of the population in the ghetto and kept expanding.

On the 22nd of September 1942 the great misfortune of expulsion arrived; everything was interrupted and the cultural building became a ruin along with all of Jewish life in Czenstochow.

Footnotes

82. Statistical Book of *Judenrat* [Jewish council] Volume II pages 154, 190.

83. Two letters from the *Judenrat* [Jewish council] to the city chief.

The Underground Movement in the Ghetto

Czenstochow was one of the few cities in Poland where a significant number of political activists of all beliefs remained after the outbreak of the war. It did not take long and the working activists began to organize underground activities that drew in not only party members, but also many nonpartisans and, chiefly, the young people.

During the early period the parties carried out their work separately. The activity by the communists was made particularly difficult because of the net that agents of the former Polish secret police began to spread over the communist workers who were watched by them during the days of the *Sanacja* [political movement founded by followers of Józef Piłsudski]. The first communist victim was Leyzer Silman. Silman was known in the Jewish labor circles under the name "Gandhi." Silman survived many years in the *Sanacja* jail and then in the Bereze [Kartuska] camp for his communist activities. He was active again when he left Bereze Kartuska. On the first day of September 1939 he was arrested and sent away to a German concentration camp.

Many communist workers were forced to hide for a certain time and then leave Czenstochow because of the net that was spread around them. Leibish Frank, the well-known communist engineer, among others had to do the same thing.

Yet, despite the frightening terror, the communists organized. The pioneers of the renewed communist activity in the underground were: the old members of the S.D.K.P.L. [Social Democracy of the Kingdom of Poland and Lithuania – Marxist party]. Maks Opatowski, the former secretary of the Czenstochower Tailor Workers Union, as well as the tailor worker Srul Dreksler, the painter worker Yankl Wajnrib and A. Sztajnbrecher – all old communists. Many others joined with them. At the beginning of 1942, they made contact with the newly emerging Polish Workers' Party (P.P.R.) through Imialek, the Polish communist and joined in spreading the [party] obligations – *dar narodowy* [national gift] – to collect money for the purpose of carrying out an active struggle against the occupier.

The Bundists also joined the activity early. The first task was to burn the archive. During the burning, a fire broke out in the premises at Piłsudski Street 17. It did not take long and the premises were in flames. The firemen and the Germans appeared who extinguished the flames, but no trace of the archives remained.

During the month of November 1939, a group of Bundists, Futurists and *Skifistn* [members of the *Socialistishe Kinder Farband* – Socialist Children's Union] gathered at the Jewish cemetery, divided themselves into smaller groups and decided that a party committee should lead the conspiratorial work. A member of the party committee was placed at the head of that particular group. The second and the last large meeting of the Bundists took place in the same location in February 1940 (the first meeting took place during the burial of Michal Szimkowicz, the tragic utopian fatality and the second during the burial of the old Bundist, Moshe-Leibe Szimkowicz, the tailor worker who died a natural death). Among other things it was decided at the second meeting to smuggle the large Culture League library at *Aleje* 20 to Nadrzeczna Street 24 to Rayzela Berkensztat, the librarian, and to begin an illegal library there. This plan was carried out over the course of two days and the library began to serve hundreds of readers and, later, the dramatic circle as well.

In June 1940, the Gestapo intensified its search for worker activists according to a list that the Gestapo had demanded that it receive from the *Judenrat*.

At night on the 30th of April, the Gestapo and gendarmes spread out through the streets of the ghetto with a precise list of communist workers and carried out a large number of arrests. Dozens of communists were arrested then along with their family members. Family members were taken when those searched for were not found. In the morning, all of the arrestees were sent away to Auschwitz, from which no one returned. Among those who perished then were: several from the well-known Dzalowski family, the father of Meir Tenenbaum (Meir Tenenbaum was jailed for communist activity for many years. He fought in Czenstochow under the name "Majorek." He perished in Warsaw, where he was hidden with "Aryan" papers). Polya Tenenbaum, the communist youth worker and active coworker from the MOPR [*Miedzynarodowa Organizacja Pomocy Rewolcjonistom* – International Organization for Help to the Revolutionaries] (her father and step-mother who "dared" to ask for her during the arrest also were taken en route and never returned), Yitzhak Czanszinski, the democratic worker, Grunem Frank (an uncle of the communist worker, Leibush Frank), with whom Leibush Frank had hidden. The worker-activist, Yitzhak Opatszinki (he left prison before the war after serving a sentence for communist activity), and a group of communists and their closest family members as well as Czanszinksi, the former council member from the left Paolei Zion [Marxist Zionists].

From time to time intra-party conferences took place to coordinate the underground activity. Two such conferences took place in 1940: one in the house of *Machzikei haDas* [Supporters of the Law] on Nadrzeczna Street and the second in the premises of *TOZ* at Berka Joselewicza Street 3. A second party conference took place during the month of August 1941 in the garden of the former Y. L. Peretz School at Krotka Street number 22 at which the question of creating a joint organization that would have a military character was considered. No agreement was reached in this area.

The activity of the Bund in the month of July 1941 was interrupted for a certain time because of the failure of the courier from the central committee in Warsaw, Marya Szczensna, to provide instructions and literature to the Bundist organization of the entire Radom district. Szczensna was arrested at the Piotroków train station during the first half of July 1941. [A large number of] arrests were made in connection with this. Among the arrestees was Motek Kusznir, who escaped. Five young people were arrested on the spot as hostages until Motek would himself appear or until the Judenrat turned him in.

Yitzhak Czonszinski

Rayzl Berkensztat

Yitzhak Opoczinski

Polya Tenenbaum

Among these arrestees were the well-known *TOZ* officials, Aviv Rozine (the son of Yakov Rozine, an active member of the fighting group at Nadrzeczna 66), Dzjunja Rozen (active co-worker in the division of children's care at *TOZ*, a daughter of the well-known Dr. Rozen in Czenstochow) and Marian Kongrecki, a son of the manufacturer of children's carriages, Kongrecki in Czenstochow). Also arrested as hostages were: Leibl* Kusznir and Chaya Kusznir, Motek's brother and mother.

* [Translator's note: the given name Leibush has many variations, such as Leib, Leibish and Leibl and they are used interchangeably in this chapter.]

On the same day, Motek put himself at the disposal of the party committee, which decreed that he should leave Czenstochow very quickly. At the same time the *Judenrat* informed [the committee] that the Gestapo demanded that it turn over Motek. If not, all of the hostages would be shot. A second meeting of the Bundist party committee took place in the residence of the Rozine family at Warszawa no. 8. Motek, himself, also took part in these discussions. His wife, Rywka waited outside for the decision that would decide about life or death for the one closest to her. It was discussed at the deliberations, whether they should turn over an active worker to save the lives of others. There also was the question whether the committee had the right to have the life of a comrade at its disposal, whether the Gestapo would keep its word when it already had its demanded victim [in its possession]. All made an effort and no one dared to quickly give their thoughts; they felt guilty both in regard to who was sitting here and with regard to whose lives were now in the hands of the Gestapo. Motek declared that he was ready to appear at the Gestapo to keep the hostages alive. Everyone who took part in these deliberations assured him that everything would be done to rescue him from the murderers' hands. They felt that a serious error would be committed, that this was a false and detrimental decision. Motek left the meeting. His wife and comrades followed him from a distance. Motek walked slowly, stopped for a second as if he was having a discussion with himself, looked around, walked quickly for a few steps as if he were running and again began to walk slowly in the direction of Kilinski Street. The Gestapo was located there; it was rare for someone to come back from there. On the same day, the Gestapo took Motek to the prison on Zawodzie and the hostages were freed the next day. Every morning Motek was taken with the couple, Moshe and Rayzele Berkensztat in a Gestapo vehicle from the prison to the Gestapo for a "hearing" that lasted the entire day and at night they were led back into the prison.

Meanwhile, the *Judenrat* announced new demands by the Gestapo, that the old Alerbardi, a Bundist, the grandfather of a communist activist, must be turned over. Ten Jews would be shot if the demand was not fulfilled. A meeting of the Bundist party committee took place in the room of Machzikei haDas [Supporters of the Law]. Alerbardi, himself, took part in the consultations. Everyone was silent. Alerbardi was silent, too. A heavy burden oppressed them: what should they do? Who could know for how long the Gestapo would pull the chain of the victims with blackmail? Who knew how long the Gestapo would blackmail them with collective responsibility? The consultations lasted for many hours; everyone understood that the earlier agreement that Motek would appear was a grave error and it was decided no longer to repeat such a tragic mistake. Alebardi was sent away to Radomsk and from there he left on foot for Piotrków, from where comrades sent him to Warsaw where it was arranged for him to work in a people's kitchen. Fensterblau, whom the Radom Gestapo were searching for in Czenstochow, also left his hiding place and escaped to Warsaw.

The Berkensztat couple and Motek would be whipped all day with clubs
and small whips until they would faint. Then pails of water would be poured
over them and the "investigation" would begin again. The day of pain ended for
the men with them being lain down tied up with their heads under a water
pipe faucet so that every few seconds a drop of water would drip on their
heads. The torturing would end the " investigation" for Rayzele with her
breasts clamped as in a vise with the doors of a closet. After such
"interrogations," all three lay broken, sick and without moving in their prison
cells for approximately two weeks. During these two weeks, the Polish teacher,
who had earlier gone through the same thing and was now waiting in their
ranks to be sent to Auschwitz, took care of them. This teacher did everything
he could that was in his power as an arrestee to revive the strength of these
three flogged people. Meanwhile, there was success in bribing two political
division members of the Gestapo, Otto and Zeier, who were searching for
Hershl Prozer. Each of them received one pair of new boots, two suits and
clothing for their children. Hershl was taken to the Gestapo where he only
received blows and after he was thrown out as a "stupid Jew." Leib Kusznir
again bribed a member of the Gestapo, Willy Krebs, through which in a certain
manner (through sending in food packages) they maintained contact with the
arrestees and encouraged them.

Nine weeks later they succeeded in bribing the then consultant for political
matters at the Gestapo with 35,000 *gildn* in money and with valuable items
and they got Motek out of prison (the Birncwajg brothers helped gather the
first sum of money). At the Gestapo, Motek was considered as having been
shot according to its sentence and in Czenstochow Motek lived using the name
"Pulkowski." After this case, we proceeded to rescue the Berkensztats in the
same way. However, we only succeeded in rescuing Rayzele Berkensztat.
Moshe Berkensztat, who had already been terribly tortured, was entirely
swollen with [damaged] kidneys; he was sent to Auschwitz from which his
children received a telegram that he had died and the Gestapo informed them
that they could have the ashes of his body sent to them for a certain payment.

The underground work by groups with all political leanings started
separately at the beginning of 1942 began to be carried out jointly. However,
the situation in the ghetto kept getting worse. New edicts kept coming, each
one more severe than the other. Sad news from other ghettos sneaked in; it
felt obvious that Czenstochow also would not avoid the terrible misfortune
that had already occurred in other Jewish settlements. Contact with Warsaw

was rare. There only was success in staying in contact with Warsaw through a young Pole from the Warsaw Polish Underground movement who ordered detonators for grenades. The detonators were ordered from the Slomnicki brothers, who had organized a well-hidden mechanical workshop at Garibaldi Street, no. 11. During one of his visits this messenger brought with him only a short letter written in Yiddish that we should listen to him attentively and adjust to his instructions. He met with us at the *TOZ* premises at the New Market no. 2. He described to us in detail the destruction of the Warsaw ghetto and ended that the ghetto there looked as if after a terrible plague. He carefully said that Czenstochow would not avoid this and advised that we prepare for an open fight. The same [messenger] also gave us the addresses of the designated places in Warsaw to which we had to report if we had to escape from Czenstochow. Meanwhile, an order was issued that all the Jews must pay the taxes owed from years past by the 16th of September. Jews began to understand that the Germans were in a rush to collect the taxes before any expulsion began. The legend that Czenstochow would avoid the misfortune evaporated.

The Jews from the small *shtetlech* [towns] that surrounded Czenstochow were sent to Radomsk and then to Czenstochow. This was a clear notice to everyone that the Germans were concentrating the Jews at several locations. The apprehension and the unease spread even further. The underground workers intensified their attention and began to seek means and ways to prepare for every eventuality. At the beginning of September 1942 we learned that the city chief demanded of the *Judenrat* a precise plan for the ghetto according to housing blocks. Several days later we again learned about some kind of secret conference with General [Julian Rudolf] Boettcher from Radom and several prominent men in Czenstochow, which was concerned with Jewish matters. It was clear to us that the plan for the ghetto was called for in connection with Boettcher's visit. It already was clear to us that Boettcher, Barneman, Einrich and Blume, who held the consultations, were preparing a plan of expulsion according to the instructions that Boettcher gave them. The liaison-men from the underground groups decided to call a joint conference to build a fighting organization. This conference was designated for Yom Kippur, the 21st of September. The place where the conference was supposed to take place was the premises of *TOZ* at the New Market no. 2. Sumek Abramowicz and two comrades (communists), whose names were not given, Brener and Kusznir (Bundists), Yisroel Szimanowicz (left *Poalei-Zion* [Marxist-Zionists]),

Rywka Glanc (kibbutzim [collective communities]), Yakov Razine, Doctor Walberg, Doctor Mering and Uzer Berish Blechsztajn were supposed to take part. They also waited for a representative from the Warsaw *ZOB* [*Zydowska Organizacja Bojowa* – Jewish Fighting Organization]. The first delegates, who were supposed to open the premises, Brener and Razine, were stopped in the courtyard in front of the premises by security policemen at 10 'clock in the morning on Yom Kippur. They were beaten. They were freed after about two hours, thanks to the intervention of the Jewish drivers who did business with these German policemen. Alas, the already too late designated conference did not take place and the expulsion-action that began on the same night of the 21st to the 22nd of September 1942 lasted for five weeks and was carried out with inconceivable cruelty, not encountering any organized resistance. The very intensive underground activity that was going to be transformed into an active resistance movement did not succeed in establishing its cadres. The greatest number of those who were drawn into this work perished in Treblinka with the majority of the Jews from the large Czenstochower community.

Only a few of them had the luck of taking part in the Treblinka revolt, such as: Wilinger, Lubling and so on. Among the most important organizers of the Treblinka revolt was Moshe Langner, whom as a punishment the German murders hung there with his head down and he – already hanging – after everything, called out for revenge and thus breathed out his soul.

During the course of the expulsion, a few surviving activists and the tragically small number of surviving young people began to organize fighting groups, which later grew into a force in the so-called "small ghetto." This group carried out activities there until the liquidation of the "small ghetto" and later in the *HASAG** camps as well.

*[Translator's note: *HASAG* – Hugo Schneider AG, a German munitions manufacturer that maintained factories in Czenstochow labor camps using slave labor.]

Demographic Relationships

a. Structure

The actual number of Jews in Czenstochow was always more than the number of Jews recorded at city hall. This could be explained by the fact that not all Jews, particularly the poor, complied at the proper time in reporting their newborn children. Significantly, during the occupation years, the actual number of Jews amounted to more than the number of Jews reported. This is because the refugees and even the regular residents who returned from their wandering during the start of the war period did not report because, "Let us just see how things will look." Mainly, they did not want to appear on any list so as to avoid for as long as possible the multiple taxes that were placed on everyone by the *Judenrat* at every opportunity as well as to avoid carrying out the duty of forced labor. Later, the order arrived from the city chief that no Jew could be registered without his permission. Very few Jews asked the city chief for permission to register, fearful of the consequences for arriving in the city illegally.

We rely on two sources to deal with the structure of the occupation years:

on a report from the statistical office at city hall (letter no. A-891/1/47 of the 18th of February 1947 and

on the statistical yearbook of the *Judenrat* for 1940, (Roczniki Statystyczne [Statistical Yearbook] volume 2). We have to consider both of them with great reservations.

That we must deal with them with reservations will be corroborated by the following facts: the statistical office at the city hall noticed in the government report that the number of unreported Jews during the occupation years grew between 10 and 20 percent. In the same report it was presented (see the further tables) that there were 34,920 registered Jews; a year earlier, that is, in June 1941, the supply office at the city hall gave out food allocations for 37,667 Jews. In a letter no. 41/3365, the city chief reported again on the 5th of August 1941 to the chief of the Radom district that there were 164,567 residents in Czenstochow, of them 37,667 Jews. On the 16th of January 1942 the city chief again shared with Radom (letter no. 6107) that approximately 40,009 Jews were present in Czenstochow.

The statistical office of the city hall stated in the above-mentioned report the number of registered Jews in Czenstochow according to the following table:

Year and month	Number of Jews	Men	Women
January 1939	28,486	13,692	14,794
January 1940	31,758	14,727	17,031
January 1941	33,921	15,634	18,187
July 1942	34,920	16,122	18,808

The supply office at the city hall gave food allocations in 1941 according to the following table:

Month	For how many souls
February	34,193
March	35,072
April	37,309
May	37,518
June	37,667

From June 1940 to the end of 1941 the numbers fluctuated by only a few hundred.

At the end of 1940 the statistical office at the *Judenrat* closed the files of the Jews in Czenstochow and carried out an analysis of the age, sex, education and profession of the 32,744 Jews who comprised the files. This research ended at the beginning of March 1941 and provided the following results:

Age	Male	Female	Together	Percent
0 – 4	917	845	1,762	5.39
5 – 9	1,240	1,200	2,440	7,45
10 – 14	1,474	1,373	2,874	8.69
15 – 19	1,606	1,663	2,874	9.98
20 – 29	2,497	3,103	5,599	17.10
30 – 39	2,909	3,275	6,184	18.89
40 – 49	1,879	2,376	4,255	13.00
50 – 59	1,498	1,701	3,199	9.90
60 – 69	949	1,057	2,006	6.00
70 and older	505	678	1,183	3.60
	15,474	17,271	32,744	100.00

Forty-one non-Polish citizens and 20 converts were counted among the general number, 32,744.

To the stated numbers from the ages 10-14 and 15-19, as well as 50-59 and 60-69 must be added a certain criterion, because to avoid the obligation of forced labor, a certain number of young people from the age of 14, reported as younger and Jews younger than 60 gave older ages. The exact opposite occurring in 1942 because the obsession arose then to be "hidden" at the temporary workplaces and everyone then wanted to be considered in the category of being capable of working.

In carrying out the analysis of the educational standing of the 32,744 Jews, the Statistical Office of the *Judenrat* took into consideration that children up to the age of 10 had received no education because of the specific situation and, therefore, were not counted in any category. Jews 10 years old and older were considered; this consisted of 28,542 people. Of them, 3,782, that is 13.29 percent were illiterate, of them 1,454 men and 2,328 women; 14,401, that is 50.45 percent, who could read and write, of them 7,236 men and 7,164 women; 5,858 finished elementary school, that is 20.51 percent, of them 2,727 men, 3,131 women; there were 2,653 with a middle [school] education, that is 9.28 percent, of them 1,054 men, 1,599 women; there were 394 with higher education, that is 1.38 percent, of them 252 men, 142 women; those with informal educations – 1,454, that is 5.09 percent, of them 594 men, 860 women.

When the statistical report about the Jewish population was compiled in 1940, the Statistical Office at the *Judenrat* eliminated children up to age 10 and considered the number 28,542.

Deducted from this were all economically passive elements, 9,479 women who were in the majority busy with running a house and 5,089 male and female students. The general number of economically active who worked to earn a living made up 13,974. There were 4,765 artisans, 3,295 workers, 1,959 traders and merchants, 662 manufacturers, 1,531 without designated trades, 1,088 officials, 272 free professions [medicine and law] were among this number of the economically active. The rest consisted of agricultural workers, musicians and so on. The statistics from the same office look different in 1941; that is illustrated in diagram number 58.

According to all probabilities the *Judenrat* statistical office used and studied the pre-war professions of everyone because in 1940 the Jews could not be employed in any agricultural work or in the free professions, which included 43 lawyers, and it was then known that lawyers could not be employed in their profession. The same can be said of teachers because only a small number of gymnazie [secondary school] professors led illegal student groups and from this drew a means of support. Another proof that the statistical office at the *Judenrat* used and studied pre-war employment for everyone is the fact that on the 9th of May 1942 the city chief received a telegraphic demand from the chief of the Radom district to give the exact number of artisans in Czenstochow. The *Judenrat* provided a list of artisans who were employed in their trades, which consisted of the following:

	Men	Women	Combined
Textile artisans	255	322	577
Metal artisans	505	12	517
Teachers	192	5	197
Construction	100	1	101
Wood	187	3	190
Hairdressers	83	11	94
Combined	1,322	354	1,676

In 1942, as we see from the provided table, the *Judenrat* circles estimated that when there already were approximately 48,000 Jews present in Czenstochow, 1,676 artisans were employed at their trades. True, constant changes took place in the Jewish population, but not in such great proportion as between 4,765 artisans in 1940 and 1,676 in 1942 when the number of Jews was much larger. The economic structure of the Jewish population from the beginning of the war to the large deportation kept changing. The tempo of change was dependent on the German edicts on the Jewish population in the city itself and on the increase in the number of Jews in the city, which was mostly a consequence of the resettlements carried out by the Germans in surrounding *shtetlech* [towns], as well as their special *aktsias* [actions, usually deportations] to make some towns *judenrein* [cleansed of Jews] and a number of the local residents were taken to the Czenstochow ghetto.

b. Natural Movements

According to the statements of the *Judenrat* statistical office it appears that in 1940 504 weddings took place. Ninety-eight of them fell in the first half of the year and 406 in the second half of the year. The greatest number of weddings took place in the month of December – 169. This phenomenon [occurred] in the second half of 1940 when a rumor spread that the rabbinate would have the right to provide a wedding ceremony until the 31st of December 1940 and that there would be an interruption in the right of the rabbinate for an entire two years after this period.[85]

Age of those married in 1940

Age	Women	Men
Up to age 19	15	3
20 – 24	182	113
25 – 29	211	229
30 – 39	86	147
40 and higher	10	12
Total	504	504

This consisted of approximately 16 weddings for every 1,000 members of the population. The same office showed that before the war, there were 7.8 weddings for every 1,000 members of the population.[86]

According to statements by the statistical office at the city hall, in 1939 260 weddings took place. In 1940 – 500, in 1941 – 284 and during the first quarter of 1942 – 78.

The *Judenrat* statistical office [said] that 351 children were born in 1940; of them, 170 boys and 181 girls. That made 10.7 for every 1,000 [residents]. The same office showed that in 1936-1938 there were 18.9 born for every 1,000 members of the Jewish population.[87]

The statistical office at the city hall indicated that births among the Jewish population were: in 1939 – 339, in 1940 – 480 and in 1941 – 281 and in the first three months of 1942 – 66.[88]

The statistical office at the city hall indicated that births among the Jewish population were: in 1939 – 339, in 1940 – 480 and in 1941 – 281 and in the first three months of 1942 – 66.[88]

In a report about mortality among the Jewish population the *Judenrat* statistical office states that in 1940 260 men and 243 women died. The 503 people who died amounted to approximately 16 cases of death for each 1,000 [people] in the population. It is noticed that in comparison to the years 1936-1938, the mortality rate increased by 5.7 for each 1,000.[89]

The statistical office at the city hall again provided the following steady progress of mortality and the natural increase among the Jewish population:

Year	Mortality	Nat. Increase
1939	298	+41
1940	537	+57
1941	958	− 677
1941 first quarter	310	− 244[90]

The numbers given, both when it talks about the structure and about the natural movement, cannot be accepted as absolute because in the specific conditions in which the Jewish population lived it was impossible for the above-mentioned office to be able to learn everything precisely and to record it.

From that which is provided we see that on one side the births kept decreasing and the cases of death increased. This throws a certain light on the conditions of Jewish life in Czenstochow during the occupation years from 1939 to the 22nd of September 1942, when the German murderers began to carry out their "deportation" decree across the entire Jewish settlement in Czenstochow.

On the Eve of Liquidation

The life of the Jews in the ghetto was difficult. The *Judenrat* sent out notices, demands and decrees every few days that began with the refrain: "At the order of the regime..." Such announcements and decrees always brought anxiety. The anxiety would be felt particularly when direct edicts appeared from the occupying regime that always began with threats of persecutions or the death penalty.

With the anxious mood, which kept getting more anxious with the arrival of 1942, there arrived an insecurity that everyone wanted to deny. News went from ear to ear that the Jews were being gassed somewhere; they were being taken in vehicles and in such a manner the Germans were annihilating the Jews from the small *shtetlech* [towns]. It was reported that a Jew who escaped to Czenstochow from a small *shtetl* outside Lodz said very secretly that he, himself, had buried his wife and child who had perished in such a manner [as described above]. All of the news was repeated many times and yet everyone added: "Somehow I do not believe that something like this could happen." They also spoke about this, that the young doctors who were sent to the Lublin area were deported somewhere with all of the Jews from the *shtetlech* and every trace of them disappeared. However, the families and relatives of these doctors consoled themselves, [believing] that without doubt they were deported with those Jews from the destroyed *shtetlech* and villages in Ukraine where they only were forced to do heavy labor. The mood was depressed and there began apparent acts of suicide. A certain Avner, a former teacher, deliberately left the ghetto so that he would be shot and it did happen; a certain Nachum Majmun hanged himself in the bath at Garibaldi Street 18.[91]

In spring 1942 the news about the fate of Lublin exploded like a thunderbolt. The destruction of Lublin was talked about in every house, about which the Germans themselves had spoken and this caused the Jews to start thinking more about the fate of the Czenstochow ghetto. Meanwhile, the Gestapo increased the terror and the frequent murders. The Gestapo shot three Jews on the 18th of June 1942;[92] on the 7th of June 1942 the Gestapo entered Betsalel Walberg's shop, which was located at Orlicz-Dreszer Street, and shot the owner.[93] These cases became known in the ghetto. Still more shootings took place of which the ghetto did not know.

At the beginning of July 1942 all of the men from the age of 16 to 60 were driven out of their residences, positioned at the old market, the new market and the 1st *Aleje* where they were held for hours. The Jews interpreted this as a kind of "test selection" carried out in this manner by General Boettcher from Radom with the city chief, Dr. Franke. The unease thus kept increasing when the news about the expulsions in Warsaw began to arrive. At the same time the German *Sondergericht* [special court], which would sentence Jews to the punishment of death for leaving the ghetto, began punishment with prison and with deportation for the same sin.

At the same time, the Jews were shot for leaving the ghetto or for some other kind of "sin" without any kind of legal judgment. Thus were the 33-year old Anshl Renkszowski and Yisroel-Mordechai Szitowski shot outside the ghetto on the 12th of August 1942.[94] The terror in the ghetto itself increased horribly. On the 3rd of August gendarmes attacked the Jewish hospital on Przemyslowa, destroyed the furniture, beat the Jewish policeman, Birnholc, who served there and stole various things of value. Soldiers and members of the *Luftwaffe* attacked not only Jewish civilians in the streets, but even Jewish policemen who were in service.[95] Therefore, everyone saw the threatening danger that lay in wait for the Czenstochow Jewish community. Everyone who had the opportunity of making contact with Polish acquaintances tried to do so and firstly arranged for a hiding place for their children. In a similar manner, several arranged for a hiding place for the entire family. Meanwhile, the city chief announced that he was setting up "shops" at *Metalurgia* on Krutka Street where work would be done for internal German use and all of those who were employed there would no be affected by any deportations. He ordered machines and a payment of one and half million *gildn* from the *Judenrat* so that the Jews could work there. From the 31st of July until the 13th of August 1942, the *Judenrat*, through its officials specially designated for this purpose, confiscated from the Jews machines necessary to organize the workshops with the aid of the Jewish police and simultaneously tried to "soften" the heart of the city chief in regard to the payment of money. After long negotiations, Franke, the city chief, agreed to take the payment in three installments and he immediately received the first payment of half a million. The confiscated sewing machines, brush machines and fur workshops were set up in *Metalurgia*. Jewish leaders were designated for each separate workshop and a separate director was responsible for all workshops.

The hope of those who were not employed at the so-called "secure temporary workplaces" now turned to the "shops." Every worker tried to obtain the red booklet at his "temporary workplace" and have it stamped at the German work office. Such a booklet was supposed to indicate that its owner was a needed person. The lines in front of the labor office grew longer from day to day. At the courtyard at *Aleje* 12, where the *Judenrat* enrolled workers in the "shops," it was dark with the thousands of people who waited here for the "luck" to be accepted.

Doctors, lawyers, teachers, professors, female Froblists [kindergarten teachers], musicians and artists; directors, merchants, manufacturers and simple traders, who had paid not to have to work or had tried to avoid heavy labor were now transformed into shoemakers, tailors, furriers, locksmiths and brushmakers (only such "shops" were set up). There were also huge lines in front of the premises of the *Judenrat*. Here, hundreds of similar skeletons wrapped in rags with hands eaten by leprosy, pushed themselves to the windows of the *Judenrat* officials and did everything to persuade the *Judenrat* members and their officials that they – the starving, exhausted Jews driven out of cities and *shtetlech* – were not so poor, needed no help, had enough strength to work and as a necessary element they had the full right to continue to remain in the city. The officials, who were employed in the social aid division at the *Judenrat*, again began to destroy cards from the files with the names of those who had come for aid. Now, the underground political parties, in view of the emergence of the great danger, began to negotiate about united action against the occupiers.

Meanwhile, the Germans kept preparing to carry out the expulsion. On the 10th of July 1942 the security police arranged for the edges of the sidewalks to be whitewashed on the corners of every street, that the houses on every street where the ghetto ended be whitewashed up to two meters high, that the entrances of every cellar room be whitewashed and so on. The Jews interpreted this order as the Germans wanting each of them to be easier to locate in the ghetto. However, so that this order would not evoke any feelings of surprise from the Jews, it also was ordered that the squares at the new market (it was here that the selections later took place) be seeded with grass.[96] It was simultaneously reported that the Jews had the right to gather in the prayer houses during the Jewish holidays and that the leaders and commissars at all temporary workplaces had the right on this holiday day at their own discretion to free the Jewish workers from work.[97] These decrees, which were probably intended to lull the attention of the Jews to sleep, had just the opposite effect. The mistrust of German reassurances kept growing and with the mistrust grew the unease that had as its culmination the approaching Days of Awe when the city leadership began to mix less in the private matters of the ghetto (this happened after Boettcher's visit at the beginning of September when the secret deliberations among the prominent Germans in Czenstochow took place), as opposed to the security police who began to appear more in the ghetto.

All of the Jews who lived on Kawia Street were moved (during the *aktsia* the large mass grave for the thousands of Jews who were shot in the course of five weeks that the expulsion lasted was created here); the security police also threw out the Jews who lived on Garibaldi Street in the houses 26 and 28 (during the *aktsia* they organized the storehouses here for the possessions they stole). Members of the Gestapo headed by Shabelski (Shabelski was the terror of the ghetto; his name always evoked dread) began to carry out more frequent searches, beatings and looting. (After the liberation, Shabelski was sentenced to death by the Polish court in Czenstochow.) Frankowski, Dzherzszon, who always had a large dog helping, Laszinski, Kestener, Hantke ("veyser kop" [white head], Afitz ("Gorgl" [Adam's apple]), Shot ("Zigeyner" [gypsy]), who had, as was told, shot the 26-year old Jeszenowicz for crossing the boundary of the ghetto at Kocapsker Bridge at Wilson Street in March 1942, Shmid ("Cyrkowiec" [acrobat]), Kirsch ("Pesele"), as well as Klibsh and Schlosser, who were the closest and most trusted men of Lieutenant Werner, Degenhardt's representative, excelled with their savagery. Onblach, Degenhardt's chauffeur, made frequent visits to Jewish residences, beating and robbing [the residents] of everything that he liked.

The mood in the ghetto already was terrible on *Erev* [eve of] Yom Kippur. It went from person to person that there was an "annihilation commando" in the city. The anxiety grew over the course of a day. At night, they began to light the Yom Kippur candles and the ghetto was transformed into great lamentations. Formerly, Jews had the right to not work on Yom Kippur morning; now very, very few Jews made use of this right. Rumors spread that the Jewish "friends of the state" such as Gnot, Jaczombek, Herman, "Kulibejke," Beser, Szeptel, Mechtiger and others, left the ghetto and hid on the Aryan side. It was related that Paul Lange, the *chazan* [cantor], the German leader of the "furniture factory," quietly advised the Jewish workers at this temporary workplace not to go home after ending their work but to remain at their workplace overnight. The workers at the "furniture factory," "Braland," "Rawa" and at the "Horowicz and Partners" factory quickly prepared bunkers at the workplaces and smuggled in their closest family members.

The rumor spread that the chairman of the *Judenrat* had been called to the city chief and several hours had passed and we had not seen him come back. Yom Kippur night, [there was] a heavy movement of Jews in the ghetto. Everyone hurried, they ran, they looked uneasily on all sides, they stopped at corners and asked each other what they had heard and they ran further, not waiting for an answer. Degenhardt threatened the greatest repressions for various false "rumors." Degenhardt ordered the *Judenrat* and the Jewish police to calm the masses and make an end to the uneasy mood in the ghetto. Members of the *Judenrat* and policemen tried to carry out the order of the police chief. They went through the ghetto streets until late in the evening and tried to convince everyone that the rumors of a The Czitnicki did not accept the favor because he wanted to take part in the fate of all of the Jews. Whoever could, at least sent their children out to Polish acquaintances. Outside of the ghetto, the members of the Gestapo and the gendarmes kept at their work and searched for Jews who were hiding there. Rumors spread that there already were many victims from among those who were caught outside the ghetto. The Gestapo caught, among others, the young daughter of the well-known Jewish labor worker in Czenstochow, Dudek Szlezinger, who was hidden with a Polish worker. She was brought to her parents on Garibaldi Street and was shot there with her father in front of her mother. Night fell. The streets were cleaned up and a dreadful stillness began to reign in the ghetto, a stillness before a storm.

At night on Yom Kippur, the 21st of September 1942, all of the ghetto streets were filled with fascist Ukrainians and Lithuanian auxiliary police, under the leadership of the members of the Gestapo and security police and the "expulsion action" began. A frightening tragedy for the large Czenstochower community began.

Bekanntmachung

Betrifft:

Aenderung der Sperrstunde.

Für die Zeit vom 20. 6. 1942 bis 31. 8. 1942 wird die Sperrstunde in der Stadt Tschenstochau

1. für Polen von **23-5 Uhr,**

2. für Juden von **21-5 Uhr**

festgesetzt.

Wer das Stadtgebiet während der Sperrstunden ohne Passierschein betritt, wird bestraft.

Gleichzeitig wird die Polizeistunde für die polnischen Gaststätten pp. auf 22.30 festgesetzt.

Tschenstochau, den 16. 6. 1942.

Der Stadthauptmann
Dr. Franke

OGŁOSZENIE

Dotyczy:

Zmiany godzin policyjnych.

Na okres od 20. 6. 1942 r., do 31. 8. 1942 r. ustala się w mieście Częstochowie godzinę policyjną

1. dla Polaków od godz. **23 do 5-ej.**

2. dla żydów od godz. **21 do 5-ej.**

Kto przebywać będzie na terenach publicznych miasta w czasie godzin policyjnych bez przepustki, zostanie ukarany.

Jednocześnie ustala się godzinę policyjną dla polskich restauracyj na 22.30.

Częstochowa, dnia 16. VI. 1942 r.

Starosta Miejski
Dr. Franke

Sabelski before the Polish People's Court in Czenstochow

Mrs. Langner in front of the witness stand

The Large Liquidation

The morning of the 22nd of September 1942, the ghetto trembled. Jewish policemen carried the desolating news to their acquaintances that the ghetto was being surrounded on all sides by fascist Ukrainian *Hilfspolizei* [auxiliary police]. Thousands of people ran around the ghetto from room to room, from house to house, from street to street. They kissed and said goodbye. The tumult was endless. They cried, they shouted, they ran and they dragged packs with them. Some dragged packs of bed linen with them, some a backpack, some a bundle and some a few dishes. They ran as if they were pulling themselves out of a terrible fire. I, too, was chased from street to street. Here I was at the market, here at the old market, here I was on Mirowska [Street], here on Garncarksa and here I was on Nadrzeczna [Street]. Here I went with the storm to *Rynek Warszawski* [a square now named Ghetto Fighters Square]. I wanted to go back but I could not. I was prevented by the storm of people and mainly – the fascist auxiliary police who made us "understand" with the butts of their rifles that there was no way back... Warszawer Street, Krotka. The streets were blocked with people. Dozens of gendarmes and members of the Gestapo, dozens of the Polish police, hundreds of bandits from the auxiliary formation. Under the hail of blows, groups were driven to the *Metalurgia*, where the "shops" were set up. Wives were torn from husbands and children from parents. They struggled with the murderers; they wanted to go together. Whoever stood opposed, fell with a shattered skull. The same happened to those who did not let themselves be torn from their wife and child, or dared to say goodbye to their wife and child. Krotka Street was full of frightful laments. Mothers, crazy with desperation, called their lost children and fell with shattered skulls. The shouting and crying of hundreds of children who were calling their mothers tore through the air. The ranks of *Metalurgia* became even denser and longer. Human shadows with hands stretched out, which held red booklets that certified the usefulness of the person, stood darkly in the giant rows one pressed to another in front of the gates of the former metal factory. The cruel police dog, chief Degenhardt, strolled here calmly among the dense mass and pointed with his riding crop over heads and stammered: "You right, you left!" He respected no one.

Thousands of red booklets, torn, trampled, lay around and their owners were driven to the left. Dozens of the sick only in underwear left the former Peretz School, in which a hospital for infectious diseases now was set up; after them came nurses. I recognized Dzjuni Rozen, the nurse, Doctor Rozen's daughter, from afar. She was running with all of the sick. It was evident now that she did not want to leave them. A revolver resounded... A number of the sick fell near the gate of the Peretz School building, and the rest were driven to the left. Hundreds of known faces floated past my eyes. I noticed the always happy, fun-loving and energetic Riwik Slomnicki, who was now being pushed to the right by gendarmes. He pulled back under a hail of blows and went to the other side. Here, he picked up a crying little girl and moved slowly with the crowd to the left. Near me stood a young couple, near them a small child. They spoke among themselves quietly in Polish. "Dziecku nic zlego nie zrobion" (Nothing bad will be done to a child). They left the child who was immediately driven to the left. And they themselves scrambled to the tower of *Metalurgia*. I saw how Leon Rozensztajn, disheveled and wild, wrestled with two gendarmes. He fell down, stood up on his knees and pleaded with the gendarmes who were dragging him away and pushing him into *Metalurgia*. The same thing happened with Leibl Altman, who struggled to go with his wife and children. I, too, was pushed into *Metalurgia*. My red booklet "gave witness" that I was a brush-master, and it turned out that the Germans who checked the booklet thought this artisan could be of use...

* * *

The factory square was full of people and yet it was so quiet, as at a cemetery. Here served several members of the *Judenrat* such as: Kapinski, Berliner, Borzykowski, and Kurland. The Germans also brought the old man from the *chevre kadishe* [burial society], Miski, who under supervision of gendarme Ibersher had to direct the clearing away of the dead to Kawia Street where two large pits had already been dug for a mass grave. There was a terrible oppression of sadness and anxiety. We moved in the shadows or we sat frozen. A high moan was heard from another spot for several seconds, or an outbreak of crying. The frightening stillness that lasted during the first moments was interrupted. Leib Altman sat alone on a stone, hit his head with his fists and screamed: "My wife, my children! My joy-giving children!" Hela Frank, the wife of the well-known munitions worker, Engineer Leibusz Frank, sat in a corner somewhere.

She kept her three and half year old boy hidden under her dress. She related how Machl Birncwajg with the help of Mikhl Wajskop (he later was an active member of *ŻOB* [Jewish Fighting Organization]) brought her to the "furniture camp" after the curfew to hide her and her child in a bunker. However, she was driven from there. She had lived for three years with the hope of finding her husband who left for the Soviet Union and now all of her hopes were shattered. Leon Rozensztajn sat on some sort of old rusted kettle and looked ahead expressionless with eyes wide open. At every step another dejected face, another insane look. They sat; they turned around as if one did not want to see the other. Two gendarmes appeared at lunchtime, looked on all sides, as if they were searching for someone. They stopped near Rozensztajn, asked him if he was the Jew who wanted to go with his wife and called him to go with her. A few seconds later a shot was heard and Rozensztajn already lay in a pool of blood. This shot agitated the despondent crowd like an announcement that here their lives also were not secure. Degenhardt arrived, accompanied by gendarmes. All of the Jews were chased and ordered to stand in dense rows. Every row was looked over carefully. Whoever looked too young or too old, whoever looked weak or had a defect was immediately taken out of the row and taken away. A 14-15 year old boy stood a few rows in front of me. He was removed from the row by Degenhardt himself; then Degenhardt pointed to a middle-aged Jew with his riding crop and called out: "You are certainly his father!" The Jew struggled, but it was of no use. He had to go with the boy as his "father"... Those who believed that their lives would be secure in the "shops" and who began to look for ways to save themselves saw these illusions evaporate. The 22nd of September, the first day after Yom Kippur, ended for the Jews of the Czenstochow ghetto with several hundred murdered on the spot and 8,000 deported to Treblinka.

Earlier, the packs that those deported had with them were taken and they even were told to take off their shoes and then they were pushed into the previously prepared cattle cars. The streets: Kawia, Wilson, Krutka, Garibaldi, Rynek, Warszawski, part of Garncarska and part of Nadrzeczna, which had been populated by Jews, were now entirely emptied.

The next morning – all of the ghetto streets were heavily guarded, there was heavy gunfire in the streets from which the Jews already had been deported.

Here were killed Jews who attempted to hide and did not appear at the "selections." Frequents shots echoed in the still inhabited streets that ended the lives of those who dared to climb out of a window or to appear on a balcony.

A rumor spread a few days later that a certain number of Jews in the train wagons from the second "selection" had been sent back to the ghetto. Nervous movement began. They ran to the members of the *Judenrat*; they tried to learn something precise from the Jewish policemen, from the Polish *granat* policemen [Blue police - Polish police in the Nazi-occupied area of Poland known as the General Government], from the gendarmes. Everyone wanted to learn if someone in their family, from those closest to them and acquaintances were among the "fortunate ones." They learned from the Jewish policemen that Jews actually had been sent back to the ghetto from the train wagons, but they had the right to return only to the streets where Jews remained. A ray of hope that was full of trembling and unease for their further fate was noticed only in a few; the vastly large number were resigned [to their fate] and did not believe in miracles.

On the third day, I was summoned to go to Degenhardt's representative, to the security policeman Sapert, who served at *Metalurgia*, and in Kapinski's presence I received an order that all former leaders of the *TOZ* institutions should organize a sanitation site for the remaining Jews. A freight wagon and horses was put at my disposal and under the supervision of a gendarme, of the Polish policeman and of a Jewish policeman, I had to leave *Metalurgia* twice a day and bring the property assets from *TOZ* and from the sanitation site which was headed by the *Judenrat*. I made an agreement with my "accompanier" and for a 100 *gildn* a head, he permitted me to take Jews with me from the ghetto and smuggle them into *Metalurgia* as workers who helped me with the work that was given to me. Later, they increased the payment to a thousand *gildn* a head. Dr. Yitzhak Szperling, who showed great devotion in his work in the division of help among the Jews in *Metalurgia*, as well as with the smuggling of Jews from the streets into *Metalurgia*, was designated as the doctor at the sanitation site. (The same Szperling did not act well in the *H.A.S.A.G.*)* I encountered a "selection" during my third time in the street. They drove Jews further from Warszawer Street, from the old market, from Nadrzeczna and Garncarska. All were chased to the large square at the new market. Thousands of Jews were placed here in two long rows. Dozens of gendarmes, dozens of members of the Gestapo, *Granat* policemen, hundreds from the auxiliary formations and groups of soldiers from the *Luftwaffe* encircled this square.

*[Translator's note: *H.A.S.A.G.* is the acronym for a German metal goods manufacturer, *Hugo Schneider Metallwarenfabrik AG.* A *H.A.S.A.G.* factory was established in the Czenstochower ghetto and "employed" forced labor or prisoners from concentration camps.]

Everyone held their rifles or revolvers at the ready with their sights turned to the driven together Jews. On the left side, on the west side of the square close to the First *Aleje* stood Boettcher, general in the *S.S.*, with a group of *S.S.* officers. Several Jewish policemen and Kapinski and Kurland, two members of the *Judenrat*, also were on the square and assisted during the "selection." There was total quiet. Only Degenhardt's stammering voice was heard: "What is your profession?" And not waiting for any answer, he pointed with his riding crop over the head: "Right, left, right, left!" He decided about the life and death of everyone separately with this characteristic: "You right, you left!" This "selection" lasted almost half a day. Six thousand Jews on the left were driven to train wagons and sent to Treblinka and the several hundred Jews on the right were sent to *Metalurgia*. The streets were strewn with the murdered and, in addition, the selection square was strewn with children's strollers, rucksacks, bundles, bed linens and pots. It was empty and frightening...

Day after day, I was in the street with my companions. Calls reached us from the rooms in which there were still Jews: "Jews, give us something to eat!" Through the windows I recognized children from the *TOZ* day care locations who shouted: "What will happen to us? We are hungry!" Large placards with slogans from Dr. Franke, the city chief, shouted down from the walls on which he threatened the death penalty for hiding Jews, for providing Jews with food and for selling items to Jews.[98]

Suddenly – a new ray of hope: Gendarmes brought a group of Jews into the "shops." They had ransomed themselves for large sums of money, for jewelry and other valuable items. It was reported that Degenhardt himself had taken over from a bunker a large transport of grocery items from Glatter, a grocery firm, and, therefore, he had assured Glater [earlier spelled Glatter] that he would avoid the "selection." The *Judenrat* members who served in *Metalurgia* undertook the further "mediation" and collected the ransom money from the Jews for the security police. Jews turned over the last of their possessions. They turned over hidden and walled up treasures and even their most precious jewelry that had been passed from generation to generation, if only to save those closest to them. Sacks of gold, jewelry and diamonds were turned over to the members of the *Judenrat* and from them some to the gendarmes, but the duped Jews, sentenced to death, walked further on to the cattle wagons in which they were taken to Treblinka.

At the same time, I was forbidden to go out into the street again with my usual companions without the "accompaniment" of a member of the *Judenrat*.

It began with me going with Kurland, the member of the *Judenrat*, who apparently prevailed upon my enemies behind my back that they not allow the smuggling of Jews into *Metalurgia* because this worked against the plans of the *Judenrat*, which collected "ransom" money. Therefore, I had to be satisfied with providing food for Jews in the closed ghetto during my departure through which I managed to travel with food items that I took from the *TOZ* warehouses at Przemyslowa no. 11 and from *Machzikei haDat* [Supporters of the Law] at Nadrzeczna. Kurland did help me in this. On the 29th of September we took 10 sacks of flour from the *TOZ* warehouse at Nadrzeczna no. 36 and divided it among Jews who were still on this street. We found a man who hanged himself at Nadrzeczna 34. The Jew hung in the middle of the room on tied together towels. We looked at the suicide and recognized him as a certain Yitzhak-Hersh Rug, who came from the small *shtetl* of Wyczwe that lay near Kowel in Volyn. We met the former leader of the field kitchen, Jechiel Gamulinski, at Nadrzeczna Street, in the house of the Czorker Rebbe. He agreed to take one sack of flour for the Jews who were still in this house. We gave the remaining nine sacks of flour to Zalman Windman's bakery that was located on Nadrzeczna Street so that bread could be baked for the orphans who were at Przemsyslowa no. 6. On the same day we visited the old people's home that now was located on Nadrzeczna Street in the former inn for poor visitors. The entire courtyard appeared like one slaughterhouse. All of the walls were sprinkled with blood and the passageways were full of corpses. Corpses lay in space between the beds and in the beds, several lay in the beds and half of the bodies lay hanging down, others lay with their heads under pillows as if they had wanted to protect themselves from the bullets. In one room we found an old woman among all of the dead, who was sitting in bed, shot in the chest. She was tearing at the featherbed with her hands and murmuring something unintelligible. The gendarme who watched us pulled out a revolver and returned it to the gun holster. The Polish policeman did not want a great deal made of the old woman's suffering the agonies of death.

I was in the street again on the 2nd of October; this time I was chosen to help distribute bread among the Jews who were being sent away. I felt dizzy – so many acquaintances and those close to me... I noticed Shlomo Fiszman, the former official with social aid at the *Judenrat*, who had destroyed hundreds of cards of the beneficiaries to show that there were not many poor in Czenstochow and with this to protect them from deportation. Now, he himself also was being sent away. Here, I noticed the lawyer, Mendl Konarski, who was barely pulling himself on his sick feet and was being supported by his wife and sister-in-law; here went the activist from the "workers council" Wilinger, near him his wife and children who very frequently furnished everyone with such joy with their demonstrated capabilities, charm and childish gentleness during the public appearances of the *TOZ* day care houses. A freight wagon of children in small, white aprons with blue stripes and among them – their educators – were separated from the large crowd. Rywka Waczacha, the former kindergarten teacher in the Peretz children's home and director of the orphan's house during the war, sat on one wagon. Behind this wagon, she pulled her old mother, Szmulewicz, her husband with a fiddle under his arm and the very old man Sztajer. Thus, they led the 150 children from the orphan house on their last road. The "selection" square was cleared of the sad procession. Only the murdered remained: some of them with shattered skulls and others with perforated chests. One appeared as if he was asleep and another lay with hands and feet spread out as if they were being publicly defiled. Several hundred men remained after this "selection," who were sent to the "shops" as well as other temporary workplaces where they awaited new "selections."

A wild hunt for plunder began in the ghetto at the same time that the deportations took place; Germans swindled those surviving of their hidden goods; wagons with the possessions from Jewish residences were drawn through the streets to the prepared storehouses of the security police, which now occupied all of Garibaldi Street. Wagons with the murdered moved to Kawia Street where the security police pulled out the gold teeth from the dead and cut off fingers with gold rings that were collected in baskets and taken away. Old people, the sick and children who were forced to undress and lay in a row near a pit with their faces up, were also brought there. Gendarmes then went from one victim to the next, shot a bullet into the head of each one. Afterwards, the clothing of the murdered ones was partly given to the residents of this street who had earlier been forced to throw the dead into the mass grave.[99]

On the 4th of October, the rows of the sick came from the Jewish Hospital, which was located on Przemyslowa Street. The doctors and nurses, who served there, received an order to give the sick death injections. Only a few of them submitted to this order.

The much larger number tried to calm the sick; there were also nurses who tried to create a better mood among the sick, distributing their personal underwear as gifts among the sick women who already had ended their treatment and needed to be discharged from the hospital. On the same day all of the hospital personnel were taken to a "selection" from which the largest part was sent to Treblinka. The sick, among whom were 13 new mothers and their nursing babies, were taken to Kawia Street. Here, the gendarmes shot the older ones who were still alive after the injections in their usual "manner," laying them in a row before a grave. Ibersher himself dealt with the nursing mothers. This German murderer grabbed each nursing baby by its little feet or by its little hands, shot it and threw it in the mass grave.[100] All of the remaining sick at the hospital at Krutka 22 were annihilated at the same time.

The small factory square, where the "shops" were located was densely covered with thousands of people. There was no empty bit of space where one could move. There where one ate, there where one slept and there where one sat and cried over their great misfortune – there they had to take care of the natural needs. At every step sat people crying. In the other courtyard and corner, among boards that had been thrown there, lay a young woman who writhed in pain from cramps. Forlorn, twisting in pain and alone, she lay biting her lips, her moans held in and kneaded her stomach with her own hands. A dense group of women surrounded her so that "no evil eye" would notice this. The pregnant woman had to be her own midwife...

On the second day the gendarmes found new mothers with newborn children and took them away to be killed. Each of us was sure that the fate of the two new "arrestees" already had been sealed. To everyone's astonishment, Degenhardt ordered that a liter of fresh milk be provided to the new mothers every morning. He also demanded that a special room be organized at *Metalurgia* where she and her child would be located and also declared an "amnesty" for all of the mothers with children who enrolled to be accepted in the "shops" and from "selections." A large factory room was cleaned for this purpose on the first floor. Mothers with children, filled with unease and mistrust, suffering from hunger and exhaustion in hiding places, left discretely from the cellars, attics and holes where they lay for long days and nights in deadly fear and took a place in the prepared room where they also received food for themselves and their children.

The "comfortable" life for a few dozen mothers and their children lasted for seven days. Another "selection" took place in *Metalurgia* on the eighth day. All of the mothers and their children also were taken and sent away with a new transport of Jews to Treblinka. Many Jews appeared voluntarily for this transport because they had lost their hope of again seeing those closest to them who had been deported on the earlier transport. Ester Razine, the director of the dramatic group at *TOZ*, as well as her sister, Natka Rozencwajg, who could not leave their sister, Hela Frank and her son, Asherl, alone on their unknown last road, were among the "volunteers." "Selections" took place among other survivors at other temporary workplaces, too, such as: "Golgota," "Broland," "Horowicz and Partners" factory and the "furniture camp." The "furniture camp" temporary workplace belonged to the Shtol main squad and had a certain right to ride through the emptied ghetto and collect furniture. The Jewish "guards" of this "temporary workplace," under the leadership of the bold and energetic Machl Birncwajg, began to take from the Jewish residences, closets, couches and bullet crates, in which they had secretly smuggled rescued mothers and children from cellars and attics, for whom bunkers had been prepared under the noses of the Germans in the furniture factory itself that was located at Wilson Street no. 20-22. Seventy-three people, among them mothers and children and old people, were hidden in these bunkers during the course of the deportations and for a certain time after the deportation. The workers from this "temporary workplace" gave almost everything they received in their meager portions of food to those hidden and they would themselves be satisfied with the remainder of the meager portions.

On the first day on which the deportation began, Degenhardt wanted these temporary workplaces to be liquidated and the workers to be deported. As a result, the gendarmes took away all of the Jews and brought them to *Metalurgia.* Consequently, there was the dangerous threat not only that this group would be deported, but also that those hidden in the bunkers there would die of hunger, not having any possibility of leaving. The city chief and his representative, Linderman, who became interested in the temporary workplaces because of personal security concerns if they were to be liquidated

(Linderman "hid" here so that he would not be sent to the front) kept intervening, not even ceasing [to do so] during a public quarrel in the presence of the Jews who had been driven together to *Metalurgia*.

After a half day of intervention, Degenhardt allowed the Jews to return to the "furniture camp" with the condition that they themselves would decide how many workers this temporary workplace needed. The situation for those living in the bunkers was temporarily secure. However, there was the dangerous threat that during the "selections" that would be carried out there, the gendarmes would discover traces of the bunkers. The small children in the bunkers would make a fuss and cry. Paul Lange, Linderman's representative, served the entire day in the "furniture-camp," taking orders from various German officials and assuring that the Jewish workers carried them out in the designated time. Although a German, it appeared that he knew about the bunkers and pretended he did not. Everyone understood this and did not especially watch out for him. However, there was the threat of danger that during "selections" the gendarmes would hear a tumult or a cry and then not only those in the bunkers would perish. Therefore, Luminal [a sedative] was provided in the bunkers, which served to put the children to sleep during the days on which selections took place. A certain nurse from the Jewish hospital, Manya Altman (née Malka Kalyn) had supervision of the giving of the Luminal. Yet, there would be cases in which the amount taken was too much and the children received doses of Luminal that were too large for the individual children to be able to absorb. In such cases, the children would sleep an entire day and sometimes even more. There were children who after waking up gave the impression of being drunk and not normal. They also had to be careful that the children in the bunkers did not make noise on the days when there were no selections. On such days, Teni Wajnman and Jadzia Brener, former teachers, dug rain worms in the cellars and amused the children with the movements [of the worms]. Mainly, the teachers mentioned would calm the children with little stories. The daily telling of little stories extended hours long and when the tongue stuck to the palate and they could no longer make any sound, it was enough for the story teller to move her lips, which in moments also had the effect of calming the children. The children also were kept in the bunkers of the "furniture camp" for a certain time after the deportations. There were cases then of dysentery and diphtheria.

However, this was quickly controlled thanks to the tireless work of the nurses already mentioned, who helped the pediatrician, Dr. Zajf, from Kalicz, who was chased by the occupation to Czenstochow. Dr. Zajf would leave the small ghetto to help the children who became sick in the bunkers of the "furniture factory." He was placed in danger when smuggling himself out of the ghetto and also while returning there. The bunkers in the "furniture factory" were not really hidden; however, each selection that took place removed a certain number of Jews who were sent to Treblinka with others.

Selections also took place at the temporary workplaces where Jews were quartered as well as at other temporary workplaces where there were bunkers. Among the Jews who remained after the selections that the Germans had carried out several days earlier at various temporary workplaces, the Jews of the "Galgata" temporary workplace suffered the most.

The Germans had the largest annihilation at this temporary workplace. Of the 750 Jews housed here, they left approximately 300 men. Degenhardt did not even spare the *Aleje* 14 temporary workplace. Since the creation of the large ghetto, the Germans in the house at *Aleje* 14 assembled the best tradesmen from among the Jewish artisans. This house was located at the boundary point between the ghetto and the Aryan side. This house did not belong to the ghetto. No Jews, besides those designated by the German artisans who only worked on German orders, were supposed to be there. The residents of this house were not touched during the entire deportation action. Jews believed that nothing bad would happen to the residents of *Aleje* 14 because the Germans still needed these tradesmen for their personal use. The residents of *Aleje* 14 also believed this. Therefore, they bribed gendarmes, members of the Gestapo, as well as ordinary Germans, giving them the most beautiful and expensive jewelry that anyone possessed to bring their closest relatives and friends here. The Germans "willingly" let themselves be bribed and Degenhardt also "willingly" permitted it so that the Jews in *Aleje* 14 would console themselves with hope. After all of the selections had ended, the Germans turned to the Jews at *Aleje* 14, carrying out a selection according to all of the "rules" and those removed were taken to Treblinka.

* * *

The murderous dance of deportations lasted for five weeks. Hunger and death reigned without end. The number of Jews who were sent to Treblinka or perished on the spot reached to approximately 41,000.

More than 2,000 who perished on the spot were buried in a mass grave on Kawia Street, in a large field, that lay across the road from house no. 19. Only the hearses, which the security police put at the disposal of the old *Chevre-kadisha* member, Miski, brought 1,600 of the murdered here.[101] Degenhardt designated a separate room at *Metalurgia* for Miski. Degenhardt brought Miski's closest family members here, giving Miski the "mission" of collecting the dead and taking them to Kawia Street. Therefore, Degenhardt assured Miski that and he and his family would not be deported. After all of the selections, Degenhardt sent Miski and his family to Treblinka. When Miski reminded Degenhardt of his promise, Degenhardt answered that a word of honor does not apply to Jews. Five thousand-one hundred-eighty five Jews were left legally in Czenstochow; more than 1,000 Jews remained in hiding in various bunkers. During the deportations and for a time after the deportations, those remaining legally were housed at the following temporary workplaces: *Metalurgia, Braland* firm, Horowicz and Partners firm, *HASAG Apparatebau, HADAG-Eisenhuta, Ost-Ban,* "factory camp," *Heresbau, Golgota, Metros, Aleje* 14, storehouses of the security police and at Garibaldi Street, no 18, where the Jewish policemen and the Jewish doctors and their wives and children were quartered.

The ghetto was cleaned out; there was dead silence. Everywhere, large pictures of grandfathers and grandmothers were noticed on a balcony. Soundless, frightening melodies of death, of death and ruin, were carried through the wide open doors and windows. The orphaned walls of the *TOZ* day care houses cried, the orphans' house, that in the course of long months embraced 150 orphans and now was itself orphaned, cried.

* * *

The situation for the survivors was frightening. The most terrifying was the situation for the 856 men and 73 women who were housed in the ammunition factory, *HASAG.* [102] At night, hundreds of people, men and women, were driven into one large factory room where they were guarded by armed labor security. Machine guns with their barrels pointing at the room where the Jews were located were on the roof opposite the factory building. They had to sleep on the bare cement floors. In order to carry out their natural function, lying down, they had to first ask permission from the labor security. Pain, hunger and dirt was the daily bread here.

Only one who had enough strength to save a little coffee from the daily half-liter portion that he received for drinking could wash his face a little.

The situation for those cashiered on Garibaldi in the warehouses of the security police did not appear much different. One was shot immediately here for every small "sin." The first victim here was the young man, Czarnelias, who was caught smoking a cigarette. There was an easier regimen where the doctors and police were housed. The regimen in the "furniture camp" was not as terrible as in other temporary workplaces thanks to Machl Birncwajg and his closest assistants, who placed their lives in danger and arranged bunkers for old women and mothers and children. However, here, too, Linderman sent six men to the security police to be shot. Among these six was the tailor Flamenbaum, the well-known communist activist.

* * *

Degenhardt, the chief of the security police, led the liquidation of the Jews of Czenstochow. The *S.S.* and the police leader of the entire Radomsk district, General Dr. Boettcher, who managed the extermination of the Jews in the entire Radomsk region, conducted the entire *aktsia* [action, usual refers to a deportation]. On the 1st of November the deportation in Czenstochow officially ended and the Germans began to send the cashiered surviving Jews from the temporary workplaces to a designated small area that was located in the poorest, dirtiest and most crowded part of the former ghetto. The group cashiered in *Metalurgia* was sent first and then from the remaining temporary workplaces, according to a previously created plan. The Jews who were cashiered in *HASAG Apparatebau* were the last to be moved. On the 23rd of December 1942, this group in the worst and most miserable state was taken to an especially designated house that was located next to, but outside the newly designated living area, so that workers in the ammunition factory would not be in contact with the remaining Jews. After a while the house was combined with a new fenced-in living area that was called the "small ghetto." All of the surviving Jews were now located here and among them 35 legally surviving children of doctors and policemen. Everyone here received his number. The *Judenrat* chairman received number one and the last number, 5185, was a certain woman, Franya Najman, who was allocated to the work group at the sanitary station in the small ghetto.[103]

Everyone believed that here they would be given a little tranquility and here they could mourn their dearest and closest ones. However, here in the small ghetto, those surviving were sentenced to a further fear of death and to further "selections"…

The Small Ghetto

The northeast part of the former ghetto was designated as the living area for the more than 5,000 legally surviving Jews. Starting in September 1942, the German leaders in Czenstochow marked the area where the surviving Jews would live according to a marked plan for the ghetto, which they had checked with the *Judenrat*. This area took in several houses on Mostowa Street, the small Kacza alley, a half of Nadrzeczna, a half of Garncarska and a few houses on Spadek. The several houses on Mostowa were the end of the houses on Garncarska and Kacza that belonged to the new ghetto, but which bordered on Mostowa and the houses on Spadek also belonged to the same street, but they were located at the spot where Spadek Street cut through Kacza Street. The ghetto actually consisted of three narrow, dirty parallel-lying alleys that were fenced in with barbed wire and guarded by Ukrainian fascists under the leadership of the security police. This area was given the name "the small ghetto." The Germans began to move the surviving Jews, who were housed in various temporary workplaces, here at the end of October 1942.

The small ghetto appeared as if after a pogrom. Ripped off doors and windows. All of the window panes yellowed; broken pieces of old, poor furniture, broken children's strollers, torn pillows and featherbeds and broken glasses, single shoes, feathers and simple rags in piles. On each pile was seen human shadows lost and searching for something. Someone hid a knife, someone a spoon and someone another object. Each one showed that he had found a trace of his own home and he hid it as if it was something holy. A woman held a children's shoe and she sobbingly murmured that this was certainly her child's shoe; a woman pulled a child's chair and talked to herself: "My child, my poor child, alas..." Here and there, someone was noticed sneaking through with a hidden object under his coat or kerchief.

A father or a mother full of dread carried a doll that was found or another toy for their child who lay hidden somewhere in a bunker. Thus began the life of those who were sent from the "temporary workplaces" at *Metalurgia* or from quarantine to the small ghetto. Little by little those who lived in these streets before the deportation and hid there during the deportation began to crawl out. Many Jews, who had been hiding on the Aryan side as well as a number of those who had avoided death in cellars and attics and could no longer remain there, also began to smuggle themselves into the small ghetto with work groups. Hunger and hopelessness chased them out from their hiding places and, those of them who had the good luck to meet a working group, joined it unnoticed and in such a manner smuggled themselves into the ghetto. Many did perish in such a "trousseau." However, many saved themselves in such a manner and there already were 6,500 Jews in the ghetto at the end of 1942, of which more than 3,000 were employed in various temporary workplaces, some in the ghetto workshops, which were managed by the decreased *Judenrat*, and some were illegal and unregistered. Six and a half thousand cheerless shadows, who had stolen a bit of life from their fate, were locked in a suffocating cage.

* * *

Life in the small ghetto took on a new form, without permission to carry on an economic life of its own. Everyone had to work and drew their pitiful means of support from the *Judenrat's* kitchen that was organized at Nadrzeczna Street. The wage for the work that was paid by the temporary workplaces for each slave was taken by the security police, which was our only boss. The security police turned over a half kilo of bread each day to the *Judenrat* for one working, up to a liter of coffee for breakfast and evening bread and up to half a liter of soup for lunch. Those who did not work could not register and, of course, they could not benefit from this nourishment.

Everyone had to be on their feet in groups at five o'clock in the morning, where they endured pain, mockery and ridicule, to march under guard to their designated workplaces that were located outside the ghetto. At nine o'clock at night the sad melody of a trumpet, which ordered the going to sleep, carried across the ghetto. All of the groups were counted and inspected when marching out to work and returning.

From time to time during marching out, a resounding song was heard in the ghetto from the workers, which was not an expression of drunkenness, but joy. This sound of the worker groups masked the crying of the surviving children who were being smuggled from the outside bunkers in large bread sacks into the ghetto, where new bunkers had been prepared. The workers in the temporary workplace in the "furniture camp," who prepared four well-hidden bunkers in the house at Nadrzeczna 88, especially excelled in this action. This is an example of such a situation. At the beginning of 1942, they smuggled in a large group of children. At the gate of the "Wiliat" ghetto, at the corner of Nadrzeczna and Rynek Warszawski, where the "guard" was located, there was a larger group of security police with Degenhardt at the head [SS-Hauptsturmführer Paul Degenhardt]. The workers ordered a wagon with many packs of clothing that ostensibly belonged to them, and Machl Birncwajg, the leader of this worker group, rode on the front of the wagon... The Germans began to examine the packs and meanwhile the "singers" with the mysterious sacks crept into the ghetto and disappeared. Several such cases occurred while smuggling in food.

The number of those working in the temporary workplaces at first is not exact because there were those who did not appear for work. Among those who did not appear for work were: the members of the fighting organization who carried out their work in the ghetto itself, such as in digging tunnels for the fighting organization, the old and children who were hidden in the bunkers and just people who sabotaged the work [being done] for the Germans, although because of this there were victims from time to time. The first victim for not going to work was a Jew named Plat who was shot in the ghetto by Sametkowski, a *granat* policiant [Blue police – Polish police in the Nazi-occupied area of Poland known as the General Government]; the murder committed by the Germans of a certain Mrs. Cymerman and her 14-year old daughter remains in everyone's memory. The mother did not go to work because she fell into melancholy and the child did not work because she took care of her mother who had attempted suicide several times. A heavy impression was made on everyone of the execution of Wladek Blumenfucht, the former secretary of the commercial employees union. Wladek was very sick and could not work. On the 11th of March 1943, Degenhardt ordered that he be shot. When the security policemen came for him, he swallowed a potassium capsule. The murderers still succeeded in taking him out, forcing him to take off his clothes and shoes and then shot him.

At the end of November 1942 the S.S. and [Herbert] Boettcher, the police leader from the Radom district, carried out an inspection of the small ghetto and declared it a "labor camp." From then on, the regimen in the camp became more severe; the control became stricter and the number of those working daily was precisely recorded. The first exact list of those working at the temporary workplaces outside the ghetto was created on the 5th of December 1942. Two thousand eight hundred and thirty-two Jews then worked at 27 temporary workplaces (2,474 men and 358 women).[104] The remainder were employed in the ghetto itself and a smaller number remained hidden in bunkers.[105]

Almost every day during the march to work security policemen stood near the "shuffle" of the workers and, under the leadership of Sergeant Ibersher who became the leader of the camp, pulled people out of the rows and threw them into the former butcher shop at house 7-8. Ibersher himself, with the bent handle of his cane, caught one here, here another by the chest and pulled them into the butcher shop. [Michael] Majznerowicz, the then Polish commandant of the Jewish police, using Ibersher's example, often would make use of his cane and also take part in such *aktsias*. The Jews who were thrown into the "butcher shop" were sent away to Skarzysko and Bliżyn in larger groups and they did not return from there. Often, large groups were taken from the work places and sent away. Each deportation was accompanied by victims: several fell on the spot, others fell jumping from vehicles or from the train wagons [with bars on the windows].

Clothing from those shot, that did not have any great worth, was sent to the *Judenrat* by the security police. Such a transport of clothing, in which were found 80 pieces of men's and women's things, one pair of boots, five pairs of slippers and three single shoes, was sent over the 1st of March 1943.[106] The number of each Jew shot (every Jew in the ghetto had a number) would be given to the Jewish labor office so that the Jew who had been shot could be erased from the list of those who were in the ghetto.

The number of workers at the temporary workplace kept growing at the time the ghetto was transformed into a labor camp. Everyone believed that working at a temporary workplace was safer. There were still 2,304 men and 847 women who worked in the temporary workplaces outside the ghetto at the beginning of March 1943, after many Jews had been sent out of the camps to Skarzysko and Bliżyn.[107] The ongoing *aktsias* that the German would carry out and the escapes from the ghetto with Aryan papers led to the fact that the number of Jews had begun to decrease.

At the beginning of April 1943, when almost all of the bunkers in the ghetto itself had been liquidated, there were no more than 4,043 people in the small ghetto. (2,663 men, 1,346 women and 35 children of the police and doctors).[108]

Rumors would spread very often about a period of complete liquidation. When one period passed, they began talking about another. The nerves could not bear the constant insecurity and unease. However, the threat to life and to survival increased from day to day and from hour to hour. The determination to save a little money and means to have something with which to escape and survive the time outside the ghetto became even stronger. They stole sacks of things from the police storehouses where the looted Jewish "possessions" were located and they sold them to the Poles whom they would meet at the temporary workplaces. The Jews who worked at the security police at cleaning the destroyed former large ghetto and at sorting everything in the security police storehouses excelled at this. From there the sorted things were sent to Germany. Some Jews really did gather large treasures and with them wanted to expel the terrifying anxiety of the day before and the suffering of today. Life became lawless with these people... They ran wild [with] food and debauchery. There was the impression that the people were living in a thick, dark jungle. However, at the same time a second life developed here – a life in the bunkers and in cellars. Here sat those young people, those men and women who would not forget their feelings of revenge and the drive to continue the fight against dark, Hitlerist fascism. Young boys and girls, almost children, transformed this cellar into a forge of resistance ideas. They worked tirelessly here day and night. They created weapons. With self-sacrifice, they smuggled in bullets and dynamite that was stolen from the German ammunition factories. Individual grenades were made without experience and with bare hands. Large tunnels were prepared with exits outside the ghetto that would be necessary in cases when they had to withdraw from the battlefield. They taxed and they collected money for weapons and they "finished" traitors. The fighting group expanded and became a power that everyone in the ghetto had to take into account. The mood in the ghetto changed little by little because of what was called the fighting organization. The number of fighters grew from day to day and their preparatory work – more intensive.

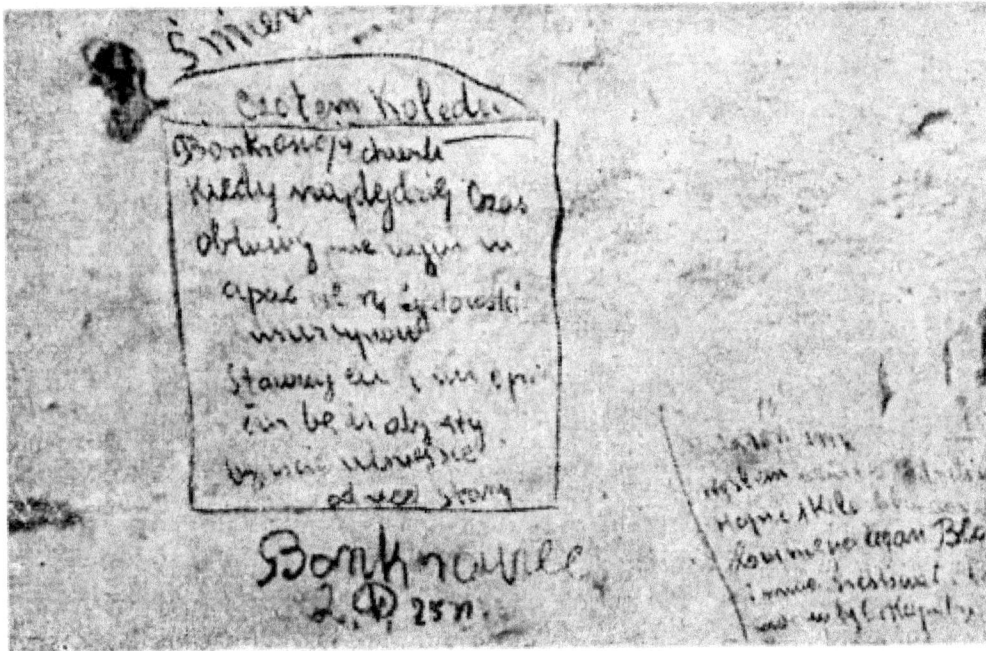

A note from a mother to her son (?)

In the cellars of the Jewish police in the small ghetto

Little was done in the small ghetto in the area of cultural activity. However, that which was done should be remembered.

A few dozen men would come together in the evening in various residences from time to time, invite several surviving singers from the former *TOZ* choir and carry out a concert. Particularly excelling in this area were the two Jakubowicz brothers, who recited and sang their own creations in which they recalled the savage events and occurrences. Several of their songs became so popular that even the Germans sang them. The most popular of their songs was: *Vuhin Zol Ich Geyn?* [Where Shall I Go?] The religious Jews also carried out certain activities. They would organize *minyonim* [prayer groups] and collectively celebrate at holiday tables. They did not miss the only Passover that they happened to live through in the small ghetto. They baked matzos and celebrated the Seder [Passover meal] collectively.

A separate chapter was the feeding location for children, which was organized in a house at Mostowa Street no. 9 where the doctors lived. A feeding location was arranged for the 35 legally surviving children of the doctors and the policemen. The wife of Kiak, the doctor of oral medicine, had the domestic [responsibilities] and the educational [responsibilities] were managed by the Froebelist teacher, Helsza Wajnrajch. Little by little, the illegal, starved and emaciated children in the bunkers began to leave their hiding places cautiously and they reported to this place for something to eat. At the beginning of November 1942, this place was visited by over 60 children. The writer of these lines headed this feeding location. The feeding location was turned into a three-class elementary school with pre-school that involved 120 children. In addition to the already mentioned [Helsza Wajnrajch], Mania Bernsztajn and Tenia Wajnman (former lecturer at the Jewish *gymnazie* [secondary school] worked as teachers there and the two female former teachers at the elementary school: Kajser and M. Zombek. The latter was a daughter of Kiak, the popular doctor in Czenstochow. The worker-activist, Herszl Frajman, the tinsmith, created a bathing room for the children from this school in the same house. Everything went according to plan until the following situation occurred: Degenhardt accompanied by Ibersher appeared on a certain day in the first half of December 1942 in the room of the Froebel [kindergarten] school. Both stopped at the threshold, looked at the children and were quiet. Finally, Degenhardt stammered (he was a little of a stutterer): *"Was machen sie denn hier?"* [What are they doing here?] Everyone was silent and was sure that a misfortune would occur. One of the doctors informed Kapinski, who came at once and began to clarify for Degenhardt that the legally surviving children were being fed here.

With his cynical, artificial earnestness Degenhardt asked Kapinski why the children look so pale. Then Ibersher spoke up that these were certainly children from the bunkers who were hungry there and had not seen any light for a long time. After a short but severe embarrassment by all, Degenhardt, to everyone's surprise, ordered that special lunches be cooked and promised weekly food allocations for all of the children, even for those who did not come to the feeding locations. From then on, all of the children did receive distributions of flour, eggs, butter, sugar and honey that was given out once a week from the storehouses of the *Judenrat* and a glass of milk for each child every day. Supervision of the school and the kindergarten was given by the *Judenrat* to the former director of the Jewish *gymnazie* [secondary school], Doctor Anisfeld, but this all was a trap. This *Gan-Eden* [paradise] for the children lasted until the beginning of January 1943. In the morning of the 4th of January 1943 we noticed that armed Germans were stationed in the ghetto. The teachers decided to send the children to their guardians because they believed that every mother or father would surely be able to hide their children better. And that actually happened; the children returned home and hid in the bunkers. However, the majority of them were discovered by the Germans with the help of several Jewish policemen. They were sent away to Radomsk with their mothers; they left for Treblinka from there. The school was liquidated; the teachers no longer wanted to be those who prepared a "more succulent" prey for the wild German animals. Anisfeld also resigned from his supervision of the children. Only 18 of the 35 legal surviving children came to the feeding place. These were the doctors' children who lived in the same house where the school was located. Later, these children also were murdered. This was on the 20th of March when the Jewish intellectuals in Czenstochow were annihilated.

The intensive preparation work for the fighting groups and the small amount of cultural work continued to be carried out and these were the only rays of light that shone in the saddened work camps.

The security police, upon whom the S.S. and police leaders in Radom had entrusted exclusive control over the Jews in the labor camps in Czenstochow, kept "bestowing" upon the prisoners one edict after another.

During the second half of the month of December 1942 Degenhardt informed the *Judenrat* that all weddings that had taken place since the deportations from the large ghetto were annulled and if these couples wished to continue to live together, they must turn [directly to him] to again have a wedding ceremony in his presence. From that moment on, every couple that wanted to live together and have a legal wedding, had to turn to Degenhardt with a written request through the intercession of the *Judenrat*. Those, who received such permission, had to hold the wedding ceremony on the day that Degenhardt designated. Degenhardt would assign several weddings on the same day and at the same time; he, himself, would attend and give his "blessing." At the same time that Degenhardt gave this order, he also ordered that unmarried women and men could not live on the same street. Kacza Street was designated for women, Nadrzeczna Street for men and Garncarska, which was located between Kacza and Nadrzeczna, was designated for family people. Degenhardt took delight in giving his "blessing" even to those who had been husband and wife for a long time but did not have any marriage documents.

The security police carried on systematic annihilation work in the small ghetto. Every day brought its number of victims. Those who did not go to work were shot; those who were caught on the "Aryan" side were brought to the ghetto to be shot so that all of the Jews would know of this. Mothers who lost their minds were shot. Young children who protected their insane mothers from committing suicide were shot. Men who were caught on the "women's" street were shot. Workers in groups marching to the temporary workplaces were shot because labor security or a gendarme who guarded these groups on the way to the temporary workplaces had some sort of suspicion about them.

Those on whose cheeks tuberculosis-fever blossomed were shot. Other seriously ill people were shot and so on. All of these "small *aktsias*" brought devastation in the already destroyed camp life. The great destruction brought with it larger *aktsias* that would be prepared with true German precision. Such an action took place at the beginning of January 1943.

On the 4th of January 1943 at 10 o'clock in the morning, the gendarmes and fully armed Ukrainians were placed in large numbers outside of the ghetto. The ghetto was shocked. There were murmurs as in a beehive. They ran from place to place. They looked at one another with eyes full of fear. They hurried uneasily and there was the impression that everyone did not want the guards outside to notice them. There were questions: "What will happen next? What more will they do with us?"

At the same time, gendarmes strolled calmly with helmets on their heads, right near the wire, and looked with nonchalance at those who were now coming from the ghetto. Suddenly, the ghetto was filled with Ukrainian fascists, security police and *granat policiant* [Blue police – Polish police in the Nazi-occupied area of Poland known as the General Government]. They divided into groups and accompanied by Jewish policemen began to cross the ghetto. Terrible noises and shouts carried from one corner of the ghetto to the other. Older people, mothers with children and children alone were pulled from the rooms, from the cellars and attics; some indifferent, let themselves be led, others threw themselves on the ground and struggled with their teeth and nails. One of the bunkers at Nadrzeczna 88 was discovered with the help of the Jewish policeman, Lesler, and the children and their mothers and grandmother were led out from there. Terrible cries of desperation carried from almost every house. The great lamentations and uproars were accompanied by the crack from revolvers. Everyone in the ghetto who did not work at the temporary workplaces outside the ghetto was driven out to "Warszawski *Ryneczek* [central square]" where a "selection" took place. The fighters carried out their first efforts. Mendl Fiszlewicz, who had escaped from Treblinka and, returning to Czenstochow, placed himself under the authority of the fighting group Nadrzeczna 66, shot at the gendarmes. Icchak Fajner, his closest comrade, also appeared. Both fell. Twenty-six more Jews were pulled out of the rows. Twenty-five were shot and one, M. Galster, a member of the *Judenrat*, was freed. The chairman of the *Judenrat* [saved] him through pleading. This aktisa [action, often a deportation] stopped at noon-time and then began with a stronger savagery. The director of the Jewish police, the

Polish *granat policiant* Majznerowicz, showed with great zeal that he knew the "craft" no less than his German teachers. All who were chased to the "selection square" struggled with their last strength. Holding her grandson, Rywka Frajman, who in her youth was active in the Bundist militias and in 1906 was wounded and lost a breast, now in despair because her husband was among the 25 men who were shot, was the only one who appeared at the transport to be sent away.

In addition to the more than 300 men, women and children who perished on the spot, several young fighters were sent to Radomsk under strict guard and from there to Treblinka. Iberszer, the chairman of the *Judenrat*, declared immediately after this slaughter that he and his comrades would be on a visit that day in honor of Kapinski's silver anniversary. At the start of the evening, gendarmes with Iberszer at their head appeared in Kapinski's house and demanded the long-promised meal. All of the members of the *Judenrat* took part in this reception, except for Anisfeld, who declared that he was ill and would not participate. Thus, on the 4th of January 1943, did the German hangmen and the toadies of the *Judenrat* end the bloody play in the small ghetto.

The ghetto took on a different appearance. Many prepared to escape to the bunkers that had been prepared earlier. Women and men [with grey hair] acquired hair as black as tar overnight – they made themselves look young; young, dark, charming girls and boys suddenly were blond – making themselves look "Aryan." Men allowed themselves to go through "cosmetic operations," erasing any "traces" as a Jew, which they received eight days after their birth [circumcision], so that they could smuggle themselves into Germany as "Aryans," for work in Germany. They escaped to the Polish side with false documents. Children were given to Poles, abandoned in Catholic dormitories as well as hidden in bunkers outside the ghetto. Many of those who left the ghetto were betrayed, accidentally recognized and perished. The urge to escape did not lessen.

February 1943. It was related from ear to ear that Jews who had relatives in Palestine would be traded for Germans who were located in England. No one where knew these rumors originated and no one made an effort to discover how true they were. As [if grabbing at a] straw, they latched onto the ray of hope. The hope was strengthened even more when the *Judenrat* actually began to register everyone who had relatives in *Eretz-Yisroel*. They stood in rows in the hours they were free of work and registered, giving the addresses of relatives in Palestine.

Those who did not have relatives "borrowed" them from acquaintances and also registered. The registration lasted for two weeks and suddenly ended. Hundreds of slaves survived another disappointment. Days of smaller selections arrived. Degenhardt and his devils searched the ghetto again and decreased the number of working people, sending out the "unnecessary ones" to Skarzysko. Both of the Botszan brothers (the sons of the publisher of the *Czenstochower Zeitung* [Czenstochow Newspaper] – Berl Botszan) and Leib Fogel, the lawyer and his brother Avraham, both sons of the *Agudah* [Orthodox political party] worker, Mendl Fogel were among those deported. (Leib Fogel escaped from the transport to Treblinka during the great expulsion, stayed in Warsaw for a time and was active in the Polish Socialist Party there. He arrived in the small ghetto from Warsaw in the month of August 1943.) Avraham Fogel also was active in the underground movement in the large ghetto and in the small ghetto. He also was one of the three who took upon themselves the recording of every incident – Jewish members of Degenhardt's entourage tried to convince him [Degenhardt] to release the Fogel brothers and the Botszan brothers; Helenka Tenenbaum, the "Queen Esther" of the small ghetto, tried. No intervention helped. Degenhardt declared that their diplomas were a sufficient crime and they did not have anything more to do in Czenstochow. The greater number of those sent out to Skarzysko perished. The Botszan brothers also perished (one of typhus and the other trying to escape). Avraham Fogel also was felled by a bullet. Leib Fogel perished when he refused to work and threw himself at the torturers with his bare hands. Terribly beaten by a foreman, lying on the ground, he still exclaimed against the murderers with his last strength and was finally shot by Batenschlager, the German camp leader there, who later, at the end of 1944, was the camp leader of the Czenstochower concentration camps: *HASAG-Pelcery* and *HASAG-Warta*.

The news of the deaths of these four young men, who were descended from old, esteemed, well-known families, arrived in the ghetto and made the very demoralized mood that reigned without end in the small ghetto even more difficult.

The 17th of March 1943. The Gestapo arrested a Jewish boy (a son of the Kongrecki family), who was hidden with his mother and small sister in the bunkers in the "furniture camp" at Wilson Street 34. Six Jewish fighters, who had their support location there, were unexpectedly attacked and taken away. On the 19th of March they were shot during a struggle with the armed enemy at the Jewish cemetery. Mrs. Kongrecki and her small daughter were shot on the same day in their bunker and the arrested boy and his father, Jecheskel Kongrecki, were murdered in the cellars of the Gestapo.

On the 20th of March 1943, Purim – a sunny, beautiful day. The arrival of spring was felt. Some kind of longing gnawed and the threat to life became stronger. A group that worked in the ghetto appeared outside often and threw jealous glances over the wires in the direction of Warszawer Street which was now on the "Aryan" side. However, the mood was heavy in the cellars of the Jewish fighting organization. They constantly had received so many wonderful reports from their six fighting comrades who had their base at Wilson Street 34 and now they had been murdered. The families of the six who had been murdered did not yet know of their misfortune, were crying, running around, seeking a rescue for their children and people tried to console them that a miracle could happen. The doctor families wanted to bring their children a little bit of a holiday and today celebrated the birthday of one of the prettiest children in the ghetto – of the small Lili Winer. The children played, sang and danced. The small Lili especially celebrated. The black velvet little dress, the white, long socks on her slender little feet and the large, snow-white ribbon in her thick, blond hairs on her head gave her a special charm. Lili then shone completely; today was her holiday; today they celebrated her seventh birthday. The guests could not take their eyes off the delicate and splendid birthday child. The children played without end and did not become tired; they unloaded their until now pent up childish energy. The guests – the doctors – gathered in another room and talked about the fate of the Jews.

Almost every one of them described everything in dark colors, waiting for another one to brush away his idea with his hand so that in such a manner it would be a little easier on the soul. Playing also changed for the children. Now they stood in a circle and played *"amol iz geven a Sorale, a Sorale a kleyn..."* [There once was a Sorale, a small Sorale]. All of the children sang and Lili and her little brother wandered in the forest looking for their mother. The children sang further, quieter and quieter: *Ryneczek* [It is dark in the woods, crying is heard.]

Suddenly, a new order from Degenhardt went through the ghetto: all members of the *Judenrat*, all doctors, engineers, lawyers and the intelligentsia with diplomas needed to appear at once with their families on the now so sadly, well-known Warszawski *Ryneczek* [central square], because they had to leave for Palestine today. The ghetto was terribly agitated anew. They did not believe and a thought sneaked in – and perhaps?... The members of the *Judenrat*, doctors, engineers and their wives and children hurried to the designated place full of unease. Lili, too, with her parents and small brother hurried. Lili's father was then also considered an intellectual. He was a well-known doctor... Hundreds of men, women and children agitatedly moved around the Warszawski *Ryneczek*. They searched for a salvation in all of the corners with their glances. Large trucks stood in the distance at Warszawer Street. The vehicles did not move and yet everyone began to feel the threatening danger. Several tried various ways to turn away from the net of death into which they had fallen. Doctor Falk tempted his luck. Doctor Lewin also tempted his luck. They tried to hide in a gate where the Germans would carry out executions of Jews [and] to leave the city for the forest from there. They did not succeed. They were noticed and led back. The members of the *Judenrat* tried to use their acquaintance with the gendarmes, but without success. One member of the *Judenrat*, Zelig Rotbard, ran from one gendarme acquaintance to another and begged that they at least permit his daughter, the 20-year old Fela, to return to the ghetto. However, he was insulted and ridiculed. Everyone had to enter the vehicles. Armed gendarmes appeared from various hiding places. More vehicles arrived with armed gendarmes and auxiliary police.

The vehicles moved from the spot and traveled at a great speed in the direction of the Jewish cemetery. The victims obviously saw death before their eyes. The 20-year old Wladek Kapinski was the first to spring from the moving vehicle. Others sprang down after him, but only six men succeeded in escaping from death. Among those escaping, in addition to Wladek, was the leader of the Jewish labor office in the small ghetto – Bernard Kurland. The remaining 127 men [*] – the small remnant of the intelligentsia with [university] degrees – were brought to the Jewish cemetery. The entire cemetery was filled with camp guards and Ukrainian auxiliary police. All of the victims were forced into the room for purifying the dead. Here, they were forced to take off their clothes. The 20-year old Fela was the first to be taken out. She stood in front of a large grave, face to face with two gendarmes. The gendarmes did not dare to do anything. A short opportunity... This opportunity was interrupted by the camp guards. A crack from a rifle and Fela lay in the throes of death, face to the earth. Both gendarmes exchanged glances, turned over the still moving body in its last anguish, looked at it for a time, looked at each other and went on to their further "holy service." Those remaining in the room for purifying the dead were taken out in pairs. The oldest were "finished" first. The German hangmen had time for the children. They wanted to play with the children a little. But they were children and the gendarmes themselves were still fathers... Children were picked up with one hand by their small hands, by their small feet or by the hair and with the second [hand] they aimed at their small heart or into their bodies. It did not matter that all of the children did not die immediately. No matter, Mother Earth covered even those who could still cry out their last Ma...

The small Lili was the last. All her clothing was removed. Only the large white band on her small head – a vestige of her holiday – was left for her. Lili stood before the grave; her large sky-blue eyes strayed from one murderer to another. It is difficult to characterize what was reflected in the eyes of the small, delicate child. The gendarmes, already saturated with blood, did not move to lift a hand to shoot. Each was waiting for the other to end that day's bloody game.

[*] [Translator's note: the text states that there were 127 men, but the further text mentions women and children.]

A longer pause... Iberszer, the tall, wide-boned camp leader, strode quickly and cut short the embarrassment of his comrades. He aimed his revolver at the chest of the young Lili with the exclamation: "For the Führer and Fatherland." The crack of the revolver and Lili closed the chain of 127 victims on her seventh birthday.

One hundred and twenty-seven people filled a new mass grave, where a little later an unknown hand laid a broken stone from a defiled headstone on which he engraved: "Czenstochower Jewish Intelligentsia, Purim, the 20th of March, 1943."

The ghetto was crushed; no one was seen in the streets. Only the gendarmes were running wildly and robbing the houses of those just annihilated. Every one of them hurried to take even more from these residences before Degenhardt would come to seal them.

Some days later, the Gestapo got a trace of the escapees. Five people were captured in their hiding places. Bernard Kurland was granted amnesty by Degenhardt and brought to the ghetto to continue to head the work and the remaining four, already locked in chains, wrestled with the Gestapo murderers and perished near the grave of the 127.

After Bernard Kurland was brought to the ghetto, Iberszer turned to him to provide for him an evening meal because of the "mercy" that he [Kurland] had been allowed to live. Iberszer became drunk and boasted of his "humanity." He related that he had seen how they sprang from the vehicles and escaped. Other gendarmes shot at them. Adults fell on the spot; children fell; however, he had not fired. He saw Kurland spring from the auto and also did not fire at him. He remembered then that he also had a family, that he also was a father of children and he could not raise his hand to shoot. He became more drunk and spoke about the execution of the 127 that took place after this at the cemetery, about the "game" with the children and about the death of the small Lili Winer. He said that it "hurt" him in his heart, but what could he do, that it was a war and everything was being done for the Führer and fatherland.

Iberzher became more drunk and related that at the order of the other doctor, [Herbert] Boettcher from Radom, similar *aktsias* had taken place against the Jewish intelligentsia on the same day in Radom, Piotrkow and Tomaszów Mazowiecki.

23rd April. Nadrzeczna 66, the youngest fighting group, sent several young people out to carry out diversionary actions. They left the ghetto with the workers at the *Ost-Ban*, were stopped on the way and three of them perished on the spot. The Gestapo and security police came; they took every second worker from this temporary workplace and shot them.

The first of May, six o'clock in the morning. The groups assembled according to the temporary workplace, stood, as always, in rows and marched to the gate of the ghetto. No one was permitted to leave. [Those in] the rows moved, moved back and remained standing, waiting for a further order. The group had a strong feeling of anxiety. The official order that everyone should remain in the ghetto and wait for further orders came an hour later. Even the workers at the ammunition factory remained in the ghetto. The temporary workplaces at which only Jewish workers were employed were completely inactive. The "Jewish problem" was everywhere. These events were observed in various ways. Several believed that this was the arrival of the liquidation of the ghetto; others waved this idea away with their hands and consoled themselves that this was no more than a means to assure that no Jews meet with Poles at the workplaces on the 1st and 3rd of May [May Day, a worker's holiday, and Constitution Day in Poland]. This was the first time all of the fighting groups got on their feet and deployed in an organized manner at their designated locations. The anxiety grew from minute to minute. They could not remain in the houses. No food was being smuggled in and only that which the *Judenrat's* kitchen had arranged was given out. However, no one was worried about this because everyone felt that a danger was approaching. Doctor Walberg, who was now outside the ghetto, let them know that he had precise information that this time nothing would happen. Mechl Birncwajg, who was outside the ghetto, gave the same information in writing. The mood did not ease and several people smuggled themselves out in garbage cans that were removed from the ghetto. They began to smuggle a little bit of potatoes and bread in the same cans.

On the 4th of May in the morning the trumpet that called the workers was heard again. The mood was eased a bit and the days began to drag with their "normal" and tragic path of life.

The regimen in the ghetto became stricter. Kestner and Laszinski, the camp leaders, were designated as supervisors over political matters at the security police. Both knew Polish very well and thus had better opportunities to hear and orient themselves as to what was happening in the ghetto. It was known that their assignment was to find out all threads of the fighting organization. The fighting organization strengthened its vigilance, carried out frequent roll calls of the groups and observed the conduct of the Jews who met with the two camp leaders. The situation of the Jews on the Aryan side also became more difficult. The hunt for Jews who were on the "Aryan" side as well as Jews who were hiding in bunkers outside the ghetto greatly increased. Many of the captured Jews were shot outside the ghetto or brought to the well-known *Ryneczek* "central square" and murdered there. There were also cases when such Jews were allowed into the ghetto without any punishment. Such cases occurred during the last weeks of the liquidation of the small ghetto. Jews from the bunkers and from the "Aryan" side began to smuggle themselves into the ghetto with the marching workers from the temporary workplaces. The soil under their feet burned and they did not want to perish alone. The number of Jews in the ghetto thus began to increase in a significant way, but the danger of death in the ghetto also increased.

The 8th of June 1943, an attack of the security police on the Jewish workers in the "furniture factory." Degenhardt led this action himself. Mechl Birncwajg particularly felt the danger personally and disappeared at the last minute. A security policeman found his mother, Bajla Birncwajg, in the second courtyard near the toilet and shot her on the spot. Ferszter, the carpenter, also was shot and another worker in the carpentry workshop we later found with a smashed in skull among the boards lying around in the first courtyard of the "furniture camp."

Lazinski, the camp leader, showed best the "art" of reaching a target with one shot. A security policeman in the other courtyard of the "furniture camp" recognized Mechl's wife, Hania Birncwajg (the daughter of the Zionist worker, Avraham-Lozer Szajnfeld), and stopped her. A false "identity card" was found in the cabinetmaker's workshop. A girl, Saba Rozenzaft, to whom the "identity card" belonged, was found out. She was also placed separately. We all stood in a long row and shook everything out of our pockets into a basket that had been set up for us by the security police. The searches ended. We stood after everything in a long row in uneasy waiting for further events. The wagon on which Hania and Saba sat ringed by security police traveled along the entire row. Mechl hid in a bunker in the "furniture factory" and only a few of his closest comrades knew where he was. They advised him to leave Czenstochow because he had had a certain "cosmetic" operation and, in addition, he still had "Aryan" papers. Therefore, outside Czenstochow he could pass for a Pole. Mechl did not want to leave Czenstochow until he saved his wife from murderous hands. Hania and Saba were held in prison for two days and then shot. Later, Motek also perished. A second misfortune came a few days later; a bunker was discovered with Jews in the Horowicz and Partners factory. One group of them perished and a second group was taken to the ghetto.

The next day, on the 9th of July, after the events at the "furniture camp," Franke, the city chief, turned with a confidential letter to Kundt, the governor of the Radom District, with a request to deport the remaining small number of Jews. In this letter Franke indicated that after the 4th and 5th of June, he brought to their attention that the presence of the few thousand Jews in Czenstochow was, in his opinion, unwanted by all of the national groups. In this letter Franke cited two justifications for why the continued presence of the Jews in Czenstochow was impossible: 1. "The Jews are an element that spreads dissatisfaction in every sense among the non-German population.

9. Juni 1943.

Herrn
Gouverneur K u n d t

Amt für Innere Verwaltung
Sei/Schl.

R a d o m

Einschreiben!
Vertraulich!

Sehr verehrter Herr Guverneur!

Wie ich Ihnen bereits anlässlich Ihres Besuches am 4.
und 5. d. M. dargetan habe, wird die Anwesenheit von
mehreren Tausend Juden in Tschenstochau von allen Be-
völkerungskreisen als äusserst abträglich angesehen. Ich
bitte darum, dass die Insassen des jüdischen Wohnbezirks
raschest aus Tschenstochau ausgesiedelt werden. Die beson-
deren Gründe für meine Bitte sind ausser den sonstigen
allgemeinen ungünstigen Wahrnehmungen noch zwei Dinge,
die die Anwesenheit der Juden in Tschenstochau auf die
weitere Dauer für unmöglich erscheinen lassen.

1.) Die Juden sind hier das Element, das die Unzufrieden-
heit an den gegenwärtigen Verhältnissen in jeder Hin-
sicht an die nichtdeutsche Bevölkerung heranzutragen
versucht. Wenngleich die Absonderung der Juden den
Vorschriften entsprechend durchgeführt wird, kann doch
nicht vermieden werden, dass hier und da immer noch
Berührungsmöglichkeiten mit der nichtdeutschen Bevölkerung gegeben sind.

2.) Ich habe den dringenden Verdacht, dass die Juden zu
einem wesentlichen Teil an den unruhigen Verhältnissen
der letzten Zeit in Tschenstochau ein überaus grosses
Mass Schuld tragen. Diese Wahrnehmung ist mir von
vielen Seiten der deutschen und polnischen Bevölkerung
mitgeteilt worden. Es ist so, dass sowohl durch propagan-
distische Hetz- und auch durch aktive Tätigkeit die Juden
die öffentliche Ruhe zu zerstören versuchen. Darüber-
hinaus versuchen sie durch Greuelpropaganda die Belange
der Feindmächte in diesem Raume in jeder Weise zu
fördern.

2.) Der Einwand, dass die Juden in der Kriegswirtschaft
bzw. Kriegsfertigung ein nicht zu verachtender Faktor
sind, möchte ich dahingehend richtigstellen, dass der
Arbeitseffekt der jüdischen Arbeiter von allen einschlä-
gigen Kreisen als äusserst minimal bezeichnet wird.
Durchschnittlich beträgt die tägliche Arbeitsleistung eines Juden nur etwa ein Drittel der Leistung eines normal-
en polnischen Arbeiters. Natürlich ist den Betriebsführern
das Vorhandensein von wenig brauchbaren Kräften immer noch lieber als gar keine. Ich glaube jedoch, dass
das Arbeitsamt bei entsprechender Weisung in der Lage
ist, in sehr kurzer Zeit den Personalausfall durch Zu-
weisung nichtdetscher Arbeitskräfte wettzumachen.

Heil Hitler!
Der Stadthauptmann
m. d. F. d. G. b.:
Stadtrat

In the cellars of the Jewish police in the small ghetto

Even when they could isolate the Jews according to all of the rules, they would not be able to prevent the Jews from coming in contact with the non-German population. Franke underlined at the end of this statement that he had a strong suspicion that the Jews carried a great guilt in the unease that recently had held sway in Czenstochow. "The Jews wanted to disturb the public calm through agitation and through active measures." Thus Franke ended his statement. 2. "As for the belief that the Jews were necessary as workers for the war economy" – the city chief wrote, "I state that the talent of the Jews is minimal because the strength of the Jewish worker is one third of that usually shown by the Polish worker. Naturally" – the city chief further wrote in his second statement – "for the [labor] manager, the Jewish worker was better than nothing, but I believe that our labor office would provide other non-German strengths in a short time."109. The fate of the rest of the Jews in the small ghetto teetered on the scale. There was a quiet but bitter struggle between the city chief, who since the great expulsion had lost his power over the Jews, and, therefore, wanted the complete liquidation of the Jews in Czenstochow so "his" city would be *judenrein* [clean of Jews] and the [labor] manager and the security police, who were interested in keeping a few Jews here so that they could show that they themselves were needed in Czenstochow and in such a manner "protect themselves" and not have to go to the front. (In September 1942 during the deportation action, we witnessed an argument between Linderman, a representative of the city leadership, and Degenhardt, who was triumphant in that he had the exclusive right to control the Jews. Now again, everyone knew that the city chief wanted to make Czenstochow Judenrein and Liht, the leader of the ammunition factory, *HASAG-Pelcery*, intervened in Radom that they leave him the Jews because the Jewish strength was needed here for the war economy.) Meanwhile the permanent destruction of the Jews took place.

On the 18th of June the Gestapo uncovered the bunker of the Soyke family. Those found in the bunker perished. Boruch Baum's daughter, the young Guta, who worked actively in the cultural area of *TOZ* in the large ghetto also perished here. At the same time, the hard-working Adam Walberg was dragged away and murdered. Almost two dozen workers, who were employed in the storehouses of the security police, were arrested and murdered. Doctor Walberg was called from the sanitary location in the ghetto, ostensibly to give quick medical help to a Jewish worker who had become ill in the police storehouses. He was shot on the way there. A group of workers was shot under the accusation that they "stole from" the police storehouses. They were buried with Dr. Walberg in a mass grave at the Jewish cemetery.

Death floated day and night across the small remnant of Jews in the small ghetto. Yet Jews smuggled themselves back into the ghetto from the "Aryan" side. Fathers and mothers also brought back their children from the Aryan side and from bunkers outside the ghetto. The parents felt they were nearing death and did not think it was right to leave their children as orphans in an environment unfamiliar to the children. The convicts in work camps understood and felt that they were on the last leg of their journey.

At night, on the 25th of June 1943, the small ghetto was surrounded. The bunkers of the Jewish fighting organization at Nadrzeczna 86 and 88 were attacked with grenades. Almost all of the fighters who were located there perished. The workers from the temporary workplaces, who were returning from work, were held on the *Ryneczek* "central square." Security police, members of the Gestapo, as well as Germans and Ukrainians from other police formations murdered everyone they met in the street, who they found in the houses where bunkers were located. People sprang through windows on high floors, from balconies and fell like birds shot in flight. From the bunkers, the Germans pulled out long and short weapons, grenades, various tools as well as German uniforms. Night fell, the Jews held on the *Ryneczek* "central square," were permitted to enter the ghetto. The workers from the ammunition factories were held there and they were told that they would no longer be allowed into the ghetto.

Work police from these factories came to take a new group from the ghetto for the nightshift in *HASAG*. People scrambled to go voluntarily to this work. Several did this because those closest to them remained there, others because they already saw the terrible danger that had arrived and they were searching for a means to remain alive. This aktsia was carried out by the recently nominated camp leaders, Laszinksi and Kestner, under Degenhardt's supervision. They knew every little corner of the ghetto; they knew of every hiding place and of every bunker. They knew the entrance and the exit of every tunnel and of every bunker built by the fighting organization. Their confidant, the Jewish policeman Yakov Rozenberg, had taken care to make sure they knew of this. This evildoer and traitor did not come from Czenstochow. But as soon as he appeared in the ghetto, it already was apparent that his role was secret. At first he played the role of a deaf-dumb person and wore a special yellow marking on his arm. Later he wore a band as a "useful Jew" and had the right to move outside the ghetto with a *Mogen Dovid* [Star of David] marking. He became a policeman again before the great expulsion. He gave the impression in the ghetto of an innocent person and simultaneously served in the police and was Laszinski's and Kestner's informant. A death sentence was carried out on him by the fighting organization; the sentence was carried out, but too late. The German police already had all of the threads of the fighting organization in its hands.

Newspaper clipping

On the 26th of June 1943, 10 o'clock in the morning. All of the men were driven out on the *Ryneczek* "central square." The entire square was surrounded by guards, members of the Gestapo, Polish policemen, air raid soldiers, Ukrainian fascists and work security from the ammunition factories in Czenstochow. The Germans with helmets on their heads stood fully armed. All of the remaining formations stood around the *Ryneczek* "central square" and held their guns with their gun-sights turned toward the surrounded Jews. Wagons full of corpses partially covered with sacks approached the square. Old men and fathers with children were taken, pulled out of the rows and placed separately under a special guard of the security police. The fathers stood quietly, broken and the children cried.

Rok VI.

Z Sądu Specjalnego

Kara śmierci za przechowywanie żydów

Przed Sądem Specjalnym w Częstochowie toczyła się rozprawa przeciwko małżonkom Tadeuszowi i Czesławie Bednarskim, zamieszkałym w Częstochowie, przy Alei Wolności.

Bednarscy w okresie od lutego 1943 r. do czerwca przechowywali żydów. Sojkę wraz z dwojgiem dzieci.

Oskarżeni pobrali od Sojki jako wynagrodzenie 12 tysięcy złotych.

W czerwcu 1943 roku, władze wykryły żydów u Bednarskich, po czym żydzi zostali skazani przez Sąd Specjalny na karę śmierci.

M... chowie Bednar... ... przy ... spowiadali przed Sądem Specjalnym, również zostali skazani na śmierć za świadome udzielenie żydom schronienia.

Galapagos

From the crying children's small voices was heard the small voice of Asher Szmuliewicz, an eight year old boy, "Rafalek, do not go with me, you can still stay, why should you perish, too?" Many of those who lived in the houses at Nadrzeczna 86 and 88 where the bunkers of the fighting organization were located were pulled out of the rows. They were loaded on the trucks by groups under the blows of rifle butts. Pleading cries, curses, threats came from the vehicles and there also appeared fists raised in the air. The Germans already were "working" on the vehicles with their rifle butts. The horrible uproar that came from the vehicles was mixed with the lamentations of the group of women who still stood at the wire in the ghetto. The packed vehicles traveled in the direction of the Jewish cemetery and returned sprinkled with blood for new servings.

Meanwhile, the Germans demanded of everyone under the threat of being shot to surrender everything that they had with them. Money, jewelry, gold and watches were stamped with the feet and thrown into the baskets especially provided by the security police.

The aktsia against the men ended. The lives of a group of young boys aged 12-15 whom Degenhardt wanted to send to their deaths still [hung in the balance]. Liht, the director of the ammunition factory, at the application from Bernard Kurland, declared that such young boys could be of use to him. Degenhardt filled Liht's request and gave the young boys into his jurisdiction.

The surviving men were sent to the ammunition factories: *HASAG-Apparatexbau* and *HASAG-Eisenhuta*. Then came the rows of women. Accompanied by the weeping of all of the women who stood on the *Ryneczek* "central square," old people and mothers with children were loaded into the same bloody vehicles and taken to their death. Mothers lost their children; children ran around on the square and burst into tears, called their mothers who had already been taken away to their deaths and had left their children here, thinking that although they were dying, some kind of miracle would happen at the last minute for their child...

Until the vehicles returned, the women were dragged into the "butcher shop" where they scratched on the walls, just as the men who had been imprisoned there earlier, their last thought: "I am curious if I will survive this murderous day" – Mietek Goldsztajn, or "My star is extinguished, it is very bad for me," or: "Bold bunker residents, the time of vengeance is coming." Children also were thrown in here. In the middle of the *Ryneczek* [central square] they lay a child on the ground, trembling with its hands and feet, crying and ceaselessly calling for his already deported mother. A tall, thin woman, the well-known to everyone Doctor Horowicz who held the hand of her own child approached the crying child. She lifted up the crying child from the ground, calmed it and leading both children by their small hands, she walked calmly and with an uplifted head in the direction of the bloodied autos. Degenhardt stopped her, advised her to give up the children and she alone should go to the *HASAG*. The doctor – now the mother of two children – did not react at all to his "mercy," did not abandon the children and went further. The murderer paid no more attention to her actions. Only the crowd of Jewish women on the "deportation" square accompanied with laments the tall, proud woman and the two small children, who were walking on their last road... The deportation of the women ended. All of the surviving women, as the men earlier, were taken to the ammunition factory of *HASAG-Apparatexbau* and *HASAG-Eisenhuta.*

After the deportation the Germans started the liquidation of the sick in the hospitals that were active in the small ghetto. In addition to the sick, children were hidden in the hospitals. The female Doctor Wajsberg and Doctor Szperling hid a few children there. Security police surrounded the hospital for infectious diseases and two went inside. They "quieted" the pleas and cries of the sick women with blows from rifle butts and riding crops and drove them out to the courtyard in their underwear. A series of shots from machine guns interrupted the lives of the unfortunate women. The men were driven out one by one. The crack from a revolver was heard as soon as a sick man crossed the threshold of the hospital, which made an end to his life.

One was a tall, young man, who proudly shouted out to the murderer, "Our innocent blood will not let you rest and always demand revenge! You, yourself, will perish in disgrace." The security policemen did not find all of the sick in the internists' hospital. The auxiliary to the labor security in the ammunition factory, *HASAG-Eizenhuta*, auxiliary who had always shown a human relationship to the tortured Jewish workers in their workplace anticipated [what would happen] and rescued a certain number of the sick from there.

In the morning Degenhardt declared an "amnesty" for all of those who were hidden in the ghetto if they came out of the bunkers by themselves. The Jewish policemen carried the "news" of the amnesty through the deadened ghetto. Eighty-four mothers, 60 fathers and approximately 100 children crawled out of the hiding places and reported. They were let in to the cleaned out hospital building. Here they were watched. They were permitted to console themselves with belief in the "amnesty" for two days; on the third day, the "amnesty" was broken. Thus, the Jews were again deceived.

House after house was exploded with dynamite. Hundreds of those hidden perished under the ruins. Dozens, who now emerged from the ruins were shot on the spot and burned. The Jews who sprang from the moving vehicles and did not fall from the bullets shooting after them on the 26th also met the same fate. Those rescued did not know of the fate of the remaining Jews in the ghetto. Moving around aimlessly for several days, they did not find any other way out than to penetrate back into the ghetto and, there, to be with the surviving Jews. Having escaped from death, they sneaked into the ghetto and here found death on the bonfire pile with all of those caught during the "amnesty."

The terrible life in the small ghetto ended and the cruel life in the camps of the *HASAG* ammunition factory began.

The small ghetto after the liquidation

Kestner – the liquidator of the small ghetto before the Polish People's Court

Zajnwel Weksztajn is giving evidence

The Resistance Movement in the Small Ghetto

In the month of October 1942, when the large deportation action was still occurring, four communist activists, Heniek Tencer, Daniel Warszawski, Wilik Celnik and Sumek Abramowicz, already had begun to organize a fighting group. This group arose in the "furniture camp" and active workers from other parties as well as the unaffiliated joined. This group earlier had gathered money and weapons in the large ghetto under the label *Dar Narodowy* [gift to the nation]. Heniek Tencer, who was known as an active communist during the years before the war, was at the head of newly reorganized fighting group. Heniek was a grandson of the well-known Czenstochow resident, Ziser. During the school year of 1929-30, he and 11 other *gymnazie* [secondary school] students, among whom were Mietek Perec (son of the well-known dentist Ahron Perec) and two more of his friends, Olek Behn and Pruszicki, were arrested for communist activity among the school youth. He continued to be active in the communist ranks after he left prison until he was sent to Bereza [Kartuska prison]. He placed himself under the authority of the anti-Fascist underground movement at the beginning of the German occupation. As soon as the Jews began to be taken from the temporary workplaces to the small ghetto, Heniek Tencer was designated as house guardian at Nadrzeczna 88, where the workers at the "furniture camp" were supposed to live and where these workers built bunkers for the mothers, children and old people who were rescued during the deportations. Heniek was entrusted as the house guardian for two reasons:

1. that there be a responsible person in the house where bunkers were prepared, and

2, so that he would not have to go out of the ghetto for any work in the temporary workplaces and could devote himself to more underground activities.

At a certain time the house guardianship at Nadrzeczna 88 was entrusted to the writer of these lines and Heniek and his wife moved to a bunker at Wilson Street 34. From there, they left for the "Aryan" side where they continued to be active.

In the end, they perished and every trace of them disappeared. Heniek Tencer was considered the pioneer of the resistance movement that arose after the great annihilating liquidation.

At the start of 1942 the Germans began to transfer the groups of cashiered Jews from the temporary workplaces into the small ghetto. Here, every survivor took stock of the savagery that had taken place during the last five-week deportation period. The last hope that they would see those closest to them who had perhaps survived at another temporary workplace ended for a large number of them. A few surviving underground workers from the large ghetto also realized that a strong "plague" had torn out of their ranks the much greater number of the surviving activists. However, no one knew exactly what would actually happen to the tens of thousands of Jews. It did not take long and letters from Mendl Wilinger and from Lubling were read in the ghetto that they had sent from Treblinka through a Polish train conductor about the suicide of their comrade and coworker, Shimshl Jakubowicz and about the actual fate of all of the Jews who were sent to Treblinka. They ordered that everything should be done for the world to learn what was happening to the Jews there. The word "Treblinka" that first became known in Czenstochow then annihilated all hopes of those who had fooled themselves and did not accept the terrible truth...

It is difficult to record the mood that began to dominate the ghetto then. It appeared as if everyone would become apathetic and that it would not matter what would happen next. Yet, the resistance movement began to solidify themselves. At the end of November there was a meeting at the laundry run by Rozine at Garncarka Street 56 in which took part: Dr. Adam Walberg, Yisroel Szimanowicz, Jakob Razine, Wilik Celnik and the writer of these lines. It was decided at the meeting to begin collecting weapons and various tools with which they could stand against the German in case of a deportation.

It also assigned to comrades Frajman and Jachimek, as craftsmen, the preparation of scissors and pliers with which they could slash through the wire fences. In addition to this, it was decided to smuggle in benzene and to place it in all corners of the ghetto so the ghetto could be set on fire on all sides in case the fight was lost. Dr. Walberg took on the military leadership. Communists, Bundists and non-party members belonged to this group.

A group of six young girls, Risha Gutgold, Saba Ripsztajn, Polya Szczekacz, Dasha Szczekacz, Sura Gutgold and Lusia Gutgold organized a collective at Nadrzeczna 66 at the same time. These six young girls decided to draw into their collective even more young people with whom they had worked at the TOZ Świetlicys [common rooms] in the large ghetto for the aid committee and also to spread literature more young people. The collective grew quickly with their following comrades: Kuba Ripsztajn, Mietek Ferleger, Mendl Fiszlewicz, Yitszhak Windman ("Lala"). Joining later were: Lolek Frankenberg ("Francek"), Mietek Wintraub ("Marduk"), Hipek Hajman, Aviv Rozine, Marisha Rozencwajg, Polya Hirsh, Jadjsha Mass, Lunya Wojdislawska, and even later this group joined: Izidor Fajner ("Faja"), Wladek Kapinski, Harry Gersznowicz and finally – Felya Zborowska and Pinek Samsonowicz. All 23 young people were from 17 to 20 years old, of whom the larger number were communists. They immediately began to prepare a revolt. They were satisfied with only eating dry bread and saved the collected money for weapons. After they had gathered a little money, Mietek Ferleger with Szulman's help left for the Kielce area and bought two revolvers. They declared themselves a fighting group, divided themselves into "fifths" and designated Mietek as the commandant of the entire group. This was the second and youngest fighting group that arose at the beginning of December in the small ghetto and they called themselves: Nadrzeczna 66.

The third group arose later at Nadrzeczna Street, no. 70 under the name, *Kibbutz*; this was a *haHalutz* [pioneer] group that Rywka Glanc, Yehuda Gliksztajn and the *shoymer* [armed guard] Avraham Zilbersztajn led at first.

There was yet another communist fighting group composed of: Sztajnbrecher, Szwierczewski, Rajch, Sztrasberg, Yanek, Yankl Besermen and Broski.

A conference of representatives of all of the fighting groups took place at the end of December 1942. The conference took place in an atmosphere of complete understanding. The *ZOB [Zydowska Organizacja Bojowa* – Jewish Fighting Organization] was founded. A commander was elected who set as a purpose: to make contact with the general "underground" in Czenstochow itself as well as outside of Czenstochow; to procure weapons and monetary means for this purpose. All members of the group were divided into fifths [groups of five]. Chosen as the commandant of the "fifths" was Mordekhai Zilberberg – a young man who had early excelled with his energy and with a certain knowledge and while still cashiered in *HASAG* began underground activity (his pseudonym was "Mojtek"). The representative of the commandant was Simek Abramowicz. Heniek Fajsak, the *Halutz* [pioneer], was designated the liaison among all of the groups. At first the Jews in the ghetto reacted to the fighting group with a certain skepticism, several with mockery and others even with hatred. The feeling of hatred was felt by the Jews who still believed that after everything they would survive and they were afraid that the "crazy ones" would bring the end closer... Little by little the activity of the Combat Organization began to have an effect; it evoked a feeling of respect from all of the Jews and also – fear. The Combat Organization grew to such strength that everyone in the ghetto had to respect it. All of the fighting groups, that until the unification numbered approximately 70 men, grew after the unification to 300, of which 120 were constantly involved in active work. Money for weapons was gathered from taxes and "thefts." The better-situated Jews were taxed and had to pay the designated sum for a particular period of time. The Jews who did not fulfill the demands were arrested and were only freed when their relatives paid the demanded sum. "Thefts" were carried out endlessly in the security police's warehouses of stolen goods on Garibaldi Street.

There also were "robberies" twice at the *Judenrat* warehouses and once – the apothecary at the *Judenrat* where chemicals useful for the grenades were found among the medicines. The "robberies" at the *Judenrat* warehouses and from the apothecary were carried out by: Avramek Czarna ("Czara"), Heniek Wernik ("Jacek"), Benianim Erenfrid, Pinek Samsonowicz and Lolek Frankenberg ("Francek"). This took place during the months of March and April 1943. Harry Pataszewicz, Avramek Kaplan, Hilel Fridman ("Chilek"), Mlodanow and others from the fighting group who proceeded to help, took part in collecting the assessments. Herszl Frazer with the help of Mosze Shmuel Landberg, Leon Fuks and a certain Guterman was busy stealing uniforms and other needed items from the security police. "Jacek" and Josek Kantor directed the digging of the underground tunnels. "Jacek" and "Bastek" directed the grenade workshop. Kaufman ("Mikrus"), the chemist, prepared the explosive material for the grenades. Michal Wajskop took care of assembling, repairing and cleaning the weapons. Designated as liaison men with *ZOB* in Warsaw were: Rywka, Hipek and "Francek."

* * *

Buying weapons was connected with great danger and sacrifice. In December 1942, Mietek Ferleger, walking on Jasnogorska Street to an agreed upon location for weapons, was stopped by "railroad security." He threw off the German after a short struggle and escaped. However, he finally was caught by the Gestapo and they tortured him for 24 hours and then shot him. This failure had a terrible influence on everyone and this was a particularly heavy blow for the group, Nadrzeczna 66, which lost a close comrade and an active and bold commander. However, it did not take away anyone's courage and the work of acquiring weapons was not weakened at all.

A similar case took place much later with "Zosha" the courier who carried weapons for the Czenstochow *ZOB*. In Czenstochow, she threw herself on a spy who persecuted her starting in Warsaw and in an uneven struggle with the Germans who encircled her, she fell.

The third case of victims during the purchase of weapons was on "Kamionka," four to five kilometers outside Czenstochow. Zilberberg, Kantor and Reni* Lenczner were sent there to receive a transport of [short barreled] rifles that were ordered for 250,000 *zlotes* through the cooperation of a weapons broker. The broker probably was an agent of the German gendarmerie. As soon as they left the designated spot with the weapons they had received, they were encircled by gendarmes and members of the Gestapo who immediately opened fire. Several Germans were wounded during the exchange of fire. Unverified news reached us that two gendarmes fell dead. Zilberberg and Kantor succeeded in extracting themselves from the German encirclement and returned to the ghetto. Renya, severely wounded, was taken alive when she already had fired all of the bullets from her two revolvers. Dying, she was tortured in the cellars of the Gestapo and did not reveal her sacred secret. All of the failures agitated the entire ghetto. Every failure was another heavy blow for the fighting group. However, the heroic conduct of the comrades who perished filled everyone with pride and inspired them to new deeds.

* [Translator's note: Reni Lenczner's name is also given as the diminutive Renya.]

* * *

The first armed, but weak, organized appearance of the fighting organization took place on the 4th of January 1943. At Degenhardt's order, all Jews who worked at temporary workplaces in the ghetto had to appear at the *Ryneczek* "Central Square." Of the command, only Mendl Fiszlewicz, of the fighting group, Nadrzeczna 66, and in whose name he was the representative in the general command, was in the ghetto. The largest number of [members] of the fighting groups in the ghetto again were from the group Nadrzeczna 66 along with several members of the general fighting group. After long consultations, with a majority of vote of the fighters, it was decided to go to the *Ryneczek* "Central Square." They did not have any weapons. The few revolvers that the organization did have then were divided among the commanders who were outside the ghetto with special tasks. Fiszlewicz had only one revolver.

Memorial to Jewish Martyrs

H.A.S.A.G

He actually took this revolver with him and his closest comrade, Izidor (Yitzhak) Fajner, took only a knife. The young fighters went to the *Ryneczek* "Central Square" with these weapons. Only Polja Szczekacz remained on watch in the ghetto.

All of the Jews in the ghetto had long been assembled in the square. The *aktsia* that Lieutenant Rohn was carrying out was already in progress. Dozens of old people, mothers and children were sealed off separately under the watch of the Ukrainian fascists. At Rohn's order, the entire group of young people was surrounded and, as a punishment which they received later like all of the Jews, they were taken over to the group of Jews who were confined. Here, the group of fighters decided to die with honor. As soon as they were taken to the square and began to stand in rows to be led away, Fiszlewicz threw himself at Rohn with the revolver and Fajner with the knife at Lieutenant Safart. Rohn was wounded in his hand and Safart turned from the square, with a slashed uniform and cut boots. Fiszlewicz's revolver jammed because the cartridge case from the bullet that he shot remained sticking out. Fiszlewicz began to fight with his teeth and nails and fell, pierced by a series of bullets that the Germans fired at him from a machine gun. Fajner, seriously wounded, also fell.

The murderers did not end their blood lecture with this; they pulled out 25 more men from the rows, divided them into two groups and shot them in front of everyone. Twenty-seven young lives were annihilated and among them: the two young fighters Fiszlewicz and Fajner, Herszl Fridman, the well-known fighter since 1905, Natan Rozensztajn the lawyer, Wernik, Szlecer, Trambacki, Haptka Sztal, Wigodzki, Zilberszac, Goldberg, Radszicki and nine more who were not all known. Not all who fell died immediately from the bullets. Several of them, among whom was Fajner, were tormented with convulsions of death for hours.

Then, after this, everyone exhaled their souls. The rest of the assembled Jews were allowed back into the ghetto. The surrounded group of Jews of about 300 people was taken to Pilsudski Street 21, where the commissariat of the Polish police was located. A group of fighters designated to be taken away, who were able to extract themselves from the encircled group of Jews during the tragic struggle, were among the 300 people. Later, Dasha Szczekaz, the young female fighter, was the only one to extract herself from the commissariat.

The command of the fighting organization did not rest. It sent tools to cut through the bars to its male and female comrades. In the morning, under heavy guard by the gendarmes, all of those held were taken to Radomsk where the expulsion of the last assembled Jews was then taking place. The fighters decided to escape along the road. Sura Gutgold was the first to escape. Jadzia Mass, who slipped and fell when running, was the second. She immediately was recaptured and the guard around the transport was greatly increased. This prevented further tries at escaping.

However, the command did not rest and sent out two emissaries, Yitzhak Windman and Zvi Lustinger, to Radomsk to bring to bear on the spot all its strength to extract their male and female comrades. The emissaries arrived in Radomsk in the very fervor of a "deportation" and it was impossible to do anything. The Ukrainians who were bribed took the money and then threatened to shoot them, if anyone tried to escape there. The female fighters decided to commit suicide and not go into the train wagons. Jadzia Mass was the first to hang herself. The second one was supposed to be Marisha Rozencwajg. The remaining Jews, who were with them, stood opposed and did not permit any further suicides. Therefore, the female fighters decided to make use of their last means – springing from a moving train. They all entered one train wagon with the tools that had been sent to them by the command in Czenstochow.

Under way they filed through the barred window openings of the horse wagon and one by one began to jump out. Others also made use of this opportunity. Only a few women, among whom was Ceshia Borkowska, the active fighter, returned to Czenstochow. The larger number were shot while jumping from the wagons and the rest perished while wandering back to Czenstochow.

* *

*

After these tragic events, the commandant decided to use more energy to procure weapons. Everyone was aware of the precise danger that lurked in buying weapons through the intercession of untrustworthy brokers who took advantage of the situation of the fighters in the ghetto and whose price for each old weapon was notorious. It was already clear that several brokers were no more than German placed spies. To be less dependent on the brokers and thus avoid surprises, it was decided to concentrate greater energy in producing grenades with their own effort.

During the late night hours when the prisoners in the ghetto, after a day of pain, insult and heavy labor, slept with a deep but uneasy sleep, shadows began to sneak quickly out of every ghetto corner and with careful movement went in the direction of an abandoned ruin of a house. Here was the workshop; here stood the forge where the forms were poured for grenades. The smoke irritated the eyes, but in every face was mirrored stubbornness, human earnestness, energy and the fervor for courageous deeds.

February 1943 – the first grenades were done. The almost grey fighters trembled with joy. The eyes of the young and even younger fighter-mechanics shone. However, doubt began to gnaw: and perhaps? Perhaps all of the work was in vain? The grenades had been finished with bare hands and without the least experience! "We must test the grenades!" – came an order. Members of the grenade group smuggled themselves out to Mirow, outside of Czenstochow, tried out the explosive force of the grenades and in the morning they brought with them a rejoicing greeting...

The "greeting" cheered up everyone. They began to feel more certain and stronger. Until now they felt as if they were hanging over a frightening abyss and now they felt firm support. They began to weave the beautiful dreams of an open fight with the Huns of the 20th century. "Now we will not go into the freight wagons like obedient sheep to the slaughter! We will not wait until the murderers come for us; we will go to them and annihilate them: blow up bridges, unscrew rails, blow up trains of the military and ammunition, killing the German criminals and perish ourselves with weapons in our hands!" – this was now the most beautiful dream of the Jewish fighter in the small Czenstochow ghetto. They took to the work with full fervor. A platoon of fighters for special assignments was trained. Leibl Cukerman, both Nasek brothers, Avramek, Czarna, both Szmulewicz brothers, "Bastek," Harri Pataszewicz, "Mikrus, "Yacek" and so on did not rest. The stole from the ammunition factories and from other temporary workplaces: aluminum, tin, carbide, quicksilver, dynamite and other chemicals that were needed for grenades. All of this was smuggled into the ghettos in small casks in which were the lunches for the ghetto kitchen for workers in the temporary workplaces.

The work was carried on in the same manner every night. Several poured out the forms, which were turned over to the mechanics and from them to those who worked in the chemical division and from there – to those who finished the grenades and even adapted the handles which were manufactured on the lathes of the "furniture camp" and in the carpenters' workshops in the ghetto itself. Young men and women, almost still children who rose here to the height of those who take upon themselves a sacred task, worked here. The work went on night after night. The finished grenades were even varnished and then they traveled to the main arsenal of tunnel no. 1 [which was] built with great effort. The workshops were disassembled and cleaned at daybreak to again be assembled with the coming of deep night and again to pour the grenades with which such beautiful hopes were bound...

At the same time, when one group of fighters was busy with manufacturing grenades, a second was busy with building underground tunnels.

The first and most important tunnel began at Garncarska Street no. 42 and had its exit outside the ghetto at the old market no. 17. The second tunnel began at Nadrzeczna no. 80/82 and had its exit in an empty field outside the ghetto at the corner of Jaskrowska Street. The tunnels also had entrances in the houses at Garncarska 40, at Nadrzeczna 86, 88 and 90. Both the entrances and the exits were well hidden and there was no danger that the "evil eye" would notice them. The work of building the tunnels went on day and night. The work was done in two shifts with up to 100 men for each shift. The young who were not yet drawn into the ranks of the Combat Organization also worked here and were ready at every call of the headquarters.

* * *

The headquarters also issued bulletins and appeals. One appeal was issued on the 1st of May and a second – to the Polish labor force about help for the Combat Organization. The bulletins were issued based on radio news. The radio was installed in the "furniture camp." The news was recorded by responsible underground workers. Important news particularly would be provided at roll calls especially called by the fighting group. Among the important news that was given at the roll calls was: the news that the Polish underground radio had provided in the second half of the month of April 1943 that Dutch women had grabbed Jewish children from the ranks and escaped with them during the expulsion of the Jews in Holland, about the course of the uprising in the Warsaw ghetto and particularly about the death of Michal Klepfisz [a chemical engineer and Bundist member of the Jewish Combat

Organization]. On the same evening, the Czenstochow Combat Organization honored the memory of the fallen Warsaw ghetto insurgent.

* * *

At the end of February 1943, "Francek," "Marduk" and Szulman were the first scouts sent out to investigate the possibilities of sending groups into the forests of Olsztyn and "Zloty Potok." They returned after two days with the view that it was too early to send a group out to the forest.

Further scouts were no longer sent out because Szulman, who was responsible for the entire Kielce area, was caught by the security police and sent to the Skarzysko camps and disappeared without a trace. A reconnaissance "group of five" was sent out to the forest at the beginning of March. This "group of five" consisted of the young fighters: Moniek Flamenbaum, Olek Hersenberg, Janek Kroyse, Heniek Richter, the son of the well-known communist activist, Dovid Richter, and Jeczik Rozenblat. Szliamek Szajn, for whom the Gestapo had been searching for a long time, joined the group. At first, they maintained contact with groups from *Gwardia Ludowa* [People's Guard of the Polish Socialist Party]. Later, they began to burn the ground under their feet because they were persecuted by the reactionary *A. K.* groups (*Armia Krajowa* [Home Army, major resistance group]). They returned from the forest and fortified themselves in a bunker in a house at Wilson Street no. 34, where the storehouses for the looted old Jewish furniture was located; this storehouse now belonged to the "furniture camp." From time to time they would make their "withdrawals" from there. Bunkers in which several Jewish families were hidden with their elders and children also were located there. Dovid Kongrecki's wife and her two children were among others who were located there. The Gestapo discovered the bunker of the six young fighters on the 17th of March 1943 because of the carelessness of Kongrecki's oldest child. They were suddenly attacked and did not have time to make use of their weapons. They were shot at the Jewish cemetery on the 19th of March.

Rywka Glanc, Hipek Hajman and Yitzhak Windman returned from Warsaw with literature and instructions at the beginning of April 1943. Rywka and Yitzhak entered the ghetto and Hipek, who was supposed to enter the ghetto with the workers at the *Enra* temporary workplace, was detained in front of *Wilot* (ghetto gate). They found literature and a *Kennkarte* [basic German identity document] on him. He was taken immediately to an arrest house at the Jewish police at Kocza Street and was handed over to the supervision of the Jewish and Polish police. He was supposed to be held here overnight to be given over to Degenhardt's disposition in the morning.

The group Nadrzeczna 66, to which Hipek belonged, had taken on themselves the task of extracting him from there. This mission was taken on by: Harry Gerszonowicz, Lokek Frankenberg, Aviv Rozine, Mietek Wajntraub and Kuba Rypsztajn. The five young fighters carried out their task perfectly and, on the same night, Hipek left for Warsaw. Weeks later, he and Yitzhak Windman, were stopped by *szmalcowniks* [Polish slang for Poles blackmailing Jews] as they were going for a transport of ordered weapons. Windman managed to disappear and the *szmalcowniks* gave Hipek into the hands of the Gestapo who sent him to the camp in Trawnik, where he perished.

* * *

The freeing of Hipek aroused the entire ghetto. The prestige of the fighting organization rose strikingly; they felt proud and simultaneously were afraid of repressions. However, no repressions came after the events of the 4th of January, because for Laszinski and Kestner – both camp leaders – who were designated as overseers of the ghetto with special authorization, as well as Morder, the German commandant of the Ukrainian ghetto guards, the matter of freeing of Hipek worried them, [they feared] the consequences for their own "carelessness." However, they began to spread a thick net to find all of the threads of the camp organization. Day by day and night by night, they themselves searched the ghetto and rummaged in every corner. Simultaneously, they began to draw into the espionage work their Jewish acquaintances, from whom they would be able to receive the most important secrets. Therefore, the organization decided to take measures against the traitors.

First, they twice warned the band, which had terrorized the Jews in the ghetto, and they extracted money from them, making use of it in a scandalous way in the name of the fighting organization. The two Szwimer brothers (the sons of a former servant in the *mikvah* [ritual bathhouse] were at the head of the band. The presented themselves as "strong ones" and did not take heed of the warnings and continued their work of terror.

A death sentence was carried out against them. A second death sentence was also carried out against the baker Motl Herman "Kulbajki," who had been long suspected of being in contact with the Gestapo and whose letter to the Gestapo had been intercepted by Mekhl Birncwajg. A corked bottle was placed in the grave of every traitor containing a piece of paper on which the reason for carrying out the sentence was written.

The work of the organization became even more difficult and more dangerous. However, no one lost his courage and everyone was ready to carry out anything that was placed on him.

* * *

During the first half of April 1943 the comrades Avramek Czarna (communist) and Manya Szlezinger (female communist) received the task of manufacturing keys that could unscrew the railroad rails. They made the tools in the ammunition factory *HASAG Apparatexbau* (Pelcery) where they worked and themselves smuggled them into the ghetto. On the 22nd of April five saboteurs left with the smuggled tools to unscrew the rails near Bleszno outside of Czenstochow through which would pass many military and ammunition transports. The saboteurs were: Aviv Rozine, Zvi Lustiger, Lolek Frankenberg, Harry Gerszonwicz and Dovid Altman. They left the ghetto with the workers of the "Ostbahn" temporary workplace. They had to "peel off" one by one and later meet in Bleszno. Here, they had to unscrew the rails and they had to wait here for the results of their little bit of work; from there they were to bring a joyful report.

Lolek was the first one who "peeled off" and he made it peacefully. Dovid Altman was supposed to be the second one. However, he was stopped by the railroad security man, Karna, a volks-Deutsch [ethnic German] from Wyczerp outside of Czenstochow. First he tried to bribe Karna; however, he immediately latched onto a second German from the railroad security. Karna withdrew from taking bribery money and both [Germans] resumed their "guard duty."

Harry opened fire on the two train guards in order to free Dovid. One of them immediately fell seriously wounded and Dovid escaped. Harry, Aviv and Zvi did not have time to escape because they were surrounded by a crowd of Germans, who shot at them from every side. Harry and Aviv fell on the spot, Zvi barricaded himself in a peasant's barn and defended himself until he was severely wounded by a grenade that was thrown [into the barn]. Alive, but seriously wounded, he was caught by the Gestapo who threw him into the same Gestapo cellar where he had previously been tortured to [get him to] reveal his comrades. Zvi did not break down and was shot at the Jewish cemetery.

As a punishment, the Gestapo and the security police shot 25 more men on the same day, that is – every second Jew who worked in the temporary workplaces, with whom the saboteurs left the ghetto. Among the 25 shot were: Yakob Mosze Gelber-Litwin, Nakhman Enzel, Berl Zeligman, Stefan Montag, Goldberg (Warszawiak), Rusin (a former student at the Y.L. Peretz school in Czenstochow) and Dudek Lewkowicz. At the same time the Gestapo found the scent of Wladek Kapinski, arrested him and shot him at the cemetery. As later related by members of the Gestapo themselves, Wladek wrestled with them during his arrest and even when he finally stood in chains before his own grave.

The blows that constantly fell on the heads of the fighters were heavy. However, everyone was full of pride as well as hatred that their comrades were perishing in this way, as they all had dreamed – in a struggle with weapons in their hands.

* * *

There were changes in the officials of the Combat Organization because of these tragic cases. Sumek (communist) often was found on the "Aryan" side and he tried to make more contact with Polish *Gwardia Ludowa* [People's Guard of the Polish Socialist Party] groups so more Jewish fighters could be sent out to the forests. Yehuda left for the villages around Koniecpol to locate bunkers there for groups sent out. "Francek," Staszek Hauze and Kheniek

Wojdislawski were designated... as the liaisons between Warsaw and Czenstochow.

Mosze Rozenberg ("Futurist" from Radomsk) and Fajgenblat (Zionist) were designated as commanders of three "fifths," which were sent out to the forests for Olsztyn and "Zloty Potok." According to later information that was brought by a messenger from the G. L. *[Gwardia Ludowa]* partisan group of the *A. K.* [Armia Krajowa – Home Army, major resistance group], all 15 men perished in a fight with the reactionary partisans of *A. K.* More than 50 men, who were divided into 10 groups, left for the forests before, during and after the liquidation of the small ghetto. The greater number of them perished in the struggle with the Germans and with the reactionary *A. K.* group. Several of them were in the well-known leftist partisan division of *Hanis* and took part in various actions against the Germans.

* * *

On the 1st of May 1943, the ghetto was closed and no one was permitted to leave for work. The fighting organization, just as the majority of the Jews in the ghetto, believed that the Germans would liquidate the ghetto and were ready to take on the fight. The weapons were divided among all of the fighting groups, which were deployed to their designated points: at the wire at Spadek Street that was in the direction of Warszawer Street, at the commissariat of the Jewish Police on Kozia Street, on Mostowa, at the entire eastern length of the ghetto near the "Warta" and at all important points in the ghetto that could have a strategic significance. The next day on the night of the 2nd of May, two notes were received: one from Dr. Walberg and the second from Machl (both were outside the ghetto) that they had exact information that this German blockade's only purpose was connected with preventing the Jews from coming together with the Poles. The notes were received by Jakob Rozine and he immediately gave them to commanders. However, the commanders did not call off the mobilization. The mobilization of the fighting organization was called off on the morning of the 4th of May when the blockade of the ghetto was withdrawn and the Jews were let out to work at the temporary workplaces outside the ghetto. However, the mood was not eased very much.

The security police and Gestapo searched among the Jewish "porters" of their acquaintance and the city chief moved heaven and earth to make Czenstochow *judenrein* [cleared of Jews]. The fighting organization again decided to constantly be in ready for an alarm and prepared intensively to take up the decisive fight. The security police and the Gestapo did find two contemptible people among the Jewish policemen who provided them with precise information about the fighting organization. The first was the Jewish policeman Rozenberg, who served Liszinski and Kestern, and the second – the policeman Plawner, who served the Gestapo.

On the 18th of June 1943 the security police, under the direction of Degenhardt himself, attacked the "furniture camp" with the purpose of eliminating Machl and his closest coworkers. The security police surrounded all of the workshops with the speed of lightning. Several security police with Degenhardt at the head entered the room in which Machl was located. No one was permitted to move from the spot where they were when the police arrived. They carried out a search and did not find any "suspects." Therefore, Degenhardt ordered that they not shoot without his order. However, Degenhardt ordered Machl to bring together all of his family members. Machl immediately realized that Degenhardt wished to kill him and his entire family. Therefore, he made use of the moment, ostensibly to bring together those closest to him and calling out: "They will not take me alive" – he disappeared. Three people were shot on the spot and the security police took two with them and later killed them.

Machl entered the square of the "furniture camp" on the same night, closed himself in a bunker of which only a few comrades knew. He was in contact only with Feywish Altman and with Michal Wajskop whom he told of the locations of hidden weapons and money. When all of the important matters already were completed, it was decided to take Machl out to stay with a Polish acquaintance with whom he had maintained contact the entire time.

Ahron Birnbaum, Chaim the barber-worker, Kobriner the painter-worker and Feywish Altman took upon themselves the removal of Machl from the "furniture camp." They took him out in a wagon in a coal basket. They stopped with the wagon on Ogrodowa Street near a paint shop, looked around to see if anyone was looking and gave the agreed upon sign. Machl came out of the basket and disappeared. A Polish woman who lived in the courtyard in which they had stopped the wagon noticed and reported it to a *granat policiant* [Blue police - Polish police in the Nazi-occupied area of Poland known as the General Government]. This policeman stopped all four comrades and transferred them to the security police. They were taken to the police station at the third *Aleje* no. 75. At the investigation they all denied [doing anything wrong] and argued that they had been sent by the old painting master, Avraham Grajcer, to receive a transport of chalk that was ordered by the "furniture camp" from the paint shop that was located in that house.

The "furniture camp" was surrounded by the security police and Degenhardt himself led the investigation. The arrestees told the writers of these lines about the manner of their defending themselves and this was told to Grajcer, the old Jewish painting master who said that they were his co-workers, that he would take all of the guilt on himself. At the cries and pleas of his children (a son and a daughter), that he not "draw a rope" onto himself, Grajcer simply answered: "I already have lived out my years and I want to be the redeemer of four young lives." During the investigation Grajcer did not break down and told Degenhardt that he sent the four men for chalk on his own and it was his fault that he forgot to give them an official note to receive the chalk; it also was his fault that they traveled unaccompanied by a German (Grajcer survived the liberation). Grajcer rescued the lives of four young men with his courageous bearing and he, himself, also got away without a punishment. The four arrestees were freed. During the liquidation of the Combat Organization in the small ghetto, one of them, Chaim the hairdresser, perished.

On the 28th of June 1943, the security police found Machl's tracks; he was hidden with a Polish family. He was arrested and shot.

* * *

Gdalya, an active member of the fighting organization was caught with literature outside the ghetto on the 16th of June. A certain Mrs. Masha Wajnberg also was arrested on the same day removing goods from the haberdashery storehouse on Garibaldi Street. All the workers who belonged to the "haberdashery" group were also arrested with her. All of those arrested were sent to Pilsudski Street to the arrest house at the commissariat of the *granat policja* [Polish police in Nazi-occupied territory]. The fighting organization decided to do everything to extract their comrade fighter from there as well as the rest of the arrestees. Herszl Prazer and Leib Cymerman were appointed to carry out the prepared plans. Herszl and Leib prepared a place to hide the arrestees if they decided to escape, sent in tools with which to saw through the bars of the window openings in the arrest cellars and simultaneously bribed the guards from the Polish *granat* policemen.

The period of escape was designated for the 23rd of June at night. However, the plan failed because of the cowardice of the arrestee, Moniek Krojze, who broke down at the last minute. That same day when their plan was discovered, that is, on the 23rd of June, Gdalya and the entire group were shot at the Jewish cemetery. On the same day the security police demanded of Doctor Walberg that he immediately report to Garibaldi Street to dispense medical help to a worker who was employed in the police storehouse who had become ill. Klipsh and Bulle, two German security police, were waiting for him at the designated spot. They greeted him with a friendly look; one of them led him to see where the "sick one" lay and the second one, who walked a few steps behind them, fired his revolver, aiming at Walberg's head. He immediately fell dead. At the same time that this happened to Walberg, the security police arrested a young Jewish couple with papers of *Volksdeutsche* [ethnic Germans], who worked as guards in the police house at the Third *Aleje* no. 75 and simultaneously worked with the Polish underground movement in Czenstochow.

While they were being taken, the man succeeded in escaping and the woman was taken to the Jewish cemetery where she was murdered with the "haberdashery" group. Walberg's body also was brought there and buried in a mass grave with the group that had been shot.

As Jewish workers, among whom was Prazer, who as a tradesman worked at the security police, later related, several security policemen boasted that they had shot "bandits" and thus gave the following history: a certain member of the *A. K.* [*Armia Krajowa* – Home Army] in Czenstochow and simultaneously an agent of the Gestapo in Radom said that Dr. Walberg was an important leader of the underground in Czenstochow and also that the couple who served as guards at *Aleje* 75 actually were Jews who were in contact with the Polish underground movement.

The fighting organization in the ghetto searched for signs of the two traitors, Rozenberg and Plawner and carried out a death sentence on them. Domb, the Jewish policeman, was also sentenced to death for his particular zeal during *aktsias* [actions, usually deportations] against Jews in the small ghetto. On the 21st of June 1943 the comrades: Avramek, Pinek, Waszilewicz, and "Baster" carried out the sentence against Rozenberg. After the liquidation of the small ghetto, the sentence against Domb also was carried out. The Gestapo itself shot Plawner after the liquidation of the small ghetto because it no longer had any need for his information.

The fighting organization decided to send out a transport of weapons to the groups that were located in the forests. Three comrades were designated for this purpose: Pinek Samsonowicz, Harri Pataszewicz and Lolek Blank. Leibush

Tenenbaum, a former member of the Peretz School managing committee and a member of the fighting organization, undertook the provision of a vehicle for this purpose.

Through the intervention of Wojdislawski and Winter, two Jewish foremen in the *HASAG*-Pelcery ammunition factory (Apparatexbau), Tenenbaum bribed the German driver of a truck that undertook driving the three comrades and their weapons. As it was learned later, the driver earlier had told everything to the Gestapo.

The three comrades left with the transport of weapons on the 24th of June. They were surrounded on the way by a horde of members of the Gestapo. While shooting at each other, Pinek fell dead, Lolek saved himself by running away and Harri fell into the hands of the enemy. They brought Harri dying into the ghetto, sat him by an open window in the building of the Jewish police and ordered that all of the Jews in the ghetto march by him. Three members of the Gestapo stood near Harri, torturing him terribly so that he would reveal who among those marching by were his coworkers.

They threw cold water on him whenever he began to pass out and continued to beat him. Winkler, a member of the Gestapo, stood out in the torturing of Harri. Harri used his last strength and did not break down. Finally, the Gestapo decided that they would get nothing from him and took him away to be shot. Tortured, Harri breathed out his soul on the way to the cemetery.

The driver also denounced Wojdislawski and Winter. Both were tortured so severely that they were broken and named Tenenbaum [as a coworker]. The Gestapo arrested Tenenbaum, tortured him and then brought him back to the *HASAG* to show him to his coworkers. To avoid suspicion, the representative of the work security leaders led him through the factory, not the Gestapo. The Gestapo got nothing from the torturing of Tenenbaum. They brought him back and shot him along with Wojdislawski and Winter.

* * *

On the morning of the 25th of June all prisoners in the ghetto were led to work in the temporary workplaces as on every day. No one sensed in advance any special changes as a result of the events of the night before. There was the impression that nothing had happened the previous night.

A number of those in the Combat Organization also left with the workers so as not to lose contact with the outside world and to further smuggle in that which was necessary to make grenades from the factories and temporary workplaces. However, the largest number of fighters still remained in the ghetto. They had to stand guard after the events of the night before! Everyone was mobilized; everyone was located in the tunnels at their designated place for roll call. The largest group was gathered in tunnel no. 1 where the weapons arsenal was located. Dozens of revolvers, dozens of grenades, two rifles, bottles with Molotov cocktails, carbide lamps and even German uniforms were there.

The weapons were divided among all of the groups and a roll call began. Marek Palman of the Warsaw ZOB [Zydowska Organizacja Bojowa – Jewish Fighting Organization] took the roll call in tunnel no. 1. Everyone was solemn. Everyone took an account of the serious situation and of the duties that each of them had taken upon themselves. They felt and they knew what would soon await the ghetto and they were prepared to oppose the approaching events.

The couriers of the groups who were already in the forest took part in this roll call. The couriers of the fighting groups in Upper Silesia also took part. They reported and they remembered the male and female comrades who had perished. The names of those comrades in the Czenstochower fighting group who perished floated up and the names also of the male and female Jewish fighters from other groups floated up. There floated up the name "Zoshya" – the pseudonym of the 19-year old seamstress, Ruchl Szabszewska, from Sosnowiec, who was one of the hardest working and boldest fighters in the Gwardia Ludowa [People's Guard – armed communist organization] group (G.L.) of Garbaty, which operated in the Kielce area. "Zoshya" was murdered near Wloszczawa by two traitors, Josef Laskowski and Czeslaw Stoliarczik, agents of the A. K. [Armia Krajowa – Home Army – the largest Polish resistance group]. (She was murdered at a moment when she was very sick.)

The name of the fallen heroes in the Warsaw ghetto floated up. Marek told about the courageous fighting comrades in the Warsaw ghetto and about the stubborn fight there. He spoke, gave out instructions and asked that [we go] in the manner of the Warsaw ghetto fighters. He called for fighting until the last bullet. We were absorbed by his descriptions and we were full of envy of the Warsaw ghetto heroes who had the great fortune to die in such a magnificent way.

The scouts brought greetings from the ghetto every 15 minutes. The ghetto was calm for the moment. All of the scouting divisions reported at three o'clock in the afternoon that the workers at the temporary workplaces had returned as normal from their work and nothing suspicious was noticed.

The mobilization was called off. One by one the fighters left the tunnel. Only the commandant, "Mojtek," who was sick, and Lutek Gliksztajn, who was guarding the weapons storehouse, remained in tunnel no. 1. It was quiet in the ghetto and the fighters did not give a thought to the fact that this might be a quiet before a storm.

Only an hour later, terrible firing from machine guns took place throughout the ghetto. The Gestapo and security police announced their arrival in the ghetto with this shooting. The houses at Nadrzeczna 86, 88 and 90 – the most important locations of the fighting organization – were surrounded and were covered with a hail of bullets. Blood flowed in the streets. The members of the fighting organization, who had left the tunnels an hour earlier, hurried back to enter [them]. They hurried to grab their weapons and pay with blood for blood, with death for death! However, they fell before they managed to enter [the tunnel]. Yisroel Avigdor Szuldhaus fell; Yosek Kantor fell; dozens of other comrades fell, unsuccessful in taking revenge for the innocently spilled blood of those closest to them, of the fighting comrades and of their parents.

The Germans attacked the tunnels with grenades. They murdered the small group of fighters who desperately resisted. Other Jews who were in the above-mentioned houses also fell. Thirty grenades, one revolver and two rifles fell into German hands. Luttek, who stood watch over the weapon storehouse, was the only one who emerged from there. Mojtek committed suicide at the last moment so as not to fall into their hands. The Germans later took revenge on "Mojtek's" body and hanged him up in the tunnel with his head down. Meanwhile, the fighters in the ghetto who were in the tunnel that had its entrance through the house at Garncarska 40 were the only ones who remained alive. This group under the leadership of Marek came out of the ghetto through the tunnel and barricaded themselves in a house at the old market no. 17. Here they waited for the enemy with their small number of weapons.

Early the next morning, on the 26th of July 1943, the whole group decided to leave their positions, taking the rescued weapons with them, to join their comrades in the forests to jointly take up the fight in relatively comfortable conditions. They began to leave the barricades in threes.

When most of them were already out and only six fighters were left under the leadership of Rywka Glanc, they were surrounded by security police and the Gestapo. The six fighters carried out an embittered defensive fight with two revolvers and one grenade. They made use of the grenade after firing all of the bullets. One member of the Gestapo fell and Lebel, the security policeman, who later gave the details of this fight to several Jewish workers who were employed by the security police in the Third *Aleje* no. 75, was wounded. The six fighters carried on their fight without weapons, but with stones and they finally all perished. Here fell: Rywka, Heniek, Polja, Dashya, Rashya and "Marduk." Few survived of those who did not perish during this fight. Marek perished later, traveling by train; "Francek" and Sumek were attacked on the "Aryan" side; Yitzhak Windman safely reached the group in Koniecpol and was murdered two weeks later when he traveled for weapons to Skarżysk [Skarżysko-Kamienna] with a certain Krzak (the news about the death of Yitzhak was brought by the same Krzak. However, the comrades believed that he had murdered Yitzhak because Krzak's statements seemed vague). Fela Zborowska, Yehuda and Bela Bram were shot by the Polish national police; Kuba Ripsztajn and Lutek Gliksztajn fell in the fight that the Koniecpoler group carried out against reactionary members of the *A. K.* [*Armia Krajowa* – Home Army].

The murderous liquidation of the small ghetto took place at the same time that the small group carried out its embittered fight at the old market 17. Dozens of Jews were shot on the spot and hundreds – were taken away in trucks to the Jewish cemetery and murdered there.

Members of the fighting organization were also among those shot on the spot and among those taken away.

Herszl Praser had been placed separately in the *Ryneczek* [central square] and was supposed to be shot. Then at the observation by a security policeman that he could be of use as a good tailor at the police workshop on Garibaldi Street, he was taken there and permitted to live. While others pleaded and wailed, Mosze Lewensztajn, already in an auto, with an upraised fist made a declaration against the murderers. At Zlota Street on the way to the cemetery, Lewensztajn, Chaim the hairdresser and other Jews tore open the trunk of the car and began to escape. Several fell on the spot under the fire that gendarmes opened on those escaping. Six of them managed to avoid the bullets. They were persecuted by Kindel, the gendarme, who had returned. The persecuted then stabbed him with his own bayonet.

The six men returned to the ghetto with the certainty that there still were Jews in the ghetto as well as several of their fighting comrades. However, there were no longer Jews in the ghetto, except for several dozen people to be shot, who were still being held. The six escapees again had fallen into the net of death and their lives were ended along with those sentenced to death.

The small ghetto in Czenstochow was liquidated on the last of the month of June 1943 and the heroic chapter of the fighting organization in the small ghetto ended. Surviving, closed in the camps of *HASAG* was a small number of Jews. A few fighters also remained alive in the forests and in the camps. This small group of surviving fighters did not cease [its activity] and continued to carry out its underground work both in the forests and in the *HASAG* camps.[110]

In the *HASAG* Camp

The approximately 4,000 still living, remaining Jews were sent to the camps of the ammunition factories *HASAG-Apparatebau* (Pelcery) and *HASAG-Eizenhuta*(Rakow) after the liquidation of the "small ghetto." These were the factories that belonged to the Polish and French joint-stock company. The Germans confiscated this factory and they converted it into ammunition factories. The security police temporarily borrowed 230 men from the ammunition factory who were housed on Garibaldi Street. At first these borrowed Jews were employed at cleaning the Jewish possessions that remained in the "small ghetto," as well as with removing the corpses that lay around here. The Jewish policemen also were employed doing the same thing. A number of the borrowed Jews were later sent to *HASAG-Pelcery*where they were murdered along with many other Jews and a number remained housed for a longer time at Garibaldi Street and worked for the Germans as craftsmen, as tailors, shoemakers, carpenters, locksmiths and sorted [things] in the warehouses of the security police.

The routne was stricter in the *HASAG-Pelcery* than in the *HASAG-Eizenhuta*. Among the German leaders in the *HASAG-Eizenhuta* ammunition camp was a higher rank police constable, Milhof, who greatly eased the fate of the Jews who were placed in his jurisdiction. During the liquidation of the small ghetto, this same [police constable] rescued the sick from the hospital and brought them to the *HASAG-Eizenhuta* factory in trucks. Later, Milhof was removed from his office and sent to the front. Glatter, the young Jewish doctor who helped him rescue the sick and in general did a great deal to ease the fate of the prisoners, was sent to another camp in Germany with all of the Jewish doctors from that camp, where he perished.

The road to Calvary for the Jewish prisoners in the *HASAG-Apparatebau* began during the large expulsion in September 1942.

From all of the temporary workplaces where the surviving Jews were housed, this was the worst. Now the larger number of the 4,000 surviving Jews was sent here. The mood here among those in the *HASAG* was an oppressed one. Some had lost their last child, some, their last relative and some, their last friend. Everyone felt alone.

At first they were dragged to the factory halls on the bare ground and food was brought from the ruined small ghetto on platforms from the food reserves that still remained there. Those in the *HASAG* assembled every night after work in the empty factory locations. Here they erected primitive kitchens from a few bricks and they cooked a few potatoes in the pots they had brought with them or a little coffee. However, not everyone had the good fortune to receive a few potatoes from a Polish worker acquaintance and not everyone brought a pot with him into the ghetto. The foremen and the work security could not bear this and the "freedom" to gather after work, and the empty factory locations were seized quickly. They continued pushing through the day with a half-liter soup, mostly made of dried beets ("sour soup" in *HASAG*-speak), with half a liter of coffee made of burned and rancid barley and 20 *deka* [a metric weight] bread per man.

The explosion of dynamite bombs reached here ceaselessly and penetrated from the houses in the small ghetto. At the same time, when the security police ripped open houses, murdering and robbing, the members of the security police Klem and his nearest trusted men: Stiglitz (a German), Kmiczikewicz (a Polish admirer, who was sentenced by a Polish court to the death penalty), Steininger (a German), Daraszenka and Paveliak (Ukrainians) left the *HASAG* for the ghetto. They searched there, looking for bunkers, murdering and robbing, taking part in mass executions. Bernard Kurland was designated as the Jewish representative, with whom the factory director established contact. Liht, the factory director had made him believe that the prisoners needed to be fed better so their productivity would be better. The factory directors arranged open bread [sales]. They themselves provided the bread. Jews bought and the directors thus had a good income from this.

Kurland also arranged for a tailoring and shoemaking workshop with the permission of the directors, as well as a laundry where Jewish craftsmen were employed, who needed to serve the prisoners. However, the routine was not eased further. Work security and foremen attacked their victims like wild animals. Groups that assembled on the square were shot at like birds. Mrs. Wolska (née Wajnrajch) fell in terrible agony from such shooting and she died in the woman's hall after more than two weeks of suffering. Here we found a worker with broken ribs that Apel, the construction foreman, had broken and here we found workers cramped in pain from being battered by work security with rifle butts.

However, the "residents of the *HASAG*" began to grow accustomed to their new hell and the feeling of deep pain began to atrophy. The thought sneaked in: perhaps? Perhaps, at least we will remain alive here? It is an ammunition factory of sorts and they still need hands to work!"

They lived here for three weeks and two days, hungry, broken, but with a glimmer of new hope. Three weeks and two days, hungry, eaten by lice and by bed bugs and tortured by work and foremen.

The 19th of June 1943. The bangs from the houses in the small ghetto were not yet stilled and here in the ammunition factory of *HASAG Apparatebau*, there was a new commotion. Every German foreman put together some sort of list of workers who were found under his supervision. The foreman Apel "Marsz" (he received the nickname from the workers because after beating someone he would shout: "Stand up and *morsz*" instead of *marsz* [march]) pointed to a worker who wore boots and boasted to another foreman that these boots would be his in the morning. Prisoners interpreted this as all of their personal clothing would be taken from them and exchanged for camp clothing; others maintained that only their boots would be taken, but not one imagined that a new misfortune was being prepared that would bring with it hundreds of victims. Between 11 and 12 on the same night, all of the prisoners were awaked from sleep and driven outside. Everyone had to march through a small alley where a "selection" took place. This time it was carried out by the factory director, Liht: by the technical director, Bretschneider; by the political officer, Arnt; by the technical manager- engineers: Spaltenholtz, Francke, Pasold; through foremen: Binter, Apel, Nicialek, Wirbac, Kehler, Walter and many other foremen. Klem, the leader of the work security, also carried out the "selections," helped by labor security [members]: Sztiglic, Szewtszenko, Daraszenka, Kmiczikewicz, Paweliak and so on. Hantke and Laszinski, the two security police, were also on the spot and [they] assisted and oversaw that everything was properly carried out. Degenhardt was at the "colony" (the directors and foremen lived here) with a larger group of security policemen. Hantke and Laszinski constantly gave instructions about how to carry out the "craft." They looked separately into each of our faces and evaluated us. Who seemed too old to them, too young or looked weak were stood apart. One "qualified" for death because he had a bald spot and a second – because he had a too beautiful and thick head of hair and appeared arrogant; another – because he wore glasses and another – because he walked a little bent; several women were pulled out of the rows because they were young and beautiful and because they were not beautiful enough. Each foreman was now an independent ruler over the life and death of his slaves. Each foreman pulled out from his group of workers those who had to go to death as "a sluggard." A young man, who wore nice boots was pulled out from among the others; Spaltenholtz pulled out the 18-year old Bialogurska from the rows and left her to stand [among those to be] killed, meanwhile calling: "You, blond, are too pretty to work; those such as you are only for amusement!" There, Klem dragged the young sanitary worker, Galster, because he gave evidence for a sick person that the other one needed a few days off from his work. At the same time, Pasold and the labor security leader turned to Galster's young wife who had turned to them to free her husband. All of those placed on the side were taken away to the "colony," which were located in the cellar-bunkers that served for holding arrested prisoners and where they would be tortured. All of the Jewish policemen in the small ghetto also were grouped and confined in these cellar-bunkers. Kurland, as the Jewish camp leader, who assisted during the selection, also was taken and thrown into a cellar-bunker.

A frightful lamentation carried through the entire factory. Those who were taken away to death now lamented; those remaining – those surviving temporarily – also cried and wailed. Two hundred sixty men now were pulled out of the ranks; 260 men were thrown into a dark cellar and spent their last night of a terrifying nightmare. Early in the morning, the foremen dragged out individual prisoners who had turned to them about the rescue of those closest to them. We saw how Spaltenholtz, among others, led the former chairman of the Lodz refugees in the large ghetto, Jaroczinski, who through Spaltenholtz tried to rescue his wife, who the night before had been thrown into a "bunker." All who naively believed that their foremen would help them pull those closest to them from the claws of death were taken to the "bunker" by the same foremen, where they shared the fate of those closest to them...

On the 20th of July 1943, 11 o'clock in the morning, dozens of people struggled to be with those closest to them in the dark cellars, to at least take a last look at their fathers, mothers, brothers, sisters or children. Factory security and foremen ran around through the factory square and searched for victims. Here, Klem led the very well-known and respected by everyone female doctor Wajsberg; a member of factory security dragged a young, good looking young man, Markowicz, in whom Klem had always shown an interest; here was dragged a small eight-year old girl, who was sneaked into the *HASAG* just a few days before, with whom even the sadistic foreman Kehler would often play: here the factory security pulled the very talented 18-19-year old Juzshek Jung ("walking encyclopedia – he was called) out of a hiding place and threw him in with those sentenced to death.

At the same time Degenhardt announced to the Jews who were housed on Garibaldi Street near the police warehouses that whoever had relatives in the *HASAG Apparatebau* and wanted to be with them could express their wish and their request would be filled immediately. Women who had husbands there reported; men reported who had wives there; mothers, sisters, brothers and children reported.

Degenhardt fulfilled their request. More than 100 men received permission and the opportunity to enter *HASAG* to be with those who were the only people left who were close to them. With joyously beating hearts, more than 100 "fortunate ones" climbed into the vehicles provided by Degenhardt for their sake. The vehicles flew quickly through the so well known Czenstochow streets: Garibaldi, Wilson Street, the Second *Aleje* and *Aleje* Wolnosci. People were taken with the hope of meeting with those nearest to them and were thrown in the dark cellars where death already floated in the air. The women and the children of the Jewish policemen finally were led away and confined in the same cellars (only the wife of policeman Kohn and her small son hid).

A terrible struggle began in the dark cellars at the "colony" of *HASAG Apparatebau*. Here not quite 500 Jews sentenced to death struggled with their German foremen and factory security; they did not allow themselves to be led to death. The struggle was a bitter one, but this time, too, the victor was the German hangman... Each victim was dazed by a hammer before being dragged out to the vehicles that were to take the victims to be shot at the Jewish cemetery. The foreman Apel "Morcz" excelled most in this "trade." (From this came his later nickname – *Hamerl* [little hammer].) "Morcz" already wore the boots he had noticed the night before on the feet of a young worker and other foremen strolled around the factory square drunk and boasted of their strength.

The still living cried quietly and the dark cellar walls of the bunkers of the arrested with some barely legible scratched out writing of the just murdered cried with them:

"Rubinku Feldman, I tell you, son, bear up well! Your mother, Ch. Feldman"

"Dear Ruwin, I go away calmly to death; do not lose hope! I kiss you! Your mother, Chana."

"I go away calmly! Yuczek Yung"

"Zosia Wigdor bids farewell to her husband Kalman; I leave calmly! Zosia Wigdor" ,"Herr Zalcberg! I believed that you would save me. I am disappointed!" (Signature is illegible, probably – Mrs. Beatus)

"I am already tired of running from death. I go away calmly. How will my children live? What will become of them? Signed – Kh. Sh."

The Jewish cemetery again increased with a mass grave of about 500 men. The German civilian foremen, the lame work security leader, Klem, and his work security and the entire factory directorate showed that they knew the sacred "religious service" no worse than the security police and the Gestapo.

Wooden barracks were then quickly erected in the *HASAG-Apparatebau* camp in an area of barely a square kilometer. This location was fenced in with barbed wire and equipped with electrical current. Observation booths were set up on the outside of the wire. In addition to this, the entire outside area was thickly guarded by work security. Long, one-story plank beds were erected in the barracks where hundreds of people slept underneath and on top one next to the other. This became the residential location for almost 3,000 men and women.

Every day brought its number of victims: someone was shot by a work security member just for amusement; someone – by a member of the Gestapo for some sin; someone for trying to escape from the camp and someone – by a foreman as a "sluggard." A child was born; it had to be murdered immediately. If someone became seriously ill, the lame work security leader also found a solution for him...

After a "selection" was carried out on the first day, there were cases of escapes from the camp. As a reprisal, six young workers were bound with wire and were kept in the square the entire day under the threat of being shot if the escapees did not return. Later, the Jewish group foremen *(kapos)* of the groups to which the escapees belonged were made responsible.

Stomach typhus broke out during the first weeks and thanks to the tireless work of Doctor Wajsberg, the young Jewish doctors: Julek Przyrowski from Czenstochow and Dr. Lunksi from Lodz as well as thanks to the nurses who were found here among the prisoners, the situation subsided so that there were no victims and the Germans did not learn of this incident. There also were individual German foremen, rare exceptions, who showed humanity toward the prisoners, such as: Hulitsh, the foreman for transport, who never raised his hand to a worker and looked away when several of the workers

carried on secret workshops and earned several *gildn* in this way; the foreman
Berger also did not hit any workers; however, he liked to go through the
barracks to look for pious Jews who prayed and laughed at them that they
"pray to a God that the American Jews had captured," and the foreman Harn
from the mechanical workshop, who even helped Jews escape from the camp
and, therefore, was arrested. Hulitsh and Harn survived and appeared as
witnesses at the indictment against the German murderous foremen from the
Czenstochow *HASAG* at the trial in Leipzig that took place during the summer
of 1949. However, the much larger number of German foremen and,
particularly the forewomen, were sadists and murderers. A particular sadism
was shown by the forewomen: Tietga Mariana, Retga Frida, Klara ("the
beautiful Klara") Marchewka and Pietrucha. Teitga Mariana with the foremen
and work police took part in the *aktsias* [actions, usually deportations] against
the Jews that were carried out in the *HASAG-Apparatebau* on the 19th of July
1943. The forewomen would stop the women at their work after 12 hours of
labor. Then the women laborers would sleep in the barracks for one or two
hours; they were awakened and sleepy, half dressed, they were led under the
watch of work security to "collect" their portion of blows for not carrying out
their work quota. The forewomen themselves would designate the number of
blows that each woman worker needed to receive and often, during the
execution of the blows, hold the designated worker by the feet or by the head.
"The beautiful Klara" became well-known with her threat to beat the male
workers and not only with her fists, but also with the ammunition boxes.
Spaltenholtz was not satisfied with only blows and leading the guard, but he
also forced them to help with the same actions [administrating blows].

Martin Kehler would murderously beat the workers, lead the guard to the
flogging and cut off the hair of women for every small "sin." He would torture
Polish workers in another manner. He would ostensibly lead them to the bath.
There, he would soap them up and rub their bodies with a floor brush. In his
relationship to the Jewish workers, Gustav always would show that he was a
devoted member of the N.S.D.A.P. (*Nationalsozialistische Deutsche
Arbeiterpartei* – National Socialist German Workers Party] and he, himself, sent
40 workers to death during the July "selection." Walter Frosse would
especially ill treat women. Johannes Nikke tortured the workers and was not
satisfied with the usual number of 25 lashes during the whippings; for him
the usual number of lashes was 50. He especially severely beat a certain
Walman with a rubber club. Certain groups of workers would receive a free
day every other Sunday. Nikke would then take this group out of the barracks

and force them to wash the cement floors in the factory halls. To wash these floors they received used, thin gloves as rags, which had previously served to check the bullet cartridge cases. Therefore, the "free" Sunday became frightening days for the women workers who were thrown within his reach.

Apel and Fasold showed the most sadism. Apel beat everyone who came under his hand for no reason. He attacked workers and beat them with everything that came to him at that moment: with a board, with a piece of iron, with a hammer. He mainly beat them in the stomach and in the sexual organs with his fists. Fasold ("Boxer") would attack workers for no reason, beat them and had no respect for women or children. The way he beat 15-year old Tuvya Nemiec remains in everyone's memory. Tuvya worked in the infantry division. He had to gather the barrels of spoiled bullet cartridge cases from the moving machines and carry them to another spot where large barrels stood for that purpose. The small, starving and exhausted Tuvya had to "stroll" this way with the heavy barrels back and forth for 12 hours. Twelve hours a day – during the day shift and 12 hours a night – during the night shift. Tuvya would walk with eyes closed from exhaustion carrying the kettles.

The way there and back already was very well known to him, so that he could allow such a "joke." Many times he felt that his feet would no longer serve him; then he put down the kettle, sat down on it and looked to the side with his eyes to see if "someone" was coming. However, there were moments when his eyes were pasted and Tuvya began to dream. Fasold caught him in such a "crime." He lifted Tuvya from the kettle by his ear, boxed him with his right hand in his left cheek; Tuvya wobbled to his right and before he was able to fall, he felt a second blow in the right cheek. Fasold grabbed him by his feet, lifted him in the air and quickly carried him away. Tuvya strained to lift his arms so that they would not be dragged along the cement floor. He lifted his arms and pressed them to his sides, but they fell down powerless and dragged further along. Fasold stopped at a not-full barrel of bullet casings with his victim and threw him in with his head down. Only half his body went into the barrel. Fasold, crazy with his superior power over the small boy, began to press Tuyva's sexual organs with one hand and began to press the second half of his body deeper into the barrel. Tuvya's screams reached the workers who stood at the machines and the noise of the machines was surpassed by the terrible moans from the women workers. Fasold roused himself from his wildness, looked around as if he was searching for the "arrogant" women who dared to interrupt his sadistic pleasure and quickly left the factory hall. From then on, the small Tuvya's tired feet would no longer fully obey and fulfill their duties.

Every day or night brought other dismal news: here work police fired into the women's barracks when it was dark and there were victims; here, Hauzner, the foreman, shot a woman because she was "lazy" at work; there, a member of work security shot a boy because he spent to much time in the toilet; here, Klem led away the sick to the Jewish cemetery where the labor security shot them; there, a drunk foreman entered the women's hall, chose the youngest girl and took her away for an entire night; here, a member of the Gestapo led someone away and that person never returned; there, three young workers were arrested for "stealing" a few pieces of bread and they were murdered; here, Stiglitz (representative of labor security) beat a woman with his stick until she began to faint and then she was dragged away and shot; here, Michal Skalenko, a member of the labor security, beat Liberman, dragged him to a cellar bunker and there, with Stiglitz's help, tortured him to death. They stopped believing that they would survive and they only posed the question: who [would perish] earlier and who later? From time to time smaller groups of prisoners were put into unfinished barracks and from there they were taken to the death camps.

* * *

The days in the camps were "monotonous," although there were frequent shocks. Every day at five o'clock in the morning, everyone had to be at the count (roll call). The Jewish camp leader and his aids carried out the count in the presence of labor security and foremen. Each *kapo* announced the number of "prisoners" for which he was responsible and presented the certificates from a doctor for the sick in their group who were missing from the count. Stiglitz created a circus: for being a few seconds late to the roll call; he forced the men who were late to throw their hats on the roof until they remained lying there. After that, the "guilty ones" had to scramble up there to take them down. For the same sin, he forced older women to choose young boys from the rows and kiss them. For similar "sins," he forced young girls to do the same thing with older Jews [men]. Those who were late also were registered so that after 12 hours of work, they themselves should report to labor security guards and there "collect" up to 25 lashes. Several returned with only a "kratke" [number sign] (marks on the buttocks) and others wandered from the guard immediately into the hospital.

During the roll call young work security members tried out their skill at riding bicycles. Zig-zagging, they rode over the toes of the prisoners while they stood in a straight row. If any of those suffering dared to murmur, they received his judgment on the spot or later at the guardhouse.

At the same time, outside the camp, a strenuous hunt for Jews took place in the city. The city leadership organized a special Jewish incendiary exhibition under the title, "the Jewish World Plague," where the Jews were presented as terrible criminals. Inflammatory leaflets and calendars were distributed with caricatures that presented the Jews as swindlers, criminals, communists and as those who ruled the world. Poles, with whom Jews were found hiding, were sentenced and shot. A note arrived at the camp from Avraham Kaplan, the formerly active *ŻOB* member who was hiding with a Pole, stating that his situation was difficult and that some way should be found for him to enter the *HASAG*. However, news was quickly received that the active *ŻOB* member and other Jews were murdered in a bunker by a band of robbers, at the head of which stood the well-known anti-Semitic merchant, Walaszczik, who led the boycott and picket activities against Jewish merchants before the war (the Polish People's Court administered the earned sentence to the murderer). Jews, who had no way out to the "Aryan side," smuggled themselves into the camps with groups of Polish workers who, meanwhile, lent the Jews work cards of Polish workers who had gotten sick. In general, it must be remembered that Polish workers smuggled in food, cigarettes and even medicines for the Jewish prisoners. The Polish communist, Imiollek, who remained in contact with the Jewish communists in the name of the *P.P.R.* [*Polska Partia Robotnicza* – Polish Workers' Party], actively helped. The Jews who smuggled themselves into Rokow in this manner, remained there because Milhof immediately took them into the list of the Jewish prisoners and the other Germans did not know. It was worse for those who smuggled themselves into Pelcery. They were given over to the Gestapo, where they perished, by work security members.

The terrible situation of the Jews who were hidden on the "Aryan side" eliminated the desire of those in the *HASAG* to escape from the camp, although the situation there was also terrible. Machl Wajskop, the *ŻOB* [*Żydowska Organizacja Bojowa* – Jewish Fighting Organization] activist who wanted to join his fighting comrades in the Koniecpol forests, was among the escapees from the camp. He did not reach his goal and perished on the road.

The negative phenomena can be observed that at the same time: whoever could make use of foul language felt "stronger" and a "competition" developed in the area. They even taught "tasty" jokes to Stiglitz. The small Gliksman, who became a favorite of Stiglitz because of his service of informing to the work security and also began to bully the prisoners, particularly excelled at teaching Stiglitz obscene Jewish expressions.

The greater number of the small number of Jews was transformed into a large frozen melancholy mass. The punitive labor within the large factory walls, the murderous foremen and work security; the heavy machinery at which they had to stand working for the entire 12 hours and sometimes as punishment had to remain for another shift and after the second shift they had to remain at work for 12 more hours with the group of workers to which they belonged, as well as the hunger, with which only a few could cope – brought melancholy results. One met shriveled people whose skin barely kept their bones from falling apart. One also met those who in the large *trepers* [shoes with wooden soles] or the *Holenderkes* (shoes made only of wood) barely dragged their feet swollen by hunger. Tuberculosis and other illnesses had their fat harvest here. Clothes of rags and wooden shoes, brought from other closed camps, were the normal clothing here. Clothing sorters found letters that the previous and now murdered owners placed in the pockets during the last minutes of their lives. They were caught reading the letters and perished.

Apathy and resignation spread even further and took control of even more prisoners. There were also cases of suicide. Fajerman, a young man, drowned in the small stream that flowed close to the electricity plant.

And yet a group of stubborn resistance fighters tried to do everything to drive away the despair. Political discussions arranged by the underground workers for a narrow circle would take place in the barracks as well as evenings of song and recitations. The performers at such cultural evenings or cultural Sundays were the few surviving female singers from the former *TOZ* choir and the Jakubowicz brothers.

After a time they began to endure great hardships from Herman, the work security leader. He was a *feldsher* [barber-surgeon, similar to a paramedic] by trade and he believed that he had to assist with every operation in the camp hospital. Other German prominent men would come to these operations and the doctor-surgeon had to give a "practical lecture." In these cases, the sick would receive larger doses of sleep drops so that the surgeon's lecture could last longer. Often, such "lectures" were successful; the operations were successful (the chief doctor – Szperling, the surgeon, was a capable craftsman). However, the sick one paid with his life. Szperling himself bore a little blame in such cases. In his visible submissiveness to the Germans, after ending an operation on the appendix, he would agree to open the stomach of a patient again so a late-arriving German could "assist" at the operation, demonstrating his knowledge. In the camp, they spoke a great deal about Szperling's guilt in the death of a certain Bronka Baum, who was operated on by him and because of the manner in which he operated on her, she later lay in the hospital for several days, [finally] dying. Szperling was one of the few Jews in the camp who provoked hatred to himself among the greater number of the prisoners. The prisoners seldom benefited from the large supply of medicines that were located in the camp apothecary, which had originated with the apothecary at the *Judenrat* and at *TOZ* in the large ghetto and, later, the small ghetto, as well as the medicines received from the Krakow Jewish Assistance Office; they seldom even received powders for headaches.

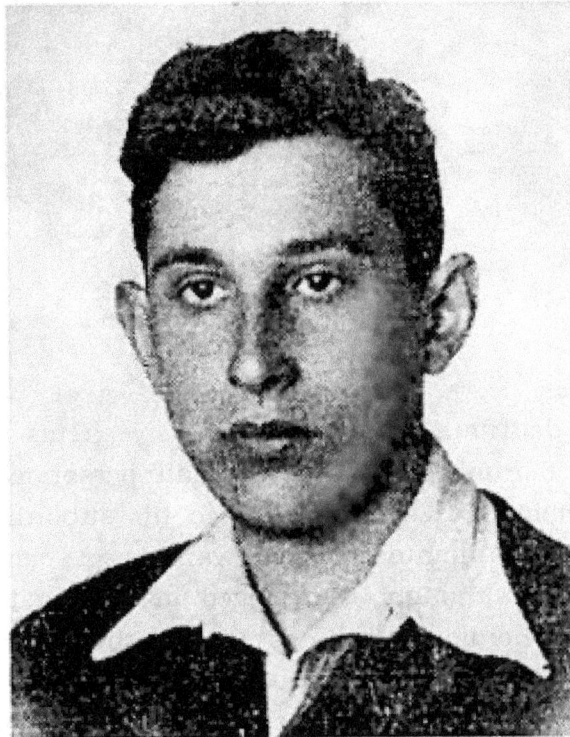

Michel Wajskop

"Zosia" Richl Szabszewski

But Szperling distributed the most expensive items to the Germans and labor security. He did not treat his subordinate personnel any better than the first German foreman; he especially bullied his subordinate Jewish doctors and nurses. His subordinate physical workers in personnel found better conditions with him although he indulged in beating them in moments of excitement; and yet he did good things, too, for their sake, particularly in the moments when he was in a good mood, he boasted to them about his ideas and achievements, unloaded his lexicon, whose variety surpassed the lexicon of the famous cursers in the camp.

* * *

Yet the tragic situation of the Jews in the *HASAG* did not kill the drive among everyone to live and also did not atrophy the human feeling of brotherly solidarity. The first, who began to send in help to the *HASAG-Apparatebau* camp, were the *Garibaldczikes* – the small number of Jews who were housed on Garibaldi Street. This group of Jews stole furniture and goods from the storehouses of the security police and sold them in various ways to the Poles. The *Garibaldczikes* taxed themselves on behalf of the Jews in the *HASAG* and sent [the sum of money] to them through designated trustworthy men: Jechiel Gamulinsk and Itcze Brener, who would divide the sum sent among those suffering from hunger and among those whom the *Garibaldczikes* had indicated to them on the list they sent. In addition to this, a group of women were organized in the camp itself that collected a weekly payment from which they began to run a kitchen for children and the sick. A great deal of initiative in this work was shown by these women: Fela Ofman and Zosia Weksztajn.

Lejzer Szidlowski

Abramek Wajskop

* * *

The connection between the Jewish underground and Warsaw ceased after the liquidation of the small ghetto. During the second month after the liquidation, Międzyrzecka, the female courier from Warsaw ("Wladka"), discovered the bunker of the fighting group in the Koniecpol forest and made contact with "Jacek" through the group that was housed in the *HASAG-Eizenhuta* camp. Through "Jacek's" intercession, "Wladek" also made contact with the Czenstochower underground workers who were in the *HASAG-Apparatebau* camp.

"Wladek" began to send money and literature into the camps. From then on the leftist underground workers in the *HASAG-Apparatebau* camp took over the coordination of the support of the illegal kitchen and enlarged it so that almost all of the sick, the children and young people benefited from it. Mrs. Dzjuba, a female Polish underground worker in Czenstochow, occasionally brought money to the camp. Mrs. Dzjuba would come into the "colony," give the money to the worker Helman and he would hand it over to the underground workers in the camp. The female cook and leader of the kitchen in the hospital was the nurse Manya Altman (née – Kalin) and the other nurses who worked there helped her. Because the sick rarely were administered the needed medicines from the camp apothecary on time, the doctors, Przyrowski and Lunski indicated which medicines were needed for which patient and they would be bought in the city and smuggled into the camp by Polish workers of their acquaintance in the factory.

* * *

The religious Jews also carried on aid work on a small scale. At the head of the religious group were: Noach Edelist and Jechiel Landau. There also were small groups of young people, former members of the Jewish Fighting Organization, who organized a collective life. At the head of this group were: Natka Wiernik (Jacek's wife), Abramek Czarna and Ruczka Dzialowska – "the Mamele" (she received the name "Mamele" for her devotion and the motherly care she showed to her comrades). Abramek and Ruczka belonged to the P.P.R. [Polska Partia Robotnicza – the communist Polish Workers' Party] group. Another group that led a collective life was a Bundist. Eli Sztajnic, Leib Leber, Josef Krojsze and the bakery worker, Betsalel Altman, stood at the head of this collective group. Jewish groups made use of their acquaintance with Polish workers who were employed in the Pelcery and Rakow factories and these workers smuggled in for the Jews food, medicines, legal German newspapers, illegal literature and everything that came from Warsaw with the couriers.

Contact among the Jews in one camp with the Jews in another camp was established with the intercession of Polish workers.

* * *

The camp routine led to those sick with high temperatures having fear of submitting themselves as sick and with their last strength they continued to stand at the machines; the pain and insults coming from each foreman and from every camp guard had to be borne; the hunger and the insecurity today and tomorrow – all of this led to strong apathy that kept spreading. However, the activity of the underground cells brought a little bit of a renewal. The moments when Soviet airplanes appeared brought in a particular renewal and belief. As soon as the factory sirens began their mournful alarm and the camp guards and the foremen escaped to the air-raid shelters, the Jews felt as if they had received a new soul; they felt somewhat freer. Several began to believe that there would be an end to the limitless troubles and others hoped that the factory would be bombed and they would have the honor to die under the factory ruins and not at the hands of the German criminals...

They could not stand still at the machines in the dark nights and also not lie in the barracks. Everyone wanted to know what was happening outside. In the barracks someone else crawled down each time from the plank beds and stealthily took a look to see what was happening outside. In the factory, every minute another worker again pulled himself from the machine and went outside discretely. They wanted to know how it looked when the large and long fiery fingers of the German searchlight tapped the dark skies searching and searching. These long, fiery fingers that searched the skies night after night threw a fear in the Germans and evoked hope in the joyful heartbeats of the Jews. And perhaps still? – many thought and consoled themselves. Perhaps still the terrible hell would end?

Everyone was sure that the Soviet "bird" would finally bring the redemption. This feeling also was strengthened with the news that the smuggled in legal and illegal newspapers daily brought about the victorious march forward of the Red Army.

* * *

Transports of Jews from the Lodz ghetto and from the temporary workplaces began to arrive in January 1944. The Jews in the *HASAG-Apparatebau* camp saved portions of their bread for those arriving. The Jews from Lodz were fortunate; they had not had as much bread as they received here for a long time. There were various opinions among those from Czenstochow in the camp and the Jews brought from the Lodz ghetto: the Lodzers believed that the *HASAG* was a paradise in comparison to the conditions that held sway in the Lodz ghetto. Here they ate enough... The Czenstochow Jews believed that the bringing of more Jews was a sign of the creation here of a new collection point where they would annihilate everyone. The labor police leader announced that those who came from Lodz had the right to write letters home and that they also could receive answers from there. The Lodzers made use of the opportunity to write home about their "luck" and they did receive answers. The Lodzers' belief in their new "luck" grew stronger and to the earlier residents of the *HASAG* the feeling that the permission to carry on correspondences was to fool the Jews from Lodz and to lure them here to be annihilated. The correspondence quickly became forbidden and the mood of those who arrived from Lodz and Plaszow became heavier.

* * *

Transports of Jews were brought from the Plaszow camp and from the Lodz ghetto at the beginning of 1944; because of this the number of Jews in the Czenstochow camps increased and two ammunition camps were created and two more camps for Jews: *Czestochowianka* and *HASAG-Warta*. The routine in the newly created camps was much more difficult than the two earlier ones. The circumstances for the *HASAG* workers in Warta were particularly severe as their situation was made more difficult by the designated Jewish camp leader, a German Jew, Jales.

The ammunition factories at Skarżysko were quickly liquidated by the Germans in July 1944 because of the offensive by the Red Army. The Jewish camps were also being liquidated there. People from there were brought to Czenstochow and a certain number of Jews from the Skarżysko camps also were sent here. The numbers of Jews increased in all four Czenstochow camps and after the departure of a certain number of the new arrivals to Germany, the complete power over the camps, *HASAG*-Warta and *HASAG-Apparatebau*, was taken over by the former German camp leader and security personnel from Skarżysko, the sadly well-known sadist and murderer, [Fritz] Bartenschlager, who while still at Skarżysko became well known for the murder of Jews and mainly for the night sprees that he would lead there. During such a "spree" he would carry out a roll call of the women, choose the youngest and prettiest, hold them an entire night at the disposal of his drunk comrades and these women would be murdered by he himself in the morning. So this sadist began to rule in the two Czenstochow camps and use his well-known torture methods.

* * *

The 20th of July 1944. Several Jews on the night shift at *HASAG-Apparatebau* came running to the barracks and reported that the masters were not watching the work very closely and kept telling secrets to each other. Others said that they overheard conversations among the masters about an assassination attempt. No one knew exactly what kind of assassination attempt this was. They did not sleep and they waited with impatience for what would happen in the morning. Early the next morning all of the Jews appeared for the roll call earlier than usual. The masters wandered around concerned and the Jews felt bolder. They already knew that an assassination attempt had been made against Hitler and these rumors went from mouth to mouth. Everyone clung to a new hope and asserted that the camp routine had become easier. Two days passed like this [with an easier routine in the camp]. They learned about everything that had happened and their hopes dissipated. They again felt the murderous camp routine and their disappointment created a tougher mood. Yet, they clung to the belief: if the Jews in Skarżysko and Plaszow camps had not been annihilated, but had just been sent over to the Czenstochow camps, the Jews in Czenstochow also would not be annihilated. Thus, the interpretations of every different event changed and, with them, the moods.

In July 1944 contact with Warsaw was completely interrupted and the aid activities stopped for a certain time. In the camp itself, the aid work was carried out with the reserves. At the end of 1944, the Warsaw Jewish underground organization again sent a courier, "Stepan," and again initiated contact with the camp underground. Letters, literature, 10,000 *gildn* of support just for Jews and a special fund for comrades who wanted to escape from the camps, were received. In addition to all of this, two letters were received about the liquidation of the Jews in the Pianke and Trawnik camps and an order that if they were not prepared for an armed appearance, the activists should escape. This was the last greeting received from outside until the moment when the Red Army occupied Czenstochow and we were liberated.

Underground Work in *HASAG* and in the Koniecpoler Forests

On the 25th of June 1943, at the same time as when the security police and Gestapo attacked the bunkers of the fighting organization in the small ghetto, all of the Jewish workers who were working in the ammunition factories were detained there and not allowed back into the ghetto. Liht, the chief director of *HASAG-Apparatebau*, carried out a roll call of all the workers and declared to them that, "The return of Jews into the ghetto would no longer be considered." Among the group of Jews being held in the ammunition factory were several active members of the fighting organization who had special jobs there in connection with the manufacture of grenades. Later, they were joined by fighters and activists in the underground movement who by a miracle were not killed during the liquidation of the small ghetto. In the forest, there also remained 23 fighters who were at three separate locations.

The fighters in the camps did not display any activity during the first two or three weeks; it was noticed that several [showed] a visible depression. And others, as if ashamed that they had survived, expressed at the rare and short gatherings their feeling of envy of those whose fate had permitted them to perish in a fight. Little by little, groups began to be created in the camps of *HASAG-Apparatebau* and *HASAG-Eizenhuta*.

The most active element – in a political sense – was the reduced communist group that consisted of about thirty people, divided into five cells. At the head of this organization stood: Sztajnbrecher, who was responsible for the work, Wajnrajch (perished later in Buchenwald), Jadza (Ita) Brener, Sztrausberg and Szwierczewski. The organization would revise political reports and carry out sabotage work in the production. Sympathizers grouped themselves around the core. Kuba Lipsztajn, the communist, was the most vigorous activist. A united front was achieved in the *HASAG*, at the head of which stood a committee of the following composition: Sztajnbrecher and Wajnrajch (Polish Workers Party), Dimand (*Hashomer Hatzair* [Socialist-Zionist]), Szimonowicz (left *Poalei-Zion* [Marxist-Zionists]) and L. Brener (Bund). The worker Josefowicz, a lock-mechanic, who excelled at sabotage work, was among the most devoted independent activists who belonged to the revolt movement here, as well as the fighters, Hilel Fridrajch, Mlodinow, Walczinscki, Prozer, Cymerman, Wernik, Jacek and so on. At first, the liaison between the camp groups and the courier from the Warsaw underground was the Polish worker, Jan Brust, who would smuggle into the Rakow factory everything that "Vladka" from Warsaw had given him and there he would turn over everything. The Jewish comrades would send out everything from here that was designated for us in Pelcery through the Polish worker Woyceck Nabialek. Woyceck would give this to his nephew, Eugeniusz Nabialek, who worked at *Pelcery*.

Eugeniusz would smuggle things in here and give it to us. The frequent searches that were carried out when the Polish workers crossed through the factory gates demanded a great deal of care. Everything went on peacefully for a long time. Once, a very strenuous search was carried out when Brust had letters and money with him. Noticing how workers standing in front of him were being checked, he withdrew from the gate and destroyed the letter. Factory security members noticed this and wanted to stop him. He began to run away. The factory security began to fire after him and Brust fell severely wounded. The letters already had been torn into small pieces and widely scattered by the wind. He swallowed several pieces of the letters that were still with him when he fell. However, the money was found on him and confiscated. "Jacek," the Jewish liaison officer, immediately learned of this and sent out a sum of money from his reserve to rescue Brust. However, his wounds were so severe that no doctor could save him. Jan Brust died a few days later. He perished at his post, tragically, helping the Jews. After this tragic case, contact was transferred to the "Pelcera." The liaison here was Mendjec, the Polish foreman, and his daughter, who had earlier been in contact with Jankl Gutman, the tailor.

Meanwhile, aid activities kept widening. So those who could not be drawn into the clandestine work could also benefit from the aid, the same security group leaders, *Kapos* [prisoners assigned by the Germans to carry out various tasks in the ghetto], who worked with the underground movement, received certain sums of money to buy bread and divide it among their groups of workers and also to procure special lunches for the sick workers in their groups. There were also such volunteers who had sums of money at their disposal and they would use it as loans to people to be divided among those suffering from need without them knowing from where the money originated to be paid back after the war. After the Jews from the Lodz ghetto arrived and, later, from Skarzysko, the aid work had to become more intensive, although the means were very limited.

Several men led by Engineer Afrat, who was an envoy from Warsaw while still in the Skarzysko camp, took part in the aid work among the prisoners from the camp. Doctor Trajwicz (from Bialystok, arrived with the Jews from the Skarzysko camp) was occupied with the aid work in the *HASAG-Warta* camp with Polya Koczol, the nurse who earlier was at [*HASAG*] Rakow and there worked with Doctor Glatter and with Wernik and Wilczinski and later was transferred to Warta where she again worked as a nurse in the camp hospital there headed by Dr. Trajwicz. Their activity was severely limited because of the routine that reigned in the Warta camp and because of the fear of the Jewish camp leader and the Jewish policemen there who ruled with an "iron fist as the Germans had ruled," as well as the inadequate means that would be sent from the Pelcery. The situation there was worse than in the rest of the camps. There could be no talk of creating a fighting group there. The routine in the Warta camp was very severe because there the camp leader of Skarzysko, Bartenschlager, knew mostly what he could do to the insecure Jewish prisoners. The routine also became more severe in Pelcery. The fight leadership in the camps of Rakow and Pelcery provided an exact account of the situation and made intensive attempts to organize the fighting fifths [groups of five members] and to prepare plans for a revolt in case of an "aktsia" [deportation]. The leadership of the fighting group in Pelcery worked out three plans: preparing tools that the "fifths" would use in fighting, disrupting the factory by igniting the dynamite storehouse and organizing a number of substantial groups where resolved fighters would be found who were ready to sacrifice their own lives, attack the work security guards at a designated moment, disarm them, control the factory for a certain time so a larger number of people could escape.

This responsibility for making special shears and pliers with insulated handles that would be able to cut the wire fence even where it was electrified was given to Adasz Sztajnbrecher, the communist. The remaining members of the leadership allotted the barracks among themselves where each one had to organize and direct a "fifth."

The comrades in Warsaw expressed their readiness to provide weapons and called for us to provide them with a way to bring the weapons into the camps. However, the searches of the Polish workers in factories became more frequent and more vigorous. Therefore, it became impossible to find among the Polish workers in Pelcery workers who would and could undertake such dangerous smuggling. "Jacek," who strongly yearned for an armed stand, declared that there was such a specialist in the *Eizenhuta*, who had found a Polish officer who had agreed to provide weapons. Later, "Jacek" advised that the same person had told him that he was an officer in the *A.K.* [*Armia Krajowa* – Home Army, the main Polish resistance movement] and he would do nothing for the Jews.

* * *

They had to give up the idea of fighting with weapons in their hands. The underground cells continued to carry on their work: meetings took place, joint conversation were arranged on the memorial days for the deportations in the large and small Czenstochow ghettos and of the Warsaw Ghetto Uprising. The press that would be smuggled in went from hand to hand and they strove to receive radio news from time to time. The radio news was received from male and female workers who would be taken by the German foremen to the "colony" to clean their residences. They attempted to catch something from the radio from time to time. In addition, Fufek Rozencwajg received radio news in the workshop where he worked in a certain manner. They were in constant contact with Warsaw. They did not wait for a courier from Warsaw in cases of need, but sent letters through Jankl Gutman to the liaison, Mędrzec, with whom the Warsaw couriers would stop and he and his daughter or wife would send them to Warsaw to Maria Borkowska at Krochmalna 83.

On a certain day work security attacked the barracks in the *HASAG-Pelcery* camp and confiscated all of the collected tools as well as the tools from all of the artisans who would make various things to sell. There were no reasons given for such searches that were repeated several times. However, all of the tools were taken and a decree also was issued that no tools could be found in the barracks square or in the barracks themselves, even those that were necessary to clean [the barracks].

* * *

On the 4th of November 1944, during the search of the Polish workers upon their departure from the *Pelcery* factory, letters were found on Eugeniusz Nabialek that had been sent by Natka Wernik to "Jacek" at "Rakow" and he was arrested. The second contact person, Wojciech Nabialek, was also arrested in connection with this. The letters that were found on Eugeniusz led to the trail of Natka and Jacek, who were arrested. Both Nabialeks were sent to the Gross Rosen concentration camp where Wojciech perished. Jacek and Natka also were deported. Eugeniusz Nabialek, Jacek and Natka survived. All three were saved by the Red Army.

* * *

The fighting mood of the prisoners in the camps changed during the last months before the liberation. The bringing of the Jews to Czenstochow from the Skarzysko and Plaszow camps, which was instigated by Germans, that the Jews were to make room for various people in the camps, caused many to forgot the sad experiences they had been through up to then and was interpreted as a sign that they [the Germans] would not kill any more Jews. We [reported] to the comrades in Warsaw about the atmosphere among the prisoners and about the changing relationships in the camps. The answer from the central party authorities was that we should not have any illusions because the politics of the German fascists in relation to the Jews had not changed in general and if there was no prospects of entering into open struggle, the activists should escape from the camp.

Because of the danger of collective responsibility, it was decided that the most active should not escape and it also was understood that there would be no possibility of entering into an open fight.

Contact with Warsaw was broken in August 1944 because of the Warsaw Uprising. However, in a few days messengers again were sent to Czenstochow and to Konicepol. The usual couriers from Warsaw renewed contact with Medrzec's daughter and constantly asked after the "health" of her relatives.

Becalel Altman, who was taken out of the camp every morning as a good baker to be a baker outside baking bread for the Germans, became the contact man with the new messenger from Warsaw. The bakery, where Altman would bake the bread, was the meeting point for him and the messenger from the Warsaw underground.

* * *

In December 1944 we were convinced of the truth of the warnings from the comrades in Warsaw that the German politics in relation to the Jews had not changed. *S.S.* members came who took over the entire management of the Jewish camps. The routine became a great deal worse from when [Georg] Bartenschlager had ruled. It became impossible to move from the factory square to the barracks. Only entire labor groups could march out from the barracks to work in closed ranks after the roll call and march into work. It also became impossible to continue to run the kitchen for the sick and the children who had to make sure that the *S.S.* not notice them. The *S.S.* had a certain Goldsztajn to help them, whom they brought from the Plaszow camp.

This person brought everything to them and beat the prisoners no less than the *S.S.* members themselves. Therefore, the aid activity from outside was entirely interrupted. On the spot, they [the aid activities] were still carried out with the last reserves, but in a limited amount until the 15th of August 1945, when the Red Army neared the gates of Czenstochow and the former prisoners became the bosses of their own lives and freedom.

* * *

The 28 fighters who were located in the Koniecpol forests did not sit with idle hands during the time in which we carried out our activities in the camps. They carried out attacks on Germans and German guards to obtain weapons and food for themselves. Each of their attacks was well organized and was successful. However, they maintained that they would not carry out any larger actions against the Germans and looked for ways and opportunities for mutual contact with Polish partisan groups and to join them.

However, great anti-Semitic *A.K.* bandits under the name *Orzel* [eagle] were in the Koniecpol area. The Jewish fighters in Koniecpol, not knowing the character of these bandits, began to carry out negotiations about joint actions against the Germans. The exact location and terms of the first meeting were discussed. Several Jewish partisans, with Kuba Ribsztajn at the head, were chosen and waited at the designated place and time for the Polish partisan delegation. Ten partisans arrived with revolvers and automatic weapons. Kuba and his comrades, not suspecting the Polish partisans of anything bad, went toward them with joy and earnestness, not even removing their revolvers from their pockets. As soon as they were face to face, the members of *Orzel* opened fire on the Jewish group. Several of the already wounded Jewish partisans succeeded in escaping death. All of the rest perished on the spot.

The Jewish fighters in Koniecpol became more cautious after this occurrence. They then assembled bunkers [on the property of] certain Poles and would only leave them at night to carry out attacks on their own at designated points where there were Germans. Even in the bunkers, the small group of Jewish fighters did not have any rest from the reactionary A.K.-bands. The members of *Orzel* searched for the bunkers of the remaining Jewish partisans. After a while, a large group of them attacked the bunker in which were located: Jehuda Gliksztajn, Bela Zbarowska and Bela Bram.

All three were successful in escaping from the murderous hands and disappeared in the forest. The members of the *Orzel* organized a chase after them. The *granat* policemen [Blue police – Polish police in the Nazi-occupied area of Poland known as the General Government], who served in Koniecpol, came to their aid. The three Jewish fighters were surrounded in a narrow area of the forest where they were captured under fire from automatic weapons used by the *granat* policemen and they perished.

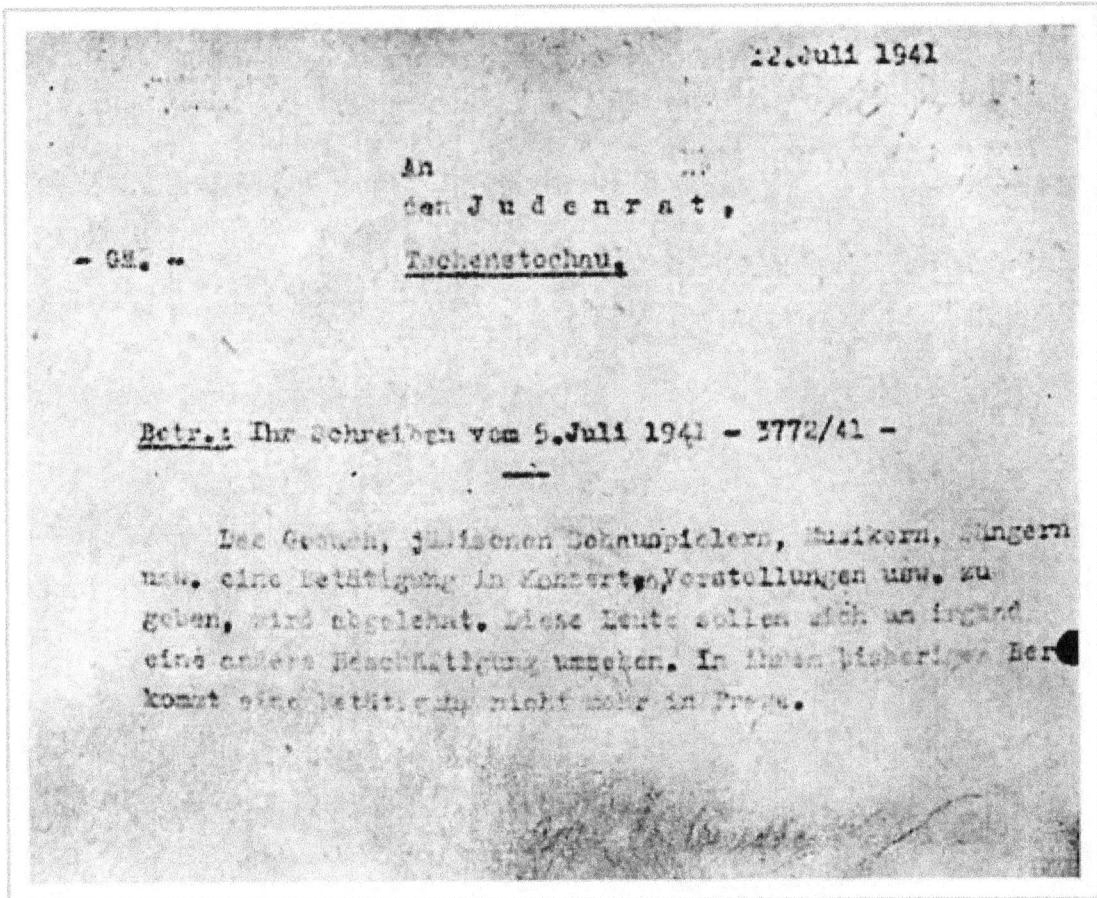

A 1941 order sent to the *Czenstochower Judenrat*

A Polish leftist partisan division of Hanis also was located in the Koniecpol area; several members of the Jewish Fighting Organization joined this partisan group, which accepted them in a fraternal and comradely manner. Here, the *ŻOB* [*Żydowska Organizacja Bojowa* – Jewish Fighting Organization] members had their first opportunity to demonstrate their exploits and sacrifice. Lejzer Szidlowski particularly excelled here. Lejzer came from Amstow. On the 25th of September 1942, when the expulsion of the Jews from Amstow began, his family members hid in a bunker where, as Lejzer later said, they were murdered because of a robbery. Lejzer then carried with him the idea of suicide. This feeling disappeared suddenly when he was drawn more strongly into the work of *ŻOB* in the small ghetto. His external appearance made it possible for him to move more freely as an "Aryan" than others and to carry out very dangerous missions for the organization. He already was trained in his "trade" of carrying out the tasks laid on him by the organization, that even when he was stopped near *Wilot* (ghetto gate) when he had a weapon on him, he turned around in a deft manner and smuggled and carried the weapon into the ghetto. Lejzer showed a great deal of heroism with his boldness both in the ranks of *ŻOB* and the ranks of the Gwardia Ludowa [People's Guard]. Lejzer, already wounded, also excelled greatly in the fight against the Germans carried on by the "Hanis" Group in the area of the village, Święta Anna (near Koniecpol). He fell in 1944.

Amstew expulsion (Mstow) 25th September 1942

The most secure bunker near Koniecpol, where the fighters maintained themselves, was in the village of Michałów.

There they were in the Polish family Pindeliak's house, where the wife, Celina Pindeliak, stated that 15 members of *ŻOB* under the leadership of Boliek Gewercman were with them. The same woman said that only eight of the 15 survived. At the end of January 1945 several of them arrived in Czenstochow and Gewercman, their representative, began to take part in the building of a renewed Jewish community in Czenstochow.

The Last Days of the Czenstochower *HASAG* Camps

On the 14ᵗʰ of December 1944 the camps in Czenstochow were taken over by members of the *S.S.* The routine in the camps, as was said grew a great deal more severe. Boettcher, the *S.S.* general and police leader of the Radom district, also often began searching the camps. They had to report for the roll call by barracks. That is, all residents of each barrack had to stand in front of their barrack for the roll call and wait until everyone was counted. Then they had to march in closed ranks from the camp to the factory square to work. Goldsztajn, the Jewish camp leader, stood at the gate of the camp among the *S.S.* members and received reports. Each *kapo* [prisoner assigned by the Germans to carry out various tasks in the ghetto] had to go at the head of his group of workers and call out to Goldsztajn: "Kapo so and so (here he had to call out his name), how many prisoners." The men had to remove their hats while marching past Goldsztajn. Those who were a little late in calling out their names or the number of prisoners, as well as those who called out too quietly and not clear enough would [be dealt with by] Goldsztajn, so that even the members of the *S.S.* maintained that he acted even worse than they. The clothing of the prisoners was again marked with red stripes with a specially prepared paint and special camp clothing *(pasiakes)*. The food also became more meager and the time for eating, that earlier was also limited, was completely eliminated.

The *kapos* had to distribute the food among their workers in the halls of the factories and [the workers] also were not permitted to leave their machines when receiving the food and while eating the workers had to watch over the movement of the machines. Contact with the outside world was stopped entirely and the contact between the camps in Czenstochow itself also ceased. The mood of the prisoners was very tense. They still looked for ways to learn something. From time to time they succeeded in receiving a German newspaper from Polish workers, which they smuggled in despite very thorough searches while going through the gates of the factory. The meager news that the German newspapers still gave about the victories of the Red Army encouraged and created the belief that the freedom so longed for would shortly arrive.

Monday, the 15ᵗʰ of January 1945, 10 o'clock in the morning. Members of the *S.S.* came to the barracks location in the *HASAG-Apparatebau* camp and began to whistle. Goldsztajn immediately came running and stood at attention. He received an order to wake up all of the men from the night shift and assemble them at the square near the hospital. His order was carried out. The men from the night shift were chased to the designated square. Whoever was late received the appropriate "lecture" from Goldsztajn. All of those assembled stood at attention and waited with extraordinary nervous tension for what would happen. The *S.S.* and the work security stood fully armed both at the barracks location and around the outside of the wire. Liht, the factory director, arrived and gave a speech to the assembled Jews that they had to be sent to another camp in Germany, because the Germans wanted to protect the Jewish prisoner from the Bolshevik "danger" that was approaching Czenstochow... Liht simultaneously stressed that the prisoners would first be bathed in the places they would enter and then they would receive other clothing and be taken to work in such locations where no "evil" would happen to them. Therefore, he warned that all had to be obedient and ready to prepare to leave. After this speech by the director everyone was sent to the barracks to prepare their bundles for the departure.

The barracks immediately were surrounded with armed labor security and it would have been extraordinary if anyone could have wormed their way out from this encirclement. Wagons were placed at the factory square on the same day and everyone being held was taken away under heavy guard.

New transports and new laments from the survivors. Husbands, wives, brothers and sisters of those deported reported voluntarily and asked to be sent with a transport of women so that they would not be torn away from their only surviving relatives. At the same time, all of the prisoners in the camps, *HASAG-Eisenhuta* and *HASAG-Czestochowianka*, were taken away.

A rumor spread among the remaining Jews in the *HASAG-Apparatebau* and *HASAG-Warta* camps, who were getting ready to be sent out that the Germans already had escaped from Kielce and that the liberation army was already in the *shtetlekh*: Włoszczowa and Koniecpol. Jews no longer wanted to remain in the barracks and searched for hiding places in the factory square because they wanted to avoid the fate of being deported. Suddenly, the earth began to tremble from bombardments. The German foremen became apprehensive. The bombardments increased from minute to minute and we already saw the distant columns of flames. The Germans became more anxious. The Jews also were tense. They believed that the Germans wanted to blow up the ammunition factories and that they would perish under the ruins. Some of the Jews gathered in the bunkers so as not to perish under the ruins of the factories and others actually hid in the factory halls so as to perish on the spot and not to be dragged away by the Germans. Night fell. The bombardments increased. The Jews who were in the barracks of *HASAG-Pelcery (Apparatebau)* were encircled by labor security under the leadership of the labor security leader Herman and were ordered to go with them. Only approximately 400 people allowed themselves to be terrorized by labor security and actually were taken away. The remainder of the Jews in the barracks escaped to the factory square and became the bosses there. The Germans now withdrew from the factory in haste. The Jews broke into the "colony," armed themselves, opened all of the stores and also became the bosses here.

They looked for Germans: they looked for factory security [men]; the feeling of revenge boiled. The Jews in the Hasag-Warta camp also did not allow themselves to be taken away, listening to the call of the local community workers headed by Dr. Trajwicz.

In the morning of the 17ᵗʰ of January 1945, Jews also come to the square of *Kolonie* in the "Pelcery" [labor prison] from the "Warta" [labor prison]. They hugged, they kissed and they cried. We cried from sorrow, we cried from joy. We noticed with surprise that the feeling of sorrow and of farce was much stronger than the joy that we survived.

Approximately 5,200 of the 11,000 Jews who were in the Czenstochow camps during the last months remained [alive]. The rest were dragged away to the camps of Buchenwald and Gross Rozen during the last days before the liberation, where the greater majority perished.

On the 17ᵗʰ of January 1945, the Soviet liberation army already was in Czenstochow. Five thousand two hundred men opened the gates of the concentration camps and exited to freedom. Five thousand two hundred slaves with death sentences hanging over their heads over the course of five years won back their lives and freedom.

Of the 5,200 Jews who were liberated in Czenstochow, 1,518 were Czenstochower residents before and after the outbreak of the war, of whom 1,240 were born in Czenstochow. The Jews from outside [Czenstochow] little by little left Czenstochow, traveling to their birthplaces. The majority of the Czenstochower residents remained in the city and began rebuilding their lives on new foundations in the newly created free, People's Poland.

List of Jewish Doctors in Czenstochow
Who Perished During the German Occupation

Augenfisz Rayzl from Plock, perished with a 13-year old child in Treblinka.

Broniatowski Ayzyk from Sosnowiec, perished with his wife and 12-year old child in Treblinka.

Bram Arnold, where he perished has not been established.

Blumenfeld Dovid, perished in Czenstochow with his wife and two children in 1943 during the deportation of the Jewish intelligentsia.

Bernsztajn Nisen Uzer, where he perished has not been established.

Bolotne Shmuel of Bendin, perished in Majdanek.

Bartczinski Juliusz, perished in Czenstochow during the deportation of the Jewish intelligentsia.

Epsztajn Bernard, perished in Czenstochow with his wife and two children during the deportation of the Jewish intelligentsia.

Falk Chaim, perished with his wife and 6-year old child in Czenstochow during the deportation of the Jewish intelligentsia.

??ksztajn Stefan, perished in Czenstochow with his wife during the deportation of the Jewish intelligentsia. [The first letters of the surname are missing in the original text].

Glatter Leyzer, perished in Buchenwald.

Gutman Leon, perished in Czenstochow in the small ghetto, on the 27th December 1942.

Grunwald Kruza, perished in Czenstochow during the deportation of the Jewish intelligentsia.

Horowicz Irena, perished in Czenstochow with a 3-year old child during the liquidation of the small ghetto.

Halleman Moshe and Halleman Miriam (husband and wife), perished in Czenstochow with their 6-year old child during the deportation of the Jewish intelligentsia.

Igel Henrik, of Rawa Ruska, perished with his wife and two adult children in Czenstochow during the deportation of the Jewish intelligentsia.

Krauskop Hersh, perished with his wife and two children in Treblinka.

Kagan Dovid, perished in Czenstochow with his wife and 12-year old child during the deportation of the Jewish intelligentsia.

Kajak Moshe Feytl, perished with his wife and 10-year old child in Czenstochow during the deportation of the Jewish intelligentsia.

Lewin Mietczyslaw, perished in Czenstochow with his wife during the deportation of the Jewish intelligentsia.

Lewin Shmuel Leib, of Aleksandrow near Lodz, perished in Majdanek.

Lipinski Yudl, perished in Czenstochow with his wife during the deportation of the Jewish intelligentsia.

Lipinski Zigmund, perished with his wife and child in Czenstochow during the deportation of the Jewish intelligentsia.

Prafart Sholem, perished in Czenstochow with his wife and 8-year old child during the deportation of the Jewish intelligentsia.

Rozen Naftali, perished during the deportation of the Jewish intelligentsia in Czenstochow with his wife and 10-year old child.

Szafer Szajdliner Rayzl, perished with her two children in Treblinka.

Sziker Alfred, perished with his wife and 11-year old child in Czenstochow during the deportation of the Jewish intelligentsia.

Szajnic Mordekhai, perished in Czenstochow with his wife during the deportation of the Jewish intelligentsia.

Trauner Henrik of Buczacz, perished with his wife and 8-year old child in Treblinka.

Tenenbaum Berl and Tenenbaum Yakhet (husband and wife), perished with their 10-year old child in Treblinka.

Tarbeczka Dovid, perished in Ludmir (Vladimer Volinsk).

Walberg Adam Ayzyk, perished in the small ghetto in 1943.

Winer Eliash, perished in Czenstochow with his wife and 2 children during the deportation of the Jewish intelligentsia.

Warmund Wolf, perished in Czenstochow with his wife and 2-year old child during the deportation of the Jewish intelligentsia.

Wajsberg Ruchl, perished in Czenstochow in the HASAG camp.

Zandsztajn Hilary, perished in Czenstochow with his wife and 15-year old son during the deportation of the Jewish intelligentsia.

Zand Yakob and Zand Rywka (husband and wife) perished in Warsaw with their 6-year old child.

Zandberg Yehezkiel, perished in Czenstochow during the deportation of the Jewish intelligentsia.

Zajf Yosef from Kalisz, perished with his wife and 7-year old child in Czenstochow during the deportation of the Jewish intelligentsia.

Gajzler Hiplit, where he perished has not been established.

Goldman Leon, where he perished has not been established.

Lewkowicz Tankhm, where he perished has not been established.

Sobol Wladislaw, where he perished has not been established.

Konarski Adam, where he perished has not been established.

Dentists

Broniatowski Artur, perished in Treblinka.

Broniatowska Tisa, perished in Treblinka, with her 6-year old child.

Brandes Ester from Chelm, perished in Treblinka with her 5-year old child.

Bem Gitl, perished in Treblinka.

Blajwajs Lotta, perished in Treblinka.

Cymerman Gitl, perished in Treblinka.

Epsztajn Bayla Rywka, perished in Treblinka.

Frenk Helena from Krzepice, perished in Treblinka, with her husband and two children.

Grin Mordekhai, perished in Treblinka, with his wife and two children.

Korngold Rywka from Plock, perished in Treblinka with her two children.

Kartuz Ruchl, perished in Treblinka with her 8-year old child.

Lampel Yehudis from Lodz, perished in Treblinka.

Lewkowicz Leah, perished in Treblinka with her 12-year old child.

Minc Amalia, perished in Treblinka.

Rozenowicz Mikhal, perished in Treblinka.

Zalcberg Eugenia, perished in Treblinka.

Map of Czenstochow

Names Index

Please note that the page numbers at the right are the page numbers in the original Yiddish Yizkor book, not the page numbers of this book.

Surname	Given Name	Title	Notes	Page
DRAHABERG		City commissar		6
RIDIGER		Chief of civil managing committee		6
ZIMNIAK	A.	Vicar-General/Suffragan Bishop, Czestochowa		6
KRIGER		Gestapo Chief in Czestochowa		7
SZABELSKI		Volksdeutsch [ethnic German] member of the Gestapo		7
GRANEK	Yudl			8
AMBRAS		Chief of gendarmes		8
CANGREL		Hauptwachmeister [warrant officer]		8
KABAK		Hauptwachmeister [warrant officer]		8
PELTA			husband and wife	9
BARIMHERCIK		General		9
KAWA			war invalid owner of cigarette kiosk	10
DEREGOWSKI	Stanislaw			10
DITMAN		Hauptscharführer [squad leader]		10
ASZ	Moshe			11

ASZ	Nuchem	Rabbi		11
ASZ	Moshe			12
BROMBERG	Leib			12
BERLINER	Nusan-Dovid			12
KROJCER	Ahron-Josef			12
KAPINSKI	Leib			12
KONIECPOLER	Dovid			12
BESERGLIK	Mordechai			12
BRANDLIEWICZ	Ziskind			12
GERICHTER	Jechiel			12
ICEK	Wolf			12
GRYNFELD	Nakhman			12
KLAJNPLAC	Josef			12
BRONIATOWSKI	Josef			12
LEWIT	Jakob			12
LEWKOWICZ	Shmuel			12
NAJFELD	Maurici			12
NIEMEROWSKI	Shmuel			12
RODAL	Natan			12
ROTBARD	Zelig			13
ROZINER	Jakob			13
RUCZEWICZ	Michal			13
SLONIMSKI	Adam			13
SZAFIR	Gershon			13
CZERIKER	Wilhelm			13
KAPINSKI	L.			13
BROMBERG	L.			13
BERLINER	N.D.			13
NOJFELD				13
GERICHTER				13

WENDLER		Dr.		13
POHORILLE				13
GITLER				13
ASZ	Lieb			13
FOGEL	Avraham			13
GAJZLER	Leon			14
GALSTER	M.			14
KOHLENBRENER	Bernard			14
PRAFART	M.			14
EPSZTAJN	Ester			14
PRUSZICKI				14
HASPNFELD	Marian			14
SAFIRSZTAJN	Maurici			14
KAPINSKI	Moshe			14
KASMAN	D.			14
RENENWETER	M.			14
RIFSZTAJN	Y.			14
KACINEL	Maurici			14
RADAL	N.			14
KONARSKI	M.			14
RAJCHMAN	W.			14
KRAKOWER	W.			14
RADAL	A.			14
POHORILLE				14
GITLER				14
ASZ				15
RAZINE				15
BESERGLIK				15
BRANDLEWICZ				15
BRONIATOWSKI				15

GRYNFELD				15
KLAJNPLAC				15
NIEMIROWSKI				15
RUCZEWICZ				15
SZAFIR				15
LEWIT	Y.			15
ANISFELD	Wolf			15
BORZYKOWSKI	Dovid			15
GALSTER	Maurici			15
GITLER	Jeremy			15
KAC	Shmuel			15
KACINEL	Maurici			15
KAPINSKI	Moshe			15
KURLAND	Bernard			15
PAHARILLE	Shimon			15
PRAPART	Maurici			15
ZANDSZTAJN	Hilary			15
WAJNRIB	Shmuel			15
KAPINSKI	Leib			16
BROMBERG	Leib			16
POHORILLE	Shimon			16
BERLINER	Nusan-Dovid			16
GERICHTER	Jechiel			16
GITLER	Jeremy			16
ROTBART	Zelig			16
KOHLENBRENER	Bernard			17
KOHLENBRENER				18
WENDLER				19
KADNER				20
LASH		Dr.		20

WENDLER		Dr.		21
WENDLER				22
FRANKOWSKI		Lieutenant colonel of gendarmerie		24
WENDLER				25
KADNER				25
LEWKOWICZ	Mordechai			28
DOLF		Major		28
KOHN				28
KOHN				29
LIPSZIC			from Radom	29
KAWAN			war invalid	29
KURLAND	Bernard			29
PANTOFEL			83 year old tailor	29
PANTOFEL	Avraham		hairdresser	29
PANTOFEL	Moshe		locksmith	29
DOLF				30
BORZYKOWSKI	Dovid			30
KURLAND	Bernard			30
PANTOFEL	Avraham			31
NIEDZIELA			from Wielun	31
TARASHENKO			Ukrainian foreman	31
GRIESHAMMER	Fritz			32
POHORILLE				32
WALBERG	Adam	Dr.		33
FRANKE		Dr.		34
GALSTER	M.			35
HELMAN	A.			35
BORZYKOWSKI				35

LANDA	Y.			35
CEDERBAUM	M.			35
JARACINSKI	Z.			35
SZTARKMAN	Y.			35
WENDLER				35
DEGENHARDT				38
RIDIGER				40
POHORILLE	Shimon		lawyer	41
ZAWADA			Volksdeutsch	41
SCHLEECHT				41
LASKI				41
WENDLER				41
MASZEWICZ		Mrs.		41
WENDLER				42
SZEFTEL	Eliash			42
BESER	Jehuda Meir			42
ROZENBERG	Yakov			42
GEOBBELS	(Joseph)			43
ROZINE	Yakov			43
ASZ	Mendl			43
ASZ	Nakhum			43
CZANSZINSKI	Yitzhak			43
RODAL	Natan			43
KAZAK	Tsesha			43
TEMPEL	Yakov			43
KOZAK	Tsesha			43
JAROCZINSKI			Lodz refugee	45
BABIACKI			Lodz refugee	45
HOSSENFELD	M.		lawyer	45
TEMPEL	Yakov			46

LIPINTKA		Mrs.		46
ROZINE	Yakov			46
BIRNBAUM	Hanka			46
WINDHAJM	Genya			46
JANOWSKA	Chana			46
HALLEMAN			pediatrican	46
BLUMENFELD	Dovid			46
ROZEN	Junya			46
ROZEN			doctor	46
KUSZNIR	Motek			46
CZANSZINSKA	Cesha			46
GLATTER	Lejzer			46
KONARSKI	Mendl			46
WALBERG	Adam		doctor	46
WALBERG			doctor	47
CHADA			Klobuck TOZ	47
GRILIAK			owner apothecary warehouses	48
KANDER			representative of city chief	49
KONARSKI			TOZ chairman	49
WALBERG				49
KAPINSKI			Judenrat chairman	49
POCHOLERA (POHORILLE)			Rasta chief	50
BORZYKOWSKI			member of Judenrat	51
KURLAND			member of Judenrat	51
GERICHTER			member of Judenrat	51

MERING		Dr.		51
WIESALOWSKI				51
PIETROWSKI (PIETRIK)				51
WAJNBERG	Laya			52
GELBER	Ruzshka			52
GINSBERG	Saba			52
WACZECHA	Rywka			52
SZIWAK	Sala			52
MASS	Jadzia			52
SZTERENSI	Ira			52
SZCZEKACZ	Polya			52
SZCZEKACZ	Dasha			52
ROZINE	Aviv			52
FAJNER	Yitzhak			52
KRISZTAL	Lili			52
HAFTKE	Stefa			52
LANDAU	Ruzsha			52
OPATOWSKA	Zosha			52
PRASZKEWICZ				52
MENDLSON		Mrs.		52
ROZENCWAJG	Lonya	Professor		52
PERETZ	[Y.L.]			53
REISEN	[Avrom]			53
(BRAHINSKY]	Mani Leib			53
RAZINE	Yakov			53
RAZINE	Ester			53
BRENER				53
BLUMENKRANC	Fishl			53
SREBRNIK	Leib			53

BORNSZTAJN	Yeshaya			53
BIRNCWAJG	Makhl			53
KURLAND	Noakh			53
KUSZNIR	Leibl			53
BLUMENKRANC	Fishl			54
BORNSZTAJN	Yeshayale			54
DZIGAN	Simon			54
WALBERG				54
KONARSKI				54
ROZINER				54
BRENER				54
FOGEL			two brothers	54
ASZ	Mendl			54
CHILWNER	Sura OKRENT			54
KUSZNIR	Motek			54
DATNER			son-in-law of Fogel family	54
BLECHSZTAJN	Uzer			54
KUSZNIR	Leibl			54
ZONDSZTAJN		Dr.		54
PRUSZICKI			Former Bank Director	55
WALBERG				55
GITLER	Jeremy			55
KACINEL		Dr.		55
POHORILLE				55
KUSZNIR	Leib			55
KOZLOWSKI				55
KRUZLER				55
CHRAPORT	Maka			55
ORCACH				55

ALECHIM	Sholem			55
BERKENSZTAT	Rayzele			56
PRUSZICKI				56
KAPINSKI				56
WENDLER				56
WALBERG		Dr.		57
JAKUBOWICZ				57
EDELIST	Henrik			57
EDELIST	Ludwig			57
GRABINER				57
BAUM	Borukh			57
BAUM	Guta			57
NODELBERG	Roma			57
POZNANSKA				57
ASZ	Nokhum	Rabbi		57
ZITENFELD	Slowaka			57
KAPIECKA	Wanda			58
GLIKSMAN		Miss		58
KOSCIUSZKO	Tadeusz			58
PILSUDSKI	Jozef			58
SILMAN	Lejzer {Ghandi]			58
FRANK	Leibush			59
OPATOWSKI	Maks			59
DREKSLER	Srul			59
WAJNRIB	Yankl			59
SZTAJNBRECHER	A.			59
IMIALEK			Polish communist	59
SZIMKOWICZ	Michal			59
BERKENSZTAT	Rayzele			59

DZALOWSKI			family	60
TENENBAUM	Meir [Majorek]			60
TENENBAUM	Polya			60
CZANSZINSKI	Yitzhak			60
FRANK	Grunem			60
FRANK	Leibush			60
OPATSZINSKI	Yitzhak		former Paolei Zion counsil member	60
SZCZENSNA	Marya			60
KUSZNIR	Motek			60
ROZINE	Aviv		son of Yakov	61
ROZINE	Yakov		daughter of Dr. Rozen	61
ROZEN	Dzjunja			61
ROZEN		Dr.		61
KUSZNIR	Leibl			61
KUSZNIR	Chaya			61
KUSZNIR	Motek			61
KUSZNIR	Rywka		Motek's wife	61
BERKENSZTAT	Moshe			61
BERKENSZTAT	Rayzele			61
ALERBARDI			Bundist	62
KUSZNIR	Motek			62
FENSTERBLAU				62
BERKENSZTAT			couple	62
BERKENSZTAT	Rayzele			62
OTTO			political division of Gestapo	62
ZEIER			political division of Gestapo	62
PROZER	Hershl			62

KUSZNIR	Leib			62
KREBS	Willy		member of Gestapo	62
KUSZNIR	Motek			63
BIRNCWAJG		Brothers		63
BERKENSZTAT	Rayzele			63
BERKENSZTAT	Moshe			63
SLOMNICKI		Brothers		63
BOETTCHER	(Julian Rudolf		General	64
BARNEMAN				64
EINRICH				64
BLUME				64
ABRAMOWICZ	Sumek			64
BRENER				64
KUSZNIR				64
SZIMANOWICZ	Yisroel			64
GLANC	Rywka			64
RAZINE	Yakov			64
WALBERG		Doctor		64
MERING		Doctor		64
BLECHSZTAJN	Uzer Berish			64
WILLINGER				65
LUBLING				65
LANGNER	Moshe			65
	Avner		former teacher	71
MAJMUN				71
WALBERG				71
BOETTCHER			General	71
FRANKE			Dr.	71
RENSZKOWSKI	Anshl			72

SZTOWSKI	Yisroel-Mordechai			72
BIRNHOLC			policeman	72
FRANKE				72
BOETTCHER				73
SHABELSKI			member of Gestapo	74
FRANKOWSKI				74
DZHERZSZON				74
LASZINSKI				74
KESTENER				74
HANTKE				74
AFITZ				74
SHOT				74
JESZENOWICZ				74
SHMID				74
KIRSCH				74
KLIBSH			DEGENHARDT's representative	74
SCHLOSSER			DEGENHARDT's representative	74
DEGENHARDT				74
WERNER			Lieutenant,	74
ONBLACH			DEGENHARDT's chauffeur	74
GNOT				74
JACZOMBEK				74
HERMAN				74
"KULIBEJKE"				74
BESER				74
SZEPTEL				74
MECHTIGER				74

LANGE	Paul			74
DEGENHARDT				75
EINHORN	Pinkhas			75
CZITNICKI				75
SZLEZINGER	Dudek			75
DEGENHARDT				76
ROZEN	Dzjunja			77
ROZEN			Doctor	77
SLOMNICKI	Riwik			77
ROZENSZTAJN	Leon			77
ALTMAN	Liebl			77
KAPINSKI			Member of Judenrat	77
BERLINER			Member of Judenrat	77
BORZYKOWSKI			Member of Judenrat	77
KURLAND			Member of Judenrat	77
MISKI			Khevre Kadishe	77
IBERSHER			gendarme	77
FRANK	Hela			77
FRANK	Leibush		engineer	77
BIRNCWAJG	Makhl			78
WAJSKOP	Mikhl			78
ROZENSZTAJN	Leon			78
DEGENHARDT				78
DEGENHARDT				79
SAPERT				79
KAPINSKI				79
SZPERLING	Yitzhak		Doctor	79
KAPINSKI				80

KURLAND				80
DEGENHARDT				80
FRANKE		Dr.		80
GLATTER				80
GLATER				80
KURLAND				81
RUG	Ytizhak-Hersh			81
GAMULINSKI	Jechiel			81
WINDMAN	Zalman			81
FISZMAN	Shlomo			81
KONARSKI	Mendl			82
WILINGER				82
WACZACHA	Rywka			82
SZMULEWICZ				82
IBERSHER				83
DEGENHARDT				83
RAZINE	Ester			84
ROZENCWAJG	Natka			84
FRANK	Hela			84
FRANK	Asherl			84
BIRNCWAJG	Makhl			84
DEGENHARDT				84
LINDERMAN				84
DEGENHARDT				85
LANGE	Paul			85
LINDERMAN				85
ALTMAN	Manya			85
KALYN	Malka			85
WAJNMAN	Teni			85
BRENER	Jadzia			85

ZAJF		Dr.	pediatrican	85
ZAJF		Dr.		86
DEGENHARDT				86
MISKI				87
DEGENHARDT				87
CZARNELIAS				88
BIRNCWAJG	Makhl			88
LINDERMAN				88
FLAMENBAUM			tailor	88
DEGENHARDT				88
BOETTCHER		General, Dr.		88
NAJMAN	Franya			88
DEGENHARDT				91
BIRNCWAJG	Makhl			91
PLAT				91
SAMETKOWSKI				91
CYMERMAN		Mrs.		91
BLUMENFUCHT	Wladek			91
BOETTCHER				92
IBERSHER				92
MAJZNEROWICZ				92
JAKUBOWICZ			brothers	94
WAJNRAIJCH	Heltsha		Froebelist teacher	94
BERNSZTAJN	Manya			94
WAJNMAN	Tenya			94
KAJSER				94
ZOMBEK	M.			94
KIAK				94
FRAJMAN	Hershl			94

DEGENHARDT				94
IBERSHER				94
KAPINSKI				94
DEGENHARDT				95
KAPINSKI				95
IBERSHER				95
ANISFELD		Doctor		95
DEGENHARDT				96
LESER			Jewish Policeman	97
FISZLEWICZ	Mendl			97
FAJNER	Yitzhak			97
GALSTER	M.			97
MAJZNEROWICZ			Director of Jewish police	97
FRAJMAN	Rywka			97
IBERSHER				98
KAPINSKI				98
ANISFELD				98
DEGENHARDT				99
BOTSZAN	Berl			99
FOGEL	Leib			99
FOGEL	Mendl			99
FOGEL	Avraham			99
TENENBAUM	Helenka			99
BATENSCHLAGER			German camp leader	99
KONGRECKI		family		100
KONGRECKI	Mrs.			100
KONGRECKI	Yekhezkel			100
WINER	Lili			100

KUNDT			governor of Radom district	106
FRANKE				107
LINDERMAN				107
DEGENHARDT				107
LIHT			leader of HASAG Pelcery	107
SOYKE		family		108
BAUM	Borukh			108
BAUM	Guta			108
WALBERG		Doctor		108
LASZINSKI				109
KESTNER				109
DEGENHARDT				109
ROZENBERG	Yakov			109
SZMULIEWICZ	Asher			110
	Rafalek			110
KURLAND	Bernard			110
DEGENHARDT				110
LIHT				110
GOLDSZTAJN	Mietek			111
HOROWICZ		Doctor		111
DEGENHARDT				111
WAJSBERG		Doctor		111
SZPERLING		Doctor		111
TENCER	Heniek			113
WARSZAWSKI	Daniel			113
CELNIK	Wilik			113
ABRAMOWICZ	Sumek			113
ZISER				113
PEREC	Mietek			113

PEREC	Ahron			113
BEHN	Olek			113
PRUSZICKI				113
TENCER	Heniek			114
WILINGER	Mendl			114
LUBLING				114
JAKUBOWICZ	Shimshl			114
ROZINE				114
WALBERG	Adam	Dr.		114
SZIMANOWICZ	Yisroel			114
RAZINE	Yakov			114
CELNIK	Wilik			114
FRAJMAN				114
JACHIMEK				115
GUTGOLD	Risha			115
RIPSZTAJN	Saba			115
SZCZEKACZ	Polya			115
SZCZEKACZ	Dasha			115
GUTGOLD	Sura			115
GUTGOLD	Lusia			115
RIPSZTAJN	Kuba			115
FERLEGER	Mietek			115
FISZLEWICZ	Mendl			115
WINDMAN	Yitzhak ("Lala")			115
FRANKENBERG	Lolek ("Francek")			115
WINTRAUB	Mietek ("Marduk")			115
HAJMAN	Hipek			115
ROZINE	Aviv			115

ROZENCWAJG	Marisha			115
HIRSH	Polya			115
MASS	Jadjsha			115
WOJDISLAWSKA	Lunya			115
FAJNER	Izidor ("Faja")			115
KAPINSKI	Wladek			115
GERSZNOWICZ	Harry			115
ZBOROWSKA	Felya			115
SAMSONOWICZ	Pinek			115
SZULMAN				115
GLANC	Rywka			115
GLIKSZTAJN	Jehuda			115
ZILBERSZTAJN	Avraham			115
SZTAJNBRECHER				116
SZWIERVZEWSKI				116
RAJCH				116
SZTRASBERG				116
YANEK				116
BESERMAN				116
BROSKI				116
ZILBERBERG	Mordechai ("Mojtek")			116
ABRAMOWICZ	Simek			116
FAJSAK	Heniek			116
CZARNA	Avramek ("Czara")			117
WERNIK	Heniek ("Jacek")			117
ERENFRID	Benyamin			117
PATASZEWICZ	Pinek			117
FRANKENBERG	Lolek ("Francek")			117

PATASZEWICZ	Harri			117
KAPLAN	Avramek			117
FRIDMAN	Hilel ("Chilek")			117
MLODANOW				117
FRAZER	Hershl			117
LANDBERG	Moshe Shmuel			117
FUKS	Leon			117
GUTERMAN				117
KANTOR	Josef			117
	"Bastek"			117
KAUFMAN	"Mikrus"			117
WAJSKOP	Michal			117
	Rywka			117
	Hipek			117
FERLEGER	Mietek			117
ZILBERBERG				118
KANTOR				118
LENCZNER	Reni [Renya]			118
DEGENHARDT				118
FISZLEWICZ	Mendl			118
FISZLEWICZ				119
FAJNER	Izidor (Yitzhak)			119
SZCZEKACZ	Polya			119
ROHN				119
SAFART		Lieutenant		119
FRIDMAN	Hershl			119
ROZENSZTAJN	Natan			119
WERNIK			lawyer	119
SZLECER				119

TRAMBACKI				119
SZTAL	Haptka			119
WIGODZKI				119
ZILBERSZAC				119
GOLDBERG				119
RADSZICKI				119
SZCZEKACZ	Dasha			120
GUTGOLD	Sura			120
MASS	Jadzia			120
WINDMAN	Yitzhak			120
LUSTINGER	Zvi			120
ROZENCWAJG	Marisha			120
BORKOWSKA	Ceshia			121
CUKERMAN	Liebl			122
NASAK	brothers			122
	Avramek			122
CZARNA				122
SZMULEWICZ	brothers			122
PATASZEWICZ	Harri			122
	"Mirkus"			122
	"Yacek"			122
KLEPFISZ	Michal			123
	"Francek"			123
	"Marduk"			123
SZULMAN				123
SZULMAN				124
FLAMENBAUM	Moniek			124
HERSENBERG	Olek			124
KROJSE	Janek			124
RICHTER	Heniek			124

RICHTER	Dovid			124
ROZENBLAT	Jeczik			124
SZAJN	Szliamek			124
KONGRECKI	Dovid		wife and children	124
GLANC	Rywka			124
HAJMAN	Hipek			124
WINDMAN	Yitzhak			124
DEGENHARDT				125
GERSZNOWICZ	Harri			125
FRANKENBERG	Lolek			125
ROZINE	Aviv			125
WAJNTRAUB	Mietek			125
RIPSZTAJN	Kuba			125
	Hipek			125
WINDMAN	Yitzhak			125
LASZINSKI				125
KESTNER				125
MORDER			German commandant of Ukrainian ghetto guards	125
SZWIMER	brothers			125
HERMAN	Motl ("Kulbajki")			126
BIRNCWAJG	Mekhl			126
CZARNA	Avramek			126
SZLEZINGER	Manya			126
ROZINE	Aviv			126
LUSTIGER	Zvi			126
FRANKENBERG	Lolek			126
GERSZNOWICZ	Harri			126

ALTMAN	Dovid			126
KARNA			Volksdeutsch [ethnic German]	126
GERSZNOWICZ				126
	Harri			127
	Dovid			127
	Aviv			127
	Zvi			127
GELBER-LITWIN	Yakov Moshe			127
ENZEL	Nakhman			127
ZELIGMAN	Berl			127
MONTAG	Stefan			127
GOLDBERG	("Warszawiak")			127
RUSIN				127
LEWKOWICZ	Dudek			127
KAPINSKI	Wladek			127
	Sunek			127
	Jehuda			127
	"Francek"			127
HAUZE	Staszek			127
WOJDISLAWSKI	Kheniek			127
ROZENBERG	Moseh			128
FAJGENBLAT				128
WALBERG		Dr.		128
	Makhl			128
ROZINE	Yakov			128
ROZENBERG				129
LASZINSKI				129
KESTERN				129
PLAWNER				129

DEGENHARDT				129
	Makhl			129
ALTMAN	Feywish			129
WAJSKOP	Michal			129
BIRNBAUM	Ahron			130
	Chaim		barber worker	130
KOBRINER			painter worker	130
ALTMAN	Feywish			130
	Makhl			130
GRAJCER	Avraham			130
DEGENHARDT				130
	Makhl			131
	Gdalya			131
WAJNBERG	Masha			131
PRAZER	Hershl			131
CYMERMAN	Leib			131
KROJSE	Moniek			131
WALBERG		Doctor		131
KLIPSH			German security police	131
BULLE			German security police	131
PRAZER				132
WALBERG		Dr.		132
ROZENBERG			Jewish policeman	132
PLAWNER			Jewish policeman	132
DOMB			Jewish policeman	132
	Avramek			132
	Pinek			132

WASZILEWICZ				132
	"Baster"			132
SAMSONOWICZ	Pinek			132
PATASZEWICZ	Harri			132
BLANK	Lolek			132
TENENBAUM	Leibush			132
WOJDISLAWSKI				132
WINTER				132
	Pinek			133
	Lolek			133
	Harri			133
WINKLER				133
WOJDISLAWSKI				133
WINTER				133
TENENBAUM				133
PALMAN	Marek			134
SZABSZEWSKA	Ruchl ("Zoshya")			134
LASKOWSKI	Josef			134
STOLIARCZIK	Czeslaw			134
	"Mojtek"			135
GLIKSZTAJN	Lutek			135
SZULDHAUS	Yisroel Avigdor			135
KANTOR	JosekJose			135
GLANC	Rywka			136
LEBEL			security policeman	136
	Heniek			136
	Polya			136
	Dashya			136

	Rashya			136
	"Marduk"			136
	Marek			136
	"Francek"			136
	Sumek			136
WINDMAN	Ytizhak			136
KRZAK				136
ZBOROWSKA	Fela			136
BRAM	Jehuda			136
BRAM	Bela			136
RIPSZTAJN	Kuba			136
GLIKSZTAJN	Lutek			136
PRASER	Hershl			137
LEWENSZTAJN	Moshe			137
	Chaim		hairdresser	137
KINDEL			gendarme	137
MILHOF			police constable	138
GLATTER			Jewish doctor	138
KLEM			security police	139
SHTIGLITZ				139
KMICZIKEWICZ				139
SHTEININGER				139
DARASZENKA				139
PAVELIAK				139
LIHT				139
KURLAND				139
WOLSKA (nee WAJNRAJCH)		Mrs.		140
APEL	"Marsz"			140
BRETSCHNEIDER			technical director	140

ARNT			political officer	140
SHPALTENHOLC			technical manager	141
FRANCKE			technical manager	141
PASOLD			technical manager	141
BINTER			foreman	141
APEL			foreman	141
NICIALEK			foreman	141
WIRBAC			foreman	141
KEHLER			foreman	141
WALTER			foreman	141
KLEM			labor security leader	141
SHTIGLITZ			labor security	141
SZEWTSZENKO			labor security	141
DARASZENKA			labor security	141
KMICZIKEWICZ			labor security	141
PAWELIAK			labor security	141
HANTKE			security police	141
LASZINSKI			security police	141
DEGENHARDT				141
BIALOGURSKA				141
GALSTER			sanitary worker	141
KURLAND				141
SHPALTENHOLC				142
JAROCZINSKI			former chairman of Lodz refugees	142
KLEM				142
WAJSBERG			female doctor	142
MARKOWICZ				142

KEHLER				142
JUNG	Juszhek			142
DEGENHARDT				142
DEGENHARDT				143
APEL	"Morcz" (Little Hammer)			143
FELDMAN	Rubinku (Ruwin)			143
FELDMAN	Ch.			143
JUNG	Juszhek			143
WIGDOR	Zosha			143
WIGDOR	Kalman			143
ZALCBERG				144
BEATUS		Mrs.		144
KLEM				144
WAJSBERG		Doctor		144
PRZYROWSKI	Julek	Doctor		145
LUNSKI		Dr.		145
HULITSH			transport foreman	145
BERGER			foreman	145
HARN			mechanical workshop foreman	145
	Tietga Mariana			145
	Retga Frida			145
MARCHEWKA	Klara			145
PIETRUCHA				145
SCHPALTENHOLTZ				145
KEHLER	Martin			146
	Gustave			146
FROSSE	Walter			146

NIKKE	Johannes			146
WALMAN				146
APEL				146
FASOLD	"Boxer"			146
NEMIEC	Tuvya			146
	Tuvya			147
FASOLD				147
HUASNER			foreman	147
KLEM				147
SHTIGLITZ				148
SKALENKO	Michal		labor security	148
LIBERMAN				148
KAPLAN	Avraham			149
WALASZCZIK				149
IMIOLLEK				149
MILHOF				149
WAJSKOP	Machl			150
SHTIGLITZ				150
GLIKSMAN				150
FAJERMAN				150
JAKUBOWICZ		brothers		151
HERMAN				151
SZPERLING			chief doctor	151
GAMULINSK	Jechiel			152
BRENER	Itshe			152
OFMAN	Fela			152
WEKSZTAJN	Zosha			152
MIEDZRZECKA	"Wladka"			152
	"Jacek"			152
	"Wladka"			153

DZJUBA		Mrs.		153
HELMAN				153
ALTMAN	Manya (nee Kalin)			153
PRZYROWSKI		Doctor		153
LUNSKI		Doctor		153
EDELIST	Noakh			153
LANDAU	Jechiel			153
WIERNIK	Natka		Jacek's wife	153
CZARNA	Avramek			153
DZIALOWSKA	Ruczka			153
SZTAJNIC	Eli			153
LEBER	Leib			153
KROJSE	Josef			153
ALTMAN	Betsalel			153
JALES				156
	"Stefan"		courier for Warsaw Jewish underground	157
LIHT				157
SZTAJNBRECHER				158
WAJNRAJCH				158
BRENER	Jadza (Ita)			158
SZTRAUSBERG				158
SZWIERCZEWSKI				158
LIPSZTAJN	Kuba			158
DIMAND				158
SZIMONOWICZ				158
BRENER				158
JOSEFOWICZ	L.			158
FRIDRAJCH	Hilel			158

MLODINOW				158
WALCZINSKI				158
PROZER				158
CYMERMAN				158
WERNIK				158
YACEK				158
BRUST	Jan			158
NABIALEK	Woyceck			158
NABIALEK	Eugeniusz			158
NABIALEK	Eugeniusz			159
BRUST	Jan			159
	"Jacek"		Jewish liaison officer	159
	M?drzec		Polish foreman	159
GUTMAN	Yankl			159
AFRAT		Engineer		160
TRAJWICZ		Doctor		160
KOCZOL	Polya			160
GLATTER		Doctor		160
WERNIK				160
WILCZINSKI				160
BARTENSHALGER			Skarzysko camp leader	160
SZTAJNBRECHER	Adash			161
	"Jacek"			161
ROZENCWAJG	Fufek			161
GUTMAN	Yankl			161
	M?drzec			161
BORKOWSKA	Maria			161
NABIALEK	Eugeniusz			162
WERNIK	Natka			162

	"Jacek"			162
NABIALEK	Wojciech			162
	M?drzec			163
ALTMAN	Betsalel			163
BARTENSHALGER	(Georg)			163
GOLDSZTAJN				163
RIPSZTAJN	Kuba			164
GLIKSZTAJN	Jehuda			164
ZBAROWSKA	Bela			164
BRAM	Bela			164
SZIIDLOWSKI	Lejzer			165
PINDELIAK			Polish family	166
PINDELIAK	Celina			166
GEWERCMAN	Boliek			166
BOETTCHER			S.S. general and leader of Radom district	166
GOLDSZTAJN			Jewish camp leader	166
GOLDSZTAJN				167
LIHT			factory director	167
HERMAN			security leader	168
TRAJWICZ		Dr.		169
AUGENFISZ	Rayzl		doctor	174
BRONIATOWSKI	Ayzyk		doctor	174
BRAM	Arnold		doctor	174
BLUMENFELD	Dovid		doctor	174
BERNSZTAJN	Nisen Uzer		doctor	174
BOLOTNE	Shmuel		doctor	174
BARTCZINSKI	Juliusz		doctor	174
EPSZTAJN	Bernard		doctor	174

FALK	Chaim		doctor	174
??KSZTAJN	Stefan		doctor	174
GLATTER	Lejzer		doctor	174
GUTMAN	Kruza		doctor	174
GRUNWALD	Irena		doctor	174
HOROWICZ	Moshe		doctor	174
HALLEMAN	Henrik		doctor	174
HALLEMAN	Miriam		doctor	174
IGEL	Henrik		doctor	174
KRAUSKOP	Hersh		doctor	174
KAGAN	Dovid		doctor	174
KAJAK	Moshe Feytl		doctor	175
LEWIN	Mietczyslaw		doctor	175
LEWIN	Shmuel Leib		doctor	175
LIPINSKI	Yudl		doctor	175
LIPINSKI	Zigmund		doctor	175
PRAFART	Sholem		doctor	175
ROZEN	Naftali		doctor	175
SZAFER SZAJDLINER	Rayzl		doctor	175
SZIKER	Alfred		doctor	175
SZAJNIC	Mordechai		doctor	175
TRAUNER	Henrik		doctor	175
TENENBAUM	Berl		doctor	175
TENENBAUM	Yakhet		doctor	175
TARBECZKA	Dovid		doctor	175
WALBERG	Adam Ayzyk		doctor	175
WINER	Eliash		doctor	175
WARMUND	Wolf		doctor	175
WAJSBERG	Ruchl		doctor	175

ZANDSZTAJN	Hilary		doctor	175
ZAND	Yakob		doctor	175
ZAND	Rywka		doctor	175
ZANDBERG	Yehezkiel		doctor	176
ZAJF	Yosef		doctor	176
GAJZLER	Hilpolit		doctor	176
GOLDMAN	Leon		doctor	176
LEWKOWICZ	Tankhm		doctor	176
SOBOL	Wladislaw		doctor	176
KONARSKI	Adam		doctor	176
BRONIATOWSKI	Artur		dentist	176
BRONIATOWSKA	Tisa		dentist	176
BRANDES	Ester		dentist	176
BEM	Gitl		dentist	176
BLAJWAJS	Lotta		dentist	176
CYMERMAN	Gitl		dentist	176
EPSZTAJN	Bayla Rywka		dentist	176
FRENK	Helena		dentist	176
GRIN	Mordechai		dentist	176
KORNGOLD	Rywka		dentist	176
KARTUZ	Yehudis		dentist	176
LEWKOWICZ	Leah		dentist	176
MINC	Amalia		dentist	176
ROZENOWICZ	Michal		dentist	176
ZALCBERG	Eugenia		dentist	176

Index

A

Abramek, 171

Abramowicz, 77, 133, 135, 202, 209, 211

Afitz, 203

Afrat, 176, 223

Alechim, 200

Alerbardi, 75, 201

Altman, 93, 101, 145, 146, 148, 170, 171, 179, 204, 205, 215, 216, 222, 224

Ambras, 6, 191

Anisfeld, 14, 113, 116, 194, 207

Apel, 157, 158, 163, 218, 219, 220, 221

Arnt, 158, 219

Asz, 10, 11, 12, 14, 19, 51, 65, 68, 191, 192, 193, 196, 199, 200

Augenfisz, 187, 224

Avner, 85

Avramek, 136, 141, 145, 150

B

Babiacki, 53, 196

Barenhercyk, 19

Barimhercik, 7, 191

Barneman, 77, 202

Bartczinski, 187, 224

Bartenschlager, 173, 177, 179

Bartenshalger, 223, 224

Bastek, 136

Baster, 150

Batenschlager, 117, 207

Baum, 68, 125, 167, 200, 209

Beatus, 161, 220

Behn, 133, 210

Bem, 189, 226

Berger, 162, 220

Berkensztat, 67, 71, 73, 75, 76, 200, 201, 202

Berliner, 10, 11, 14, 93, 192, 194, 204

Bernsztajn, 113, 187, 206, 224

Beser, 51, 89, 196, 203

Beserglik, 11, 14, 192, 193

Beserman, 211

Besermen, 135

Bialogurska, 159, 219

Binter, 158, 219

Birnbaum, 54, 148, 197, 216

Birncwajg, 64, 76, 94, 100, 104, 108, 122, 123, 145, 199, 202, 204, 205, 206, 208, 214

Birnholc, 86, 203

Blajwajs, 189, 226

Blank, 150, 217

Blechsztajn, 65, 78, 199, 202

Blume, 77, 202

Blumenfeld, 54, 187, 197, 224

Blumenfucht, 108, 206

Blumenkranc, 64, 65, 198, 199

Boettcher, 77, 86, 88, 96, 104, 108, 121, 184, 202, 203, 206, 224

Bolotne, 187, 224

Borkowska, 140, 178, 213, 223

Bornsztajn, 64, 65, 199

Borzykowski, 14, 34, 42, 47, 59, 93, 194, 195, 197, 204

Botszan, 117, 207

Brahinsky, 63, 198

Bram, 154, 180, 187, 218, 224

Brandes, 189, 226

Brandlewicz, 193

Brandliewicz, 11, 192

Braniatowski, 11

Brener, 1, 64, 65, 77, 78, 101, 169, 175, 198, 199,
202, 205, 221, 222

Brener (Bund), 175

Bretschneider, 158, 218

Bromberg, 10, 11, 14, 192, 194

Broniatowska, 189, 226

Broniatowski, 14, 187, 189, 192, 193, 224, 226

Broski, 135, 211

Brust, 175, 176, 223

Bulle, 150, 216

C

Cangrel, 6, 191

Cederbaum, 42, 196

Celnik, 133, 134, 209, 210

Chada, 55, 197

Chilwner, 199

Chliwner, 65

Chraport, 67, 199

Cukerman, 141, 213

Cymerman, 108, 149, 175, 189, 206, 216, 223, 226

Czanszinksi, 72

Czanszinska, 54, 197

Czanszinski, 51, 71, 196, 201

Czarna, 136, 141, 145, 171, 211, 213, 214, 222

Czarna ("Czara"), 136

Czarnelias, 104, 206

Czeriker, 11, 192

Czitnicki, 204

Czonszinski, 72

D

Daraszenka, 157, 158, 218, 219

Datner, 65, 199

Degenhardt, 88, 89, 91, 94, 95, 96, 99, 100, 101,
102, 103, 104, 107, 108, 113, 114, 117, 118,
120, 122, 125, 126, 129, 130, 137, 144, 148,
149, 158, 160, 196, 203, 204, 205, 206, 207,
208, 209, 212, 214, 216, 219, 220

Deregowski, 191

Dergowski, 8

Dimand, 175, 222

Ditman, 8, 191

Dolf, 33, 34, 195

Domb, 150, 216

Drahaberg, 3, 191

Dreksler, 70, 200

Dzalowski, 71, 201

Dzherzszon, 88, 203

Dzialowska, 171, 222

Dzigan, 65, 199

Dzjuba, 170, 222

E

Edelist, 68, 171, 200, 222

Einhorn, 204

Einrich, 77, 202

Enzel, 146, 215

Epsztajn, 12, 187, 189, 193, 224, 226

Erenfrid, 136, 211

F

Faharille, 47

Fajerman, 166, 221

Fajgenblat, 147, 215

Fajner, 62, 115, 135, 139, 198, 207, 211, 212

Fajsak, 135, 211

Falk, 119, 187, 208, 225

Fantofel, 34

Fasold, 163, 221

Feldman, 160, 220

Fensterblau, 201

Ferleger, 135, 136, 210, 212

Fershter, 208

Ferszter, 122

Fiszlewicz, 115, 135, 137, 139, 207, 210, 212

Fiszman, 98, 205

Flamenbaum, 104, 143, 206, 213

Fogel, 12, 65, 117, 193, 199, 207

Frajman, 113, 116, 134, 206, 207, 210

Francek, 135, 136, 143, 146

Francke, 158, 219

Frank, 70, 71, 93, 100, 200, 201, 204, 205

Franke, 38, 86, 87, 96, 123, 125, 195, 202, 203,
    205, 208, 209

Frankenberg, 135, 136, 144, 145, 210, 211, 214

Frankenberg ("Francek"), 135, 136

Frankowski, 28, 88, 195, 203

Frazer, 136, 212

Frenk, 189, 226

Frida, 162

Fridman, 136, 139, 212

Fridman ("Chilek"), 136

Fridrajch, 175, 222

Frosse, 162, 220

Fuks, 136, 212

G

Gajzler, 12, 189, 193, 226

Galster, 12, 14, 42, 115, 159, 193, 194, 195, 207,
    219

Gamulinsk, 169, 221

Gamulinski, 97, 205

Gelber, 62, 146, 198, 215

Geobbels, 196

Gerichter, 11, 14, 59, 192, 194, 197

Gersznowicz, 135, 211, 214, 215

Gerszonowicz, 144

Gerszonwicz, 145

Gewercman, 183, 224

Gilter, 66

Ginsberg, 62, 198

Gitler, 12, 13, 14, 66, 193, 194, 199

Glanc, 78, 135, 143, 153, 202, 211, 214, 217

Glater, 96, 205

Glatter, 54, 96, 156, 177, 187, 197, 205, 218, 223,
    225

Gliksman, 69, 166, 200, 221

Gliksztajn, 135, 153, 154, 180, 211, 217, 218, 224

Gnot, 89, 203

Goebbels, 51

Goldberg, 139, 146, 213, 215

Goldman, 189

Goldsztajn, 129, 179, 184, 209, 224

Grabiner, 68, 200

Grajcer, 148, 149, 216

Granek, 6, 191

Grieshammer, 36, 195

Griliak, 56, 197

Grin, 189, 226

Grunwald, 187

Grynfeld, 11, 14, 192, 194

Guterman, 136, 212

Gutgold, 134, 140, 210, 213

Gutman, 176, 178, 187, 223, 225

Gutt, 46

H

Haftke, 63, 198

Hajman, 135, 143, 210, 214

Halleman, 54, 187, 197, 225

Hantke, 88, 158, 203, 219

Harn, 162, 220

Haspnfeld, 12, 193

Hauze, 146, 215

Hauzner, 164

Helman, 42, 170, 195, 222

Herman, 89, 145, 166, 186, 203, 214, 221, 224

Hersenberg, 143, 213

Hipek, 135, 136, 143, 144

Hirsh, 135, 211

Horowicz, 89, 100, 103, 123, 129, 187, 209, 225

Hossenfeld, 54, 196

Huasner, 221

Hulitsh, 161, 162, 220

I

Ibersher, 93, 99, 108, 113, 204, 205, 206, 207, 208

Iberszer, 116, 120, 121

Icek, 11, 192

Igel, 187, 225

Imialek, 200

Imiollek, 165, 221

J

Jachimek, 134, 210

Jaczombek, 89, 203

Jakubowicz, 68, 111, 134, 166, 200, 206, 210, 221

Jales, 173, 222

Janowska, 54, 197

Jaracinski, 42, 196

Jaroczinski, 53, 159, 196, 219

Jeszenowicz, 88, 203

Josefowicz, 175, 222

Jung, 159, 220

K

Kabak, 6, 191

Kac, 14, 194

Kacinel, 12, 14, 66, 193, 194, 199

Kadner, 21, 30, 194, 195

Kagan, 188, 225

Kajak, 188, 225

Kajser, 206

Kalyn, 101, 205

Kander, 57, 197

Kantor, 136, 137, 153, 212, 217

Kapiecka, 68, 200

Kapinski, 10, 11, 12, 14, 57, 67, 93, 95, 96, 113,
   116, 119, 135, 146, 192, 193, 194, 197, 200,
   204, 207, 208, 211, 215

Kaplan, 136, 165, 212, 221

Karna, 146, 215

Kartuz, 189, 226

Kasman, 12, 193

Kaufman, 212

Kaufman ("Mikrus"), 136

Kawa, 7, 191

Kawan, 33, 195

Kazak, 51, 52, 196

Kehler, 158, 159, 162, 219, 220

Kestener, 88, 203

Kestern, 148, 215

Kestner, 122, 126, 127, 132, 144, 208, 209, 214

Kiak, 206

Kindel, 154, 218

Kirsch, 203

Klajnplac, 11, 14, 192, 194

Klem, 157, 158, 159, 161, 164, 218, 219, 220, 221

Klepfisz, 142, 213

Klibsh, 88, 203

Klipsh, 150, 216

Kmiczikewicz, 157, 158, 218, 219

Kobriner, 216

Koczol, 177, 223

Kohlenberger, 12

Kohlenbrener, 15, 16, 193, 194

Kohn, 33, 160, 195

Konarksi, 65

Konarski, 13, 54, 57, 98, 189, 193, 197, 199, 205, 226

Kongrecki, 74, 117, 118, 143, 207, 214

Koniecpoler, 10, 11, 154, 175, 192

Korngold, 189, 226

Kosciuszko, 200

Kozak, 52, 196

Kozlowski, 66, 199

Krakower, 13, 193

Krauskop, 187, 225

Krebs, 76, 202

Kriger, 5, 191

Krisztal, 63, 198

Krojcer, 10, 11, 192

Krojse, 213, 216, 222

Krojsze, 171

Krojze, 149

Kroyse, 143

Kruzler, 66, 199

Krzak, 154, 218

Kulibejke, 89, 203

Kundt, 123, 209

Kurland, 14, 33, 34, 47, 59, 64, 93, 96, 97, 119, 120, 121, 129, 157, 159, 194, 195, 197, 199, 204, 205, 208, 209, 218, 219

Kusznir, 54, 64, 65, 66, 72, 74, 76, 77, 197, 199, 201, 202

L

Lampel, 189

Landa, 42, 196

Landau, 63, 171, 198, 222

Landberg, 136, 212

Lange, 89, 101, 204, 205

Langner, 78, 90, 202

Lash, 21, 194

Laski, 50, 196

Laskowski, 152, 217

Lasz, 46

Laszinksi, 126

Laszinski, 88, 122, 127, 144, 158, 203, 208, 209, 214, 215, 219

Lazinski, 123

Lebel, 154, 217

Leber, 171, 222

Lenczner, 137, 212

Leser, 207

Lesler, 115

Lewensztajn, 154, 218

Lewin, 119, 188, 208, 225

Lewit, 11, 14, 192, 194

Lewkowicz, 11, 32, 33, 146, 189, 192, 195, 215, 226

Liberman, 221

Liht, 125, 129, 157, 158, 175, 185, 209, 218, 222, 224

Linderman, 100, 101, 104, 125, 205, 206, 209

Lipinski, 188, 225

Lipintka, 54, 197

Lipszic, 33, 195

Lipsztajn, 175, 222

Liszinski, 148

Litwin, 146

Lolek, 135, 136, 145, 146, 150, 151

Lubling, 78, 134, 202, 210

Lunksi, 161

Lunski, 171, 220, 222

Lustiger, 145, 214

Lustinger, 140, 213

M

Machl, 64, 104, 147, 148, 149

Majmun, 85, 202

Majznerowicz, 46, 47, 109, 116, 206, 207

Marchewka, 162, 220

Marduk, 135, 143

Mariana, 162

Markowicz, 159, 219

Mass, 62, 135, 140, 198, 211, 213

Maszewicz, 50, 196

Mechtiger, 89, 203

Mendelson, 63

Mendlson, 198

Mering, 59, 78, 198, 202

Miedzrzecka, 221

Milhof, 156, 165, 218, 221

Minc, 189, 226

Miski, 93, 103, 204, 206

Mlodanow, 136, 212

Mlodinow, 175, 223

Montag, 146, 215

Morcz, 160

Morder, 144, 214

N

Nabialek, 176, 178, 223, 224

Najfeld, 192

Najman, 104, 206

Nasak, 213

Nasek, 141

Nemiec, 163, 221

Nicialek, 158, 219

Niedziela, 35, 195

Niemerowski, 11, 192

Niemirowski, 14, 194

Nikke, 162, 221

Nodelberg, 68, 200

Nojfeld, 11, 192

O

Ofman, 169, 221

Okrent, 65

Onblach, 88, 203

Opatowska, 63, 198

Opatowski, 70, 200

Opatszinki, 71

Opatszinski, 201

Opoczinski, 73

Orbach, 67

Orcach, 199

Otto, 76, 201

P

Paharille, 14, 194

Palman, 152, 217

Pantofel, 35, 195

Pasold, 158, 159, 219

Pataszewicz, 136, 141, 150, 211, 212, 213, 217

Paveliak, 157, 218

Paweliak, 158, 219

Pelta, 7, 19, 41, 191

Perec, 133, 209, 210

Peretz, 63, 72, 98, 151, 198

Pietrik, 62

Pietrowski, 62

Pietrowski (Pietrik), 198

Pietrucha, 220

Pilsudski, 200

Piłsudski, 5, 70

Pindeliak, 183, 224

Pinek, 135, 136, 150, 151

Plat, 108, 206

Plawner, 148, 150, 215, 216

Pohorille, 12, 13, 14, 37, 49, 59, 66, 193, 194, 195, 196, 197, 199

Poznanska, 200

Prafart, 12, 188, 193, 225

Prapart, 14, 194

Praser, 154, 218

Praszkewicz, 63, 198

Prazer, 149, 150, 216

Prozer, 76, 175, 201, 223

Prusicki, 67

Pruszicki, 12, 66, 133, 193, 199, 200, 210

Przyrowski, 161, 171, 220, 222

Pulkowski, 76

R

R0zencwajg, 198

Radal, 12, 13, 193

Radszicki, 139, 213

Rajch, 135, 211

Rajchman, 13, 193

Razine, 14, 64, 78, 100, 134, 193, 198, 202, 205, 210

Reisen, 63, 198

Renenweter, 12, 193

Renkszowski, 86

Renszkowski, 202

Ribsztajn, 180

Richter, 143, 213, 214

Ridiger, 3, 49, 191, 196

Rifsztajn, 12, 193

Ripsztajn, 134, 135, 154, 210, 214, 218, 224

Rodal, 11, 51, 52, 192, 196

Rohn, 139, 212

Rotbard, 11, 14, 119, 192, 208

Rotbart, 14, 194

Rozen, 54, 74, 93, 188, 197, 201, 204, 225

Rozenberg, 51, 126, 147, 148, 150, 196, 209, 215, 216

Rozenblat, 143, 214

Rozencwajg, 63, 100, 135, 140, 178, 205, 211, 213, 223

Rozenowicz, 189, 226

Rozensztajn, 93, 94, 139, 204, 212

Rozenzaft, 123, 208

Rozine, 19, 51, 54, 62, 74, 134, 135, 144, 145, 147, 196, 197, 198, 201, 210, 214, 215

Roziner, 192, 199

Ruczewicz, 11, 192, 194

Ruczka, 171

Rug, 97, 205

Rusin, 215

Ruszewicz, 14

Rypsztajn, 144

S

Sabelski, 90

Safart, 139, 212

Safirsztajn, 12, 193

Sametkowski, 108, 206

Samsonowicz, 135, 136, 150, 211, 217

Sapert, 95, 204

Schleecht, 50, 196

Schlosser, 88, 203

Schneider, 1, 45, 78, 96

Schpaltenholtz, 220

Shabelski, 88, 203

Shmid, 203

Shmuel, 11, 14, 136

Shot, 203

Shpaltenholc, 219

Shteininger, 218

Shtiglitz, 218, 219, 221

Silman, 70, 200

Skalenko, 164, 221

Slomnicki, 77, 93, 202, 204

Slonimski, 11, 192

Sobol, 189, 226

Soyke, 125, 209

Spaltenholtz, 158, 159, 162

Srebrnik, 64, 198

Starszych, 58, 65

Statystynczny, 50

Steininger, 157

Stiglitz, 157, 164, 166

Stoliarczik, 152, 217

Sumek, 133, 146, 202

Szabelski, 5, 191

Szabszewska, 152, 217

Szabszewski, 168

Szafer, 188

Szafer Szajdliner, 225

Szafir, 11, 14, 192, 194

Szajn, 143, 214

Szajnfeld, 123, 208

Szajnic, 188, 225

Szczekacz, 62, 134, 139, 198, 210, 212, 213

Szczekaz, 139

Szczensna, 72, 201

Szeftel, 51, 196

Szeptel, 89, 203

Szewtszenko, 158, 219

Szidlowski, 169, 181

Sziidlowski, 224

Sziker, 188, 225

Szimanowicz, 77, 134, 202, 210

Szimkowicz, 71, 200

Szimonowicz, 175, 222

Szitowski, 86

Sziwak, 62, 198

Szlecer, 139, 212

Szlezinger, 89, 145, 204, 214

Szmulewicz, 98, 141, 205, 213

Szmuliewicz, 128, 209

Szperling, 95, 130, 167, 168, 204, 209, 221

Sztajer, 98

Sztajnbrecher, 70, 135, 175, 177, 200, 211, 222, 223

Sztajnic, 171, 222

Sztal, 139, 213

Sztarkman, 42, 196

Szterensi, 198

Szterenzis, 62

Sztiglic, 158

Sztowski, 203

Sztrasberg, 135, 211

Sztrausberg, 175, 222

Szuldhaus, 153, 217

Szulman, 135, 143, 211, 213

Szwierczewski, 135, 175, 222

Szwiervzewski, 211

Szwimer, 145, 214

T

Tarashenko, 35, 195

Tarbeczka, 188, 225

Tempel, 51, 52, 196

Temple, 54

Tencer, 133, 209, 210

Tenenbaum, 71, 74, 117, 151, 188, 201, 207, 217, 225

Trajwicz, 177, 186, 223, 224

Trambacki, 139, 213

Trauner, 188, 225

W

Waczacha, 98, 205

Waczecha, 62, 198

Wajnberg, 62, 149, 198, 216

Wajnman, 101, 113, 205, 206

Wajnraijch, 206

Wajnrajch, 112, 113, 157, 175, 218, 222

Wajnrib, 14, 70, 194, 200

Wajntraub, 144, 214

Wajsberg, 130, 159, 161, 188, 209, 219, 220, 225

Wajskop, 94, 136, 148, 165, 167, 170, 204, 212, 216, 221

Walaszczik, 165, 221

Walberg, 37, 55, 57, 65, 66, 68, 78, 86, 122, 125, 134, 147, 150, 188, 195, 197, 199, 200, 202, 208, 209, 210, 215, 216, 225

Walczinscki, 175

Walczinski, 223

Walman, 162, 221

Walter, 158, 219

Warmund, 188, 225

Warszawski, 107, 133, 209

Waszilewicz, 150, 217

Weksztajn, 132, 169, 221

Wendler, 11, 17, 21, 22, 23, 30, 42, 46, 47, 50, 67, 193, 194, 195, 196, 200

Werner, 88, 203

Wernik, 136, 139, 175, 177, 178, 211, 212, 223

Wernik ("Jacek"), 136

Wiernik, 171, 222

Wiesalowski, 62, 198

Wigdor, 161, 220

Wigodzki, 139, 213

Wilczinski, 177, 223

Wilinger, 78, 98, 134, 205, 210

Willinger, 202

Windhajm, 54, 197

Windman, 97, 135, 140, 143, 144, 154, 205, 210, 213, 214, 218

Winer, 118, 121, 188, 207, 208, 225

Winkler, 151, 217

Winter, 151, 217

Wintraub, 210

Wintraub ("Marduk"), 135

Wirbac, 158, 219

Wojdislawska, 135, 211

Wojdislawski, 147, 151, 215, 217

Wolska, 157, 218

Y

Yacek, 223

Yanek, 135, 211

Yehuda, 51, 135, 146, 154

Yung, 160

Z

Zajf, 102, 189, 206, 226

Zalcberg, 161, 189, 220, 226

Zand, 189, 226

Zandberg, 189, 226

Zandsztajn, 14, 188, 194, 226

Zawada, 50, 196

Zbarowska, 180

Zborowska, 135, 154, 211, 218

Zeier, 76, 201

Zeligman, 146, 215

Zibert, 46

Zilberberg, 135, 137, 211, 212

Zilberszac, 139, 213

Zilbersztajn, 135, 211

Zimniak, 3, 191

Zion, 72, 77, 175, 201

Ziser, 209

Zitenfeld, 68, 200

Zombek, 113, 206

Zondsztajn, 65, 199

www.ingramcontent.com/pod-product-compliance
Lightning Source LLC
Chambersburg PA
CBHW082004150426
42814CB00005BA/216